28 DAY BOOK

B
JORGENSEN
D

9/08 z

Richard F. Docter

Becoming a Woman
A Biography
of Christine Jorgensen

"Great insight about the life and social history surrounding this remarkable woman. . . . Includes a valuable discussion on the appearance and characteristics of cross dressers contrasted with transsexuals. . . . A fascinating companion piece to Jorgensen's autobiography. . . . Recommended for all libraries with anthropology, GLBT, psychology, and women's studies collections."

Library Journal

"The author provides a riveting mix of engaging narrative and scholarly research in this pioneering biography of Christine Jorgensen, the world's first transsexual celebrity. Docter pays the complex personality of Jorgensen proper respect while pulling no punches and leaves us in no doubt of her importance as a transgender pioneer. The author expertly peels away the layers of personal narrative, medical reporting, and media speculation to reveal how and why Jorgensen became the single most important transperson in the making of the modern transsexual."

Richard Ekins, PhD
Professor of Sociology
and Cultural Studies,
University of Ulster at Coleraine, UK;
Author (with Dave King) of *The Transgender Phenomenon*

"Extensively researched and informed by Dr. Docter's nearly five decades as a psychologist and scholar of transgender phenomenon. While the book is clearly an in-depth examination of Christine's life, both as George and as Christine, Docter delves more deeply into the psyche of Ms. Jorgensen than any prior works on this icon of transsexualism in America. This biography is a must-read for any serious student of transgender issues. It is accessible to both laypersons and mental health professionals alike."

George R. Brown, MD, DFAPA
Chief of Psychiatry, Mountain Home,
VAMC

"This is an easy, straightforward read. The author reveals Jorgensen's sense of not being fully appreciated for what she believed she had accomplished as a transsexual pioneer. Nor does it seem she ever felt herself to be the woman she struggled to become, in spite of hormones and surgeries. Readers are offered a closer look into her life and invited to judge for themselves."

Andrea L. T. Peterson, MDiv

The Haworth Press
Taylor & Francis Group
New York and London

Becoming a Woman
A Biography
of Christine Jorgensen

THE HAWORTH PRESS
Sexual Minorities in Historical Context

Bringing Lesbian And Gay Rights into The Mainstream: Twenty Years of Progress by Steve Endean, edited by Vicki Eaklor

Becoming a Woman: A Biography of Christine Jorgensen by Richard F. Docter

Becoming a Woman
A Biography
of Christine Jorgensen

Richard F. Docter

The Haworth Press
Taylor & Francis Group
New York and London

For more information on this book or to order, visit
http://www.haworthpress.com/store/product.asp?sku=5896

or call 1-800-HAWORTH (800-429-6784) in the United States and Canada
or (607) 722-5857 outside the United States and Canada

or contact orders@HaworthPress.com

The Haworth Press, Taylor & Francis Group, 270 Madison Avenue, New York, NY 10016.

PUBLISHER'S NOTE
The development, preparation, and publication of this work has been undertaken with great care. However, the Publisher, employees, editors, and agents of The Haworth Press are not responsible for any errors contained herein or for consequences that may ensue from use of materials or information contained in this work. The Haworth Press is committed to the dissemination of ideas and information according to the highest standards of intellectual freedom and the free exchange of ideas. Statements made and opinions expressed in this publication do not necessarily reflect the views of the Publisher, Directors, management, or staff of The Haworth Press, or an endorsement by them.

Identities and circumstances of some individuals discussed in this book have been changed to protect confidentiality.

Excerpts and information from Paul Eriksson's *Christine Jorgensen: A Personal Autobiography*, 1967, are reprinted with permission of Paul S. Eriksson.

Cover photograph of Christine Jorgensen reproduced courtesy of Paul Eriksson.

Cover design by Kerry Mack.

Library of Congress Cataloging-in-Publication Data

Docter, Richard F.
    Becoming a woman : a biography of Christine Jorgensen / Richard F. Docter.
        p. cm.
    Includes bibliographical references and index.
    ISBN: 978-1-56023-666-5 (alk. paper)
    ISBN: 978-1-56023-667-2 (alk. paper)
    1. Jorgensen, Christine, 1926- 2. Transsexuals—United States—Biography. 3. Sex change—Denmark. I. Title. II. Title: Biography of Christine Jorgensen.

    HQ77.8.J67D63 2007
    306.76'8092-dc22
    [B]

                                                                                    200603737

For my wife, Shirley, and our children:
Lloyd, Frank, Bob, and Joan.

ABOUT THE AUTHOR

Richard F. Docter, PhD, is a Stanford-trained clinical psychologist and gender researcher. During the Korean War he served as a clinical psychologist at Valley Forge Army Hospital and in the Department of Psychiatry at Fort Chaffee Army Hospital. For seven years he was engaged in both human and animal studies as an assistant professor of medical psychology (in residence) in the Department of Psychiatry, UCLA School of Medicine. After brief service as Associate Administrative Officer for Professional Affairs in the American Psychological Association, he became Professor of Psychology and Chair of Psychology at California State University at Northridge, where he served for thirty-seven years. Docter is a Diplomate of the American Board of Professional Psychology (Clinical) and a Fellow of the American Psychological Association (Division of Clinical Psychology). He is also a member of the Harry Benjamin International Gender Dysphoria Association. Over the past twenty-five years he has presented papers and been an invited speaker at more than forty transgender conventions and research conferences. He is the author of *Transvestites and Transsexuals: Toward a Theory of Cross-Gender Behavior* and *From Man to Woman: The Transgender Journey of Virginia Prince.*

CONTENTS

Foreword

Christine Jorgensen is one of those pivotal people in history. What she did was to bring about a radical change in thinking about what constitutes sex and gender. She did not do this by research but by announcing what she did to herself, proclaiming that she had, through surgery and hormones, changed from a male to a female. Though she was not the first person to do this, she was the one who became the public symbol of the possibilities of such change and it made her a media sensation. Technically, she was a castrated male whose body development was dependent upon the administration of hormones, the discovery and development of which took place in the 1920s and 1930s. Though she proclaimed herself a woman, her original surgery did not attempt to give her a vagina, and the later attempt of surgeons to make her a vagina out of intestine was not particularly successful. Such matters, however, were not the public part of her history. She was the man who became a woman, an example which thousands and thousands of others have since followed, and not only have males become women, but females have become men. There is good evidence that she saw herself as a pioneer whose path others would follow.

The story of what Christine did and how it came about is the subject of this much-needed and important book. Though Christine wrote her own autobiography, there was much information that she did not disclose and there was much in which she embroidered the truth. All sorts of myths developed about her, some of which she encouraged. Richard Docter has devoted several years to researching her past, interviewing surviving family members, friends, and professionals in a number of different fields. For example, Christine told a story of having the sex on her passport changed through the intervention of the American embassy, but the United States did not then include sex as a category to be listed on a passport, and all that happened is that the first name on her passport was changed from George

Becoming a Woman: A Biography of Christine Jorgensen
© 2008 by The Haworth Press, Taylor & Francis Group. All rights reserved.
doi:10.1300/5896_a

to Christine, which was a relatively minor change. In a sense, Christine lived in a world in which she created herself, and in the process blurred over much of her past, and even much of what took place around her. This was part of the Christine Jorgensen myth.

The myths will continue to survive since they are so deeply embedded in her story. Still, it is important to find out what really happened and what Christine was really like. This book is not an attempt to debunk Christine but to help readers understand just who and what she was. Uncovering the full story is much like uncovering the full story of individuals such as George Washington about whom many events have been told, such as his cutting down of the cherry trees, that were only symbolically true and might not have actually happened. This is what Docter has done. Through reading her biography we find the real person who somehow managed to find herself and start a challenge to concepts of sex and gender that are still being explored. It is important to have as realistic an account of her as possible. The little white lies she told and her modification of her own history need to be put in perspective as part of an accurate account of who she was. It is only through research such as Docter has done that we can begin to better understand her.

*Vern Bullough, PhD

---

*Vern Leroy Bullough was born in Salt Lake City, Utah, on July 24, 1928, and died at his home in Westlake Village, California, on June 21, 2006. He was the author of fifty-five books and hundreds of articles and book reviews.

Acknowledgments

Three Christine Jorgensen scholars, Vern Bullough, C. Jacob Hale, and Joanne Meyerowitz, helped me in many ways, both through their published historical contributions and with encouragement and counsel; their insights and grasp of the Jorgensen story and of its cultural impact are reflected throughout this book. The exceptionally generous assistance of Brenda Lana Smith, R. af D., helped to open doors, provided much documentation, and added significantly to the understanding of Christine Jorgensen, especially during the final years of her life. Brenda was referred to me by her good friend, Sister Mary Elizabeth, OSM. Sister Mary first met Christine through Jude Patton, and all three have been exceptionally helpful to me.

Several members of the Jorgensen family shared meals, showed me family photographs and letters, and provided impressions of their famous in-law. I am most grateful to each of them. My first contact with family members was with Marilyn Courtney, one of Christine's third cousins. She described her childhood holidays among the Jorgensens and the vacations and cruises she shared with Christine. Marilyn's sister, Kay Bryson, was also very helpful. Marilyn put me in touch with Stanton Bahr who had for several decades been one of Christine's closest admirers and friends, and with Vincent and Georgiana Manno who were close friends of Jorgensen's parents. My thanks go to each of them.

One of Christine's closest friends throughout her life was her cousin, Robert Andersen, who along with his wife, Amelia, did all they could to help me both by meeting with me and through many telephone conversations. Another cousin, Ann Hope Fisher, responded to my questions using e-mail. The willingness of each of these individuals to cooperate by adding to the historical record of Christine Jorgensen's life is especially important because few of her personal letters have survived. For example, the extensive correspondence between Christine and her parents during her years in Copenhagen is

Becoming a Woman: A Biography of Christine Jorgensen
© 2008 by The Haworth Press, Taylor & Francis Group. All rights reserved.
doi:10.1300/5896_b

nowhere to be found. Several libraries with Jorgensen holdings have been very helpful.

Ivan Boserup and his associates at the Danish Royal Library were of great importance to me as I reviewed their massive collection of the Christine Jorgensen papers. Within the Library's Photographic Division, Anne Dyhr was especially helpful along with many of her assistants. The library at my own academic home, California State University, Northridge, also has extensive Christine Jorgensen materials that are part of the Vern and Bonnie Bullough Collection on Sex and Gender. At Northridge, the Special Collections librarian is Tony Gardner who is both a good friend and a highly valued guide to this collection. My special thanks go to Preben Hertoft and Jesper Hamburger in Copenhagen; each of them provided unusually valuable information and documentation.

Ned Comstock of the Cinema-Television Library of the University of Southern California brought to my attention a fifty-year-old article in the *Los Angeles Times* that was very important in untangling how the Jorgensen story was initially publicized in 1952. Ned also made available the biography of movie producer Edward Small and his production records for the 1970 feature film, *The Christine Jorgensen Story*. Karen Petersen, a reference librarian at the Screen Writers Guild, helped to track down some of the facts about the makers of the Jorgensen film, as did screenwriter Malcom Marmorstein.

At Indiana University, the archives of the Kinsey Institute for Research in Sex, Gender and Reproduction retain more Jorgensen documentation than any other resource in this country, and fortunately for me, librarian Liana Zhou went the extra mile to make these materials available. Kinsey Art Curator, Catherine Johnson-Roehr also led me to Jorgensen holdings that were exceptionally valuable. In San Francisco, I received the full cooperation of the Gay and Lesbian Library and Archives and the same was true at the International Gay and Lesbian Archives in Los Angeles. John Hotchner of the Office of Passport Services, Department of State, was a great help in providing the history of information required on U.S. passports. So did Christopher Basinger, a good friend of Christine's during the final decades of her life. At the peak of Christine's 1953 publicity, transgender organizer and scholar Virginia Prince managed to arrange a personal interview with Jorgensen and her mother while they were staying at a Los Angeles hotel. Many thanks go to Virginia for her impressions of a youthful Christine Jorgensen. Several of my friends from the International Foundation for Gender Education also helped to fill out the story. Sincere thanks to Alison Laing, Yvonne Cook Riley, Jane Fee, Jill Reed, and Sheila Church. Moton Holt was an especially welcoming and cooperative contributor.

Childhood friends of Christine's generously shared their recollections. Thanks go to Donald Luedemann, Bruce Silver, Lillian Bellochi Abbott, Mary Reilly, and Danny Riley. Maureen Sullivan still lives on Dudley Avenue close to the Jorgensen home, and thanks go to her for putting me in touch with most of these folks.

I'm very grateful to others who assisted me, including Milton and Connie Diamond, Alissa Haggis, David King, Richard Ekins, Elizabeth Levitt, Mariette Pathy Allen, Sandy Thomas, Raymond Strait, Stanley Harris, Walter L. Williams, Valdis Volkovskis, Paul S. Eriksson, Gloria Hassman, Andrea Horkovelle, and Richard W. Smith. Christine Belanger enhanced the photographs I selected by using digital photo editing. I am especially grateful to Mary Beth Madden at The Haworth Press for her fine judgment as a copy editor. I also want to acknowledge my teachers and mentors: Fred Marer, Robert Gottsdanker, Calvin Stone, Leland Winder, and Wendell Wilkin.

Several people read drafts of the manuscript and provided extensive editorial guidance. I am highly in debt to the late Vern Bullough, Joanne Meyerowitz, Janis Walworth, June Bennett Larsen, C. Jacob Hale, Brenda Lana Smith, and Warren Bayless. But the person who invested the greatest effort, patience, and thoughtful criticism throughout this project and to whom I am most indebted is my wife, Shirley Long Docter.

Introduction

C. Jacob Hale

"Ex-GI Becomes Blonde Beauty: Operations Transform Bronx
Youth" blared the front-page headline of the *New York Daily News* on
December 1, 1952. The first report told the story of the transformation of a twenty-six-year-old New Yorker, George Jorgensen Jr., into
Christine Jorgensen which occurred through a series of hormone
injections and operations in Copenhagen. The story centered on
Jorgensen's attractive appearance, her happiness and optimism, and
her parents' bewildered yet loving reactions to the news. This and
similar accounts were carried around the world by the wire services,
and it literally knocked the hydrogen bomb tests at Eniwetok off the
front pages of America's newspapers.

Today, Jorgensen's name is unknown to many under the age of
thirty—even to many who are themselves transgendered—but in the
1950s her name shone as brightly as any. Worldwide fascination with
Jorgensen's story catapulted change-of-sex status from an occasional
curiosity item to a flood of newspaper ink. This not only changed the
arena of possibilities for those with cross-gendered feelings but it
also raised profound questions about the meanings of sex, gender,
and sexuality. In *Becoming a Woman: A Biography of Christine
Jorgensen,* Richard F. Docter offers us a lively account of that "pretty
blond girl in a topsy turvy new world," as the *Los Angeles Times*
styled her in 1953. Docter's book is based on interviews with many of

For useful conversations, sharing unpublished material, archival assistance, and/or
editorial help, I am grateful to Aleshia Brevard, Katherine Cummings, Aaron Devor,
Richard F. Docter, Tony Gardner, Robert S. Hill, Nicholas Matte, Joanne Meyerowitz,
Peter N. Nardi, Earl F. Nation, Jude Patton, Robert J. Pondillo, Don Romesburg, Nancy
E. Stoller, Susan Stryker, Stuart Timmons, Alicia Vogl Saenz, and Richard Wheeler.

her surviving relatives, friends, and professional associates, and extensive archival research, yet he presents a vibrant picture of her life, fully accessible to nonacademic readers. Jorgensen's story, as Docter tells it, is still fresh and important today. I am honored to introduce this book, to give you a taste of what lies in the pages ahead and to highlight the significance of Jorgensen's story.

The first articles in December 1952 suggested that Jorgensen had been a physically normal male who became, through a miracle of medical science, a white American ideal: a beautiful, glamorous, graceful, blonde woman with a tightly knit middle-class family, and a face and figure fit for the silver screen! But in Jorgensen's letter to her family, published with or excerpted in several articles, she wrote that nature had made a mistake—a glandular imbalance had become apparent at puberty—which she had had corrected. Christian Hamburger, Jorgensen's Danish endocrinologist, and his colleagues would not talk to the press. Reporters scrambled to get expert opinions from American physicians. Although they had no specific information about Jorgensen's case, many associated it with the kinds of cases that were familiar to them.

What was the truth of George's alteration to Christine? Was this science or science fiction? Could a physically normal male really become a woman? Had human dominion over nature finally gone too far? Modern medicine had recently triumphed over many diseases, but the world had witnessed the ferocious power of the atom unleashed on Hiroshima and Nagasaki, and the nation was worried about the looming possibility of its use in Korea. What did it mean for a man to be transformed into a woman? Was Christine really a woman now? Had she ever really been a man? What makes a woman a woman, what makes a man a man? Why would anybody want to do such a thing? Did very many other people want to do the same thing? What would happen to society if they did? What did "sex transformation" have to do with sexual and political deviance, especially homosexuality? There was still widespread consternation about Alfred Kinsey's 1948 report that more than one-third of American adult males had experienced orgasm with other men. Early homophile organizations were decried by law enforcement and the press, and Senator Joseph McCarthy was forging links between homosexuality and Communism in the popular imagination.

With such a tempest of questions, and so much cultural weight placed on one individual's victory over personal anguish and adversity, it was perhaps predictable that Jorgensen would receive a tremendous amount of attention, even though she was not the first person, or even the first American, to undergo hormonal and surgical sex transformation. And did she ever receive attention! Reporters sent out 50,000 words about her through the wire services between December 1 and Christmas, and many movie fans who missed this print coverage saw her story in a newsreel shown before their feature films. Despite the hydrogen bomb tests, the stalemated war in Korea, the election and inauguration of President Dwight D. Eisenhower, and Jonas Salk's research on a cure for polio, there was still space for Jorgensen in the newspapers in the new year. She was the "world's most talked about figure" by May 4, 1953, according to the *Los Angeles Times.*

Like some popular show business and sports personalities and a few politicians, Jorgensen quickly became recognizable by her first name alone. Shortly after her return to the United States in February of 1953, Jorgensen went to police headquarters in Garden City, Long Island, to get a driver's license. The *New York Journal-American* ran its coverage of this earth-shattering event under the headline "Christine After Driver's License," the *New York World-Telegram and Sun* called its story "Christine's Road Block Ends," the *New York Journal-American* reported "Christine Takes Driver's License Test—and Drives," and the *Los Angeles Times'* photo caption was headlined simply "It's Christine." At the end of the decade, when reports of Jorgensen's attempt to get a marriage license were carried across the country by the wire services, the *Los Angeles Mirror* headlined "Ex-Man Christine's Matrimony Delayed," and, across the continent, editors at the *Newark Star-Ledger* declared "Christine Can't Prove It, So. . .". Stand-up comic Whitey Roberts japed: "Christine's Danish surgeon . . . won the *no-ball* prize." Indeed, even the name "Christine" was more than enough: references to "Denmark" appeased the censors, such as the television executives who would not allow any mention of Jorgensen, while still letting comedians invoke her in their routines. Because they ad-libbed on live television, comedians were able to push the boundaries farther than network policies might have allowed, as Bob Hope and Jack Benny did in a live sketch on Benny's CBS show in the summer of 1953. Benny and Hope, in jungle explorer drag, captured a tiger that turned out to be a leopard. Hope remarked that the tiger "must have gone to a veterinarian in Denmark." The *Long Beach Independent* gave this preview of the November 4, 1954, episode of *Lassie:*

> NEAT TRICK—"Lassie" . . . gives birth to a litter of pups in the episode tonight and it is up to young Jeff Miller to set out in a storm to find a veterinarian to assist. But the neatest trick of the year is Lassie's giving birth to 10 puppies for, you know, Lassie is really a male dog and has never been to Denmark.

Christine Jorgensen jokes abounded, the tabloids ran scurrilous stories, some mainstream media were openly dubious of Jorgensen's claim to womanhood, and her femininity was under the microscope, but much of the publicity she got was complimentary.

After a false start showing a color travelogue film she had made about Denmark, Jorgensen was able to parlay the media attention into a successful career as an entertainer. Early help came from Walter Winchell, America's most influential newspaper columnist and broadcaster. Winchell had previously claimed that he had a "scoop": Jorgensen was a transvestite, not a woman at all. He had also declared her appearance suitable for the Harvard Hasty Pudding show, which are burlesque musicals full of crude jokes and collegiate puns in which all the performers are male. Despite his earlier jabs, Winchell convinced Jorgensen to appear at a Madison Square Garden fundraiser he organized and hosted to benefit the widows and families of New York firefighters and police officers killed in the line of duty. He insisted that the comics on the bill, including Milton Berle and Jackie Gleason, would refrain from getting a laugh "poking fun at her or putting a hand-on-the-hip or mincing around like a whoopsy." The next month she also appeared on dance king Arthur Murray's television show on behalf of Winchell's charity, The Damon Runyon Cancer Fund.

With the help of manager Charles Yates, who had represented Bob Hope, and former vaudevillian Myles Bell, Jorgensen developed a nightclub act in which she danced a little, sang a little, chattered a little, told a few jokes, and changed her costume any number of times behind an on-stage screen. She rapidly donned a compelling stage presence and an adept sense of timing, although she was not a very accomplished singer or dancer. One of her gag writers was Garry

Marshall, who later wrote for Joey Bishop and Jack Paar and has since made many popular hit movies and TV shows.

Always concerned with maintaining an image of respectability in terms of values embraced America's white middle-class, partly because she was acutely aware of her symbolic importance as a representative of others who shared her cross-gender feelings, Jorgensen insisted that her nightclub act remain free of tasteless and vulgar material. She admitted that prurient, exploitative curiosity was an element in drawing audiences to her shows, but was proud that they left entertained and edified rather than titillated by a display of "sex change" exotica. A careful balancing act was necessary for Jorgensen to maintain her dignity and self-respect on stage, while taking into account the audience's initial reason for attending and not boring them with pedantic lectures on the science of sex. Her repertoire included the songs "It's a Change" and "The Powder Room," which invoked the experiences that first brought her into the limelight and which made serious points about societal change while staying lighthearted and humorous. And, while Bell was reputed to be the only comedian in America who did not tell Christine Jorgensen jokes, Jorgensen quipped about herself and other performers made mild Jorgensen cracks; one went: "What's that you want to know? How did I like Christine Jorgensen? Loved her—hated him!"

Although the press coverage slowed down as the 1950s moved on, Jorgensen remained in public view for most of her lifetime. Mike Wallace commented in his 1959 interview with her that "the headlines have been telling of the comings and goings of Christine Jorgensen ever since December 1, 1952." Jorgensen enjoyed considerable, though inconsistent, success as an entertainer during the 1950s and into the early 1960s. Her earning power jumped as high as $10,000 for a weeklong engagement. She concocted ideas for success on the silver screen, but none ever panned out. Jorgensen had largely dropped from public view by the middle of the 1960s, concentrating instead on summer theater. She reemerged when *Christine Jorgensen: A Personal Autobiography* was published in 1967, and again in 1970 when the movie *The Christine Jorgensen Story,* in which she did not appear, was released—to critical disdain. This was followed by a stint on the college lecture circuit "Christine Jorgensen Sets the Record Straight," and occasional nightclub appearances in the late 1970s and the 1980s.

Her death in 1989 at age sixty-two of bladder cancer garnered extensive media coverage.

Jorgensen told her own story in 1953 in a five-part series in *The American Weekly,* a supplement to the Hearst Sunday papers, in her 1967 autobiography, and in numerous interviews and public appearances. These self-representations, however, were ultimately *unre-vealing* in many ways. Her romantic and sexual life—a topic about which she was repeatedly pressed—was fodder for speculation in gossip tabloids like *Confidential,* to well-respected newspapers.

Many other questions remain. Was there any basis for her claim that she had a glandular imbalance? Was she inspired by the examples of those who had earlier undergone medical treatment to achieve bodily and social change? Michael Dillon, a British physician whose 1946 *Self: A Study in Ethics and Endocrinology* did not disclose his own transsexual (female to male) status, advanced the thesis that when the mind cannot be made to fit the body, the body should be made to fit the mind. A book about a "change of sex" in which Danish painter Einar Wegener became Lili Elbe through medical treatments in Germany had been published in English in 1933. Furthermore, many have long doubted some aspects of Jorgensen's story as she told it herself. She claimed to have been stunned and confused when, while still in the hospital recovering from surgery in 1952, she was confronted by journalists clamoring for copy, and throughout her life she maintained a public stance of anger about this "betrayal." But there has long been speculation that she might have "dropped the dime" herself. Many have also been dubious of her claim that she did not dress in women's clothes until she had changed her sex on her passport, thereby abiding by legal and social proprieties. A history of wearing women's clothes is such a standard part of the life histories of most male-to-female transsexuals that it has seemed unlikely to many that Jorgensen would not have done so.

Docter shares the skepticism of many about Jorgensen's telling of her own story. But he still provides a sympathetic portrait of her, gives credible answers to many of the remaining questions about her, and unearths the complexities of a woman who represented herself as monochromatic despite her lifelong interest in color photography.

Jorgensen, of course, had immediate and powerful significance for others with cross-gender feelings, for to them, she was a very public example that it might be possible to realize their dreams. Furthermore, Jorgensen's charm, poise, beauty, dignity, and self-respect, and her family's acceptance, gave others reason to believe that actualizing their dreams could be compatible with living productive, respectable lives. She was flooded with letters from thousands of people interested in sex transformation for themselves, on a scale unprecedented by earlier subjects of media reports. So were her Danish physicians, other doctors whom the letter writers thought might have information or be able to help, and popular medical and sexological writers, to such an extent that some felt themselves to be under siege.

Before medical treatment in Copenhagen, Jorgensen had sought treatment in the United States without much success. She initiated her own process of transformation by obtaining female hormones, letting her hair grow longer, and wearing androgynous clothing while practicing a feminine style of self-presentation. Drawing from the work of German sexologist Magnus Hirschfeld, whose Institute for Sexual Science in Berlin had been burned by the Nazis in 1933, endocrinologist Christian Hamburger diagnosed Jorgensen as a "genuine transvestite" and vowed to help her. The medical protocol used by Hamburger and his colleagues to treat Jorgensen became known—and a source of ethical controversy—both in medicine and the general public. In the broadest outlines, this protocol consisted of three stages: extensive psychiatric and physiological examination, medically supervised treatment with female hormones to effect a reversible "chemical castration," and, when that was insufficient to relieve her distress, gonadal and genital surgeries to transform her external anatomy to that of a female. Hamburger believed that a successful outcome required not only social and bodily alteration but also formal recognition by legal authorities that a transformation had indeed been accomplished, and he helped her to gain such recognition through the issuance of a new U.S. passport. Over the next two decades, this protocol, with some minor changes, became the standard for the treatment of transsexual patients. Many, but not all, transsexuals now object to the medicalization of transsexuality because of the stigma of psychiatric diagnoses and the assault to autonomy entailed by requiring the go-ahead of mental health professionals before hormonal and surgical treatment. However, the protocol for sex transformation to which the Jorgensen phenomenon brought wide attention was an important step in the expansion of the possibilities for the use of hormones and surgeries to accomplish such changes.

As early as 1949, New York- and San Francisco-based endocrinologist Harry Benjamin had been seeking a surgeon to operate on a patient who felt driven to change sex (male to female), but he had been unable to find surgical help for her in the United States. The explosion of interest in the Jorgensen case, and perhaps the publication of English-language medical journal articles about the case by Hamburger and his associates, helped bring Benjamin success in this quest. Elmer Belt was a highly skilled and inventive Los Angeles urologist who was also renowned for the pivotal role he played in the establishment of the medical school at the University of California, Los Angeles, and as a collector of DaVinciana. In late 1953, he became the first consistent option in the United States for male-to-female genital alteration—at least for those who could afford his fees. He continued to hold this position until 1962, when he ended this part of practice at the insistence of his wife and son, Bruce, a urologist who practiced in his father's clinic. During this period, a few transsexuals, such as Hedy Jo Star in Memphis, were able to find surgeons who did not make sex conversion part of their practices. Some transsexuals resorted to self-castration as a first step toward obtaining more extensive genital surgery because legal opinion held that otherwise surgeons might be subject to prosecution for "mayhem"—just as for elective vasectomy on nontranssexual men. Belt avoided this legal risk by implanting the testicles into the abdomen.

The Jorgensen phenomenon was an important impetus to community organization. Certainly, there were social and correspondence networks of people with cross-gender feelings prior to December 1, 1952. But, Jorgensen became an immediate point of reference: "How am I like Christine?" and "How am I different from Christine?" suddenly were compelling questions, pressed both internally and externally.

During the 1950s, others who claimed to be seeking or to have obtained surgical alteration of the genitals—Ray/Rae Bourbon, John "Bunny" Breckenridge, Dixie MacLane, Charlotte MacLeod, and Tamara Rees, for example—were in the news. They all compared themselves, and were compared by journalists, to Jorgensen. Networks grew on their own. Moreover, physicians such as Benjamin and Belt brought together both transsexual patients and those with cross-gender urges who disavowed desire for transformative surgery.

At the time the news about Jorgensen hit the headlines, Virginia Prince participated in a local network of transvestites that centered around Johnny/Joan/Joanne Thornton in Long Beach and communicated with Louise Lawrence and Alvin S. Harris in the San Francisco Bay Area. The Long Beach group had published a couple of mimeographed newsletters, titled *Transvestia,* in early 1952. Prince wrote to Jorgensen and later recalled that she would have hopped onto the first ship to Europe if she could have afforded it. In 1960, Prince restarted *Transvestia* as a continuously published magazine that ran to 100 editions before her retirement as editor in 1980. In 1961, after sending invitations to every cross-dresser she knew in the Los Angeles area, she founded the Hose and Heel Society, which developed into The Foundation for the Full Personality Expression and, later, Tri-Ess, the Society for the Second Self. This grew into an international organization with chapters in many different locales, with other organizations forming as they splintered off from Prince's due to personality clashes and political and philosophical disagreements. Presently, the International Foundation for Gender Education's highest award is the Virginia Prince Award, which is given annually to one transgender person who has made a significant lifetime contribution to the transgender community over a fifteen-year span. Despite her early interest in undergoing "the Christine operation," as newswriters called it, Prince became vehemently anti-transsexual.

While Prince took great paints to distance herself and her organizations from both transsexuality and homosexuality, Reed Erickson acted upon a more inclusive vision. An eccentric multimillionaire who kept a pet leopard named Henry, he began female-to-male medical treatments with Benjamin in 1963 and founded the Erickson Educational Foundation (EEF) in 1964. EEF's goals were broad: "to provide assistance and support in areas where human potential was limited by adverse physical, mental or social conditions, or where the scope of research was too new, controversial or imaginative to receive traditionally oriented support." Although EEF placed a major emphasis on transsexuality, homosexuality and transvestism were also within its purview. To assist and support transsexuals and other gender variant people, EEF maintained an office in Baton Rouge, Louisiana, that functioned as a national clearinghouse for information and referrals. Free preliminary counseling was provided. EEF published a series of booklets about transsexuality, distributed a bibliography of reference materials and a biannual newsletter, and participated in the production of educational films.

It was not only Jorgensen's symbolic position, but also her participation in community events, that spurred community organizing. In the 1970s Jorgensen became friends with Joanna Clark (now Sister Mary Elizabeth) and Jude Patton. Working together as J2CP, Clark and Patton put out the newsletter *Renaissance,* which provided international news about gender variance from 1976 until 1983. Patton focused on educational appearances while Clark's major interest was in changing laws which hampered transsexuals in adjusting to or living in their new identities. Both provided limited peer counseling. Each summer, J2CP hosted a party; Jorgensen was often an honored guest. She also made occasional public appearances with Patton and Clark. For example, in 1974 she and Patton were "Transsexual Experience" panelists, along with two others, at the Century Plaza Hotel in Beverly Hills. With Clark, who chaired the Southern California American Civil Liberties Union's Transsexual Rights Committee, Jorgensen spoke about transsexual rights to the Southern California ACLU's Lesbian and Gay Rights Chapter in 1982.

The Jorgensen furor brought about a major increase in research about gender variance, including transsexuality. Five transsexuals participated in an early study conducted at University of California Los Angeles by psychoanalyst Frederic G. Worden and clinical psychologist James T. Marsh. Their article, published in the *Journal of the American Medical Association* in 1955, reached a negative conclusion: the subjects at first appeared to be "relatively well-adjusted persons, but, on closer inspection, it was found that they were quite disturbed." This study was linked to Jorgensen in the popular press, even though she had no connection to the Worden-Marsh research: in its coverage of this study, *Time* magazine's lead sentence referenced Jorgensen and it ran a picture of her. *The Long Beach Independent* headlined its story on the *JAMA* piece: "Note Desire to Escape All Sex Among Christine-Minded Men." Some of the study's subjects participated to advance the cause of public and medical acceptance. Dixie MacLane, who had been inspired to seek surgical transformation by the news about Jorgensen, had a more pragmatic goal: she hoped that her participation might lead to surgery at UCLA. When a committee at UCLA decided against transsexual surgery and the Worden-Marsh study was released, she felt used and betrayed by the UCLA scientists.

At the time MacLane sought surgery at UCLA, Elmer Belt's favorite nephew, Willard E. Goodwin, was the first chairman of urology at the new UCLA medical school his uncle had helped to establish. Before returning to Los Angeles to accept this appointment, Goodwin had worked at Johns Hopkins University with some of urology's most prominent practitioners. He was the last resident in urologic surgery under Dr. Hugh Hampton Young, who is generally regarded as the father of modern urology and who had a special interest in surgical alteration of the genitals of intersexed people. When the Gender Identity Research Clinic (GIRC) was established in the Department of Psychiatry in 1962, Goodwin was a member. Later, psychiatrists Robert Stoller and Richard Green were influential directors of the GIRC. The GIRC neither provided nor officially recommended surgery for transsexuals, and its professional reputation was primarily built on its attempts to inculcate traditional gender roles in order to prevent homosexuality, transvestism, and transsexuality. But the GIRC's widespread professional reputation inspired other university-based researchers to form gender identity centers, some of which—for instance, Johns Hopkins, Stanford, and University of Minnesota—did begin to perform transsexual surgery in the late 1960s and early 1970s. The Erickson Educational Foundation provided research funding to the Johns Hopkins program and to Benjamin, which enabled the 1966 publication of Benjamin's groundbreaking *The Transsexual Phenomenon.* This book served multiple functions. For transsexuals, it provided a road map on which to plot a route to medical services. For professionals, including lawmakers and public servants as well as social workers and health care professionals, it gave concrete information about how to meet the needs of transsexual citizens, clients, and patients so they could lead productive lives. For the general reading public, it framed transsexuality and crossdressing within a tradition of liberal scientific humanism.

In addition to funding physicians' research, Erickson donated substantial sums to ONE, Inc., beginning in 1964. Founded in 1952 in Los Angeles to advance acceptance of homophile men and women, ONE established three important publications, ran national and international social services out of its cramped office, and sponsored lecture series, conferences, and college- and graduate-level courses on topics related to homosexuality. A staggeringly important early accomplishment was ONE's 1958 victory against the Los Angeles postmaster in the United State Supreme Court: for the first time, mere homosexual content in a magazine was not obscene and, therefore, could be sent through the U.S. mail. When Erickson first started donating to ONE, he suggested that the corporation set up a tax-exempt, nonprofit organization to attract more donors; this became the Institute for the Study of Human Resources (ISHR), over which Erickson presided until 1977. ISHR, among its many activities, was an institutionalized vehicle through which transsexuals and cross-dressers came together with gay men and lesbians for seminars and conferences—though not always without acrimony. In 1974, for example, a notable ISHR conference on "variant sex behavior" was organized by historians Vern and Bonnie Bullough in Los Angeles. This conference brought together Christine Jorgensen, Virginia Prince, EEF's director Zelda Suplee, author and sociologist Laud Humphreys, eminent gay novelist Christopher Isherwood, and UCLA psychologist Evelyn Hooker, whose research on gay men outside of clinic settings is widely acknowledged as crucial to the change in psychiatric attitudes that resulted in the American Psychiatric Association's 1973 decision to remove homosexuality from its diagnostic manual of mental disorders. Evening entertainment options included a transvestite show. Jorgensen presented the closing lecture at ISHR's 1975 "Sex, Role and Gender" conference. The Bulloughs' association with Erickson included funding for their research on sex and gender variance and for the collection of materials on human sexuality and gender that they donated to the Oviatt Library's Special Collections and Archives at California State University, Northridge. This collection is an invaluable resource for students and scholars of transgender history, as is that at the ONE Institute, now located near the University of Southern California.

The naming of transsexuality was another important change initiated by the publicity about Jorgensen. This shift in terminology helped expand the possibilities for physical, social, and legal change of sex status. When Hamburger called Jorgensen a "genuine transvestite," he did not mean merely that Jorgensen was a man who wanted to wear women's clothes. In European medical circles, transvestism included both cross-dressing urges and cross-gender identification. Hamburger felt that the diagnosis of genuine transvestism was justified in cases of cross-gender identification that was secondary neither to homosexuality nor to fetishistic desires.

Hirschfeld had used the phrase "seelischer Transsexualismus" (psychic transsexualism) in his 1923 essay "Die Intersexuelle Konstitution." Kinsey and his colleagues had used the word "transsexual" "as one of a number of terms applied to homosexuality and embodying an 'intermediate sex' conception of that phenomenon" in their 1948 *Sexual Behavior in the Human Male.* David O. Cauldwell used "transexual" to refer to a person with a "pathologic-morbid desire to be a full member of the opposite sex" in his 1949 *Sexology* article "Psychopathia Transexualis." But it was not until Benjamin's 1953 and 1954 publications in, respectively, the *International Journal of Sexology* and the *American Journal of Psychotherapy* that the word "transsexual" started to catch on. Even then, "transsexual" did not come into wide usage outside of medical and sexological discourse until the end of decade. During the 1950s, Jorgensen and her doctors referred to her case as one of true, real or genuine transvestism. She later thought this language unfortunate, and indeed it was in the United States, since most American physicians did not have the concept of a genuine transvestite. For them, and the journalists who relied upon their authority, there were only two, mutually exclusive possibilities: either Jorgensen was a hermaphrodite or else Jorgensen was a transvestite. If Jorgensen was a hermaphrodite, there was nothing remarkable about her transformation. If Jorgensen was a transvestite, she was merely a man disguised as a woman, which, though pathological, was not unusual and certainly did not warrant all the fuss and confusion in the media; the only factor that made her case unusual was the collusion of her Danish physicians in the masquerade. In this conception, the feelings and urges that led Jorgensen to live as a woman were irrelevant.

This conception was expressed most fully in a four-part exposé by the *New York Post's* Alvin Davis that was widely advertised and featured in a number of other U.S. newspapers during April 1953. For Davis, the reason Jorgensen was physically a normal male was that Jorgensen, unlike hermaphrodites and pseudo-hermaphrodites, did not have any undeveloped female sex organs; although he did not name the sex organs in question, it is obvious from his article that he meant ovaries. Therein was a simple answer to the question, perplexing to so many in both 1952 and contemporary America, about what ultimately makes a man a man and what ultimately makes a woman a woman: it's the gonads. Testicular tissue makes a man a man, ovarian tissue makes a woman a woman.

But why Jorgensen felt an irresistible urge to wear women's clothes—and why wearing women's clothes wasn't enough for her— is precisely the heart of the matter: she felt like a woman and wanted to be one. This led immediately to a crisis among some who just wanted to be left alone to present themselves as they pleased, whether some of the time or all of the time. How were they to distinguish themselves from those like Jorgensen, those who wanted not just to be left alone but to obtain medical assistance in living lives that more accurately reflected their own feelings about themselves? Answering this question, and engendering public acceptance to be left alone, were the twin burdens of Edward D. Wood, Jr.'s 1953 film *Glen or Glenda.* The question remained alive in cross-dressers' organizations such as those headed by Virginia Prince, and in the work of physicians such as Harry Benjamin. It remains alive today, for example, in a recent controversy between the Los Angeles Police Department (LAPD), local mainstream media, and trans activists about whether a preoperative male-to-female murder victim should be counted as a transsexual "she" or a transvestite "he"—evidently the only choices for the LAPD and some local mainstream news outlets.

There is no more consensus now about how to answer these questions than there was when they became so pressing on December 1, 1952. Is it gender identity—what one feels one's own gender is? Is it gonads? Is it hormones? Is it genitals? Is it chromosomes? Is it legal status as male or female? Is it whether one is accepted socially as a man or a woman? Is it the sex to which one was assigned at birth? A combination of those factors? Something else entirely?

Who gets to decide? Is it up to biologists? Doctors? Pscyhologists? Elected or appointed governmental officials? Journalists? Society at large? The transgendered community? Each individual alone? Or, is it up to each one of us as an individual embedded within the multiple communities that make up our lives, our selves, and the meanings of bodies and our actions?

Christine Jorgensen, whether she initially meant to or not, brought these questions to the forefront of public and professional consciousness. She refused to let them die. She accepted her position in the cultural imagination as the primary symbolic embodiment of transsexuality, despite the inevitable objectification of such a position. Through her life she insisted that everyone is both female and male—an idea quite peculiar in America though not in mid-century Europe. In public she maintained her grace and her sense of humor—at least most of the time—while other people tried to answer these questions using her life and her body for their own purposes, often with little regard for her humanity.

Using the conceptual and material resources available to her, she exercised agency by adapting those resources to her own desires and thereby she changed those resources in the process. From the resources available to her she crafted an understanding of herself, rather than merely accepting a conception handed to her by medical or juridical authority figures. She stuck to her sense of herself in the face of an incredible array of forces that could have erased her had she not been so resolute, mentally quick, and dignified. She creatively used her position to expand the horizon of possibilities for us all.

Skoal, Christine!

Skoal to you as well, Richard, for bringing us so much more understanding of this influential and inspiring pioneer.

Bibliography

Archival Collections

CJC: Christine Jorgensen Collection, Danish Royal Library, Copenhagen, Denmark.

GHP: Gay History Project, in Vern and Bonnie Bullough Special Collection on Sex and Gender, Special Collections and Archives, Oviatt Library, California State University, Northridge.

HWC: Harris-Wheeler Collection, in Vern and Bonnie Bullough Special Collection on Sex and Gender, Special Collections and Archives, Oviatt Library, California State University, Northridge.

ONE Institute, Los Angeles, California.

VPC/N: Virginia Prince Collection/Newsclippings, in Vern and Bonnie Bullough Special Collection on Sex and Gender, Special Collections and Archives, Oviatt Library, California State University, Northridge.

Unauthored Sources

"Altered Ego," *Time* (April 18, 1955), in ONE Institute, Subject File "Jorgensen, Christine."

"Another Ex-GI Is Changed Into a 'Woman' in Denmark," *San Francisco Chronicle,* February 25, 1954, in VPC/N, Box 1/6.

"Another 'Man' Changes Sex, Name to Dixie," *Keyhole* (December 1st Issue, 1955), n.p., in ONE Institute, Subject File "MacLane, Dixie (Earl)."

"Angeleno Who Switched Sex Has Name Changed," *Los Angeles Times,* November 9, 1955, in VPC/N, Box 5/6.

"Army Vet Changes to Blonde Female, N. Y. Paper Says," n.p., December 1, 1952, in VPC/N, Box 1/6.

"Arthur Murray Party . . . Tonight," Advertisement, *New York Times,* April 5, 1953.

"Becoming of Two Men," *The Advocate* 41 (July 3, 1974): 14.

"Breckinridge in Hollywood," *San Francisco Examiner,* May 15, 1954, in VPC/N, Box 1/6.

"Bronx 'Boy' Is Now a Girl," *New York Times,* December 2, 1952.

"'Bunny' Buys Marching Cad," *San Francisco Examiner,* May 16, 1954, in VPC/N, Box 1/6.

"Cal. Millionaire Tells Plans for Sex Change Movie," *Los Angeles Herald and Express,* May 8, 1954, in VPC/N, Box 5/6.

"Changes Sex," Photograph with caption, *Los Angeles Daily News,* December 2, 1952, in VPC/N, Box 1/6.

"'Charlotte', Once Charles, Returns to Dyersburg," *Huntsville Times,* May 13, 1954, in VPC/N, Box 1/6.

"Charles is now Miss Charlotte," *Daily Sketch,* February 24, 1954, in ONE Institute, Subject File "Transsexuals VI."

"Christine After Driver's License," *New York Journal-American,* February 25, 1953, in VPC/N, Box 1/6.

"Christine Can't Prove It, So. . .," *Newark Star-Ledger,* April 4, 1959, in ONE Institute, Subject File "Jorgensen, Christine."

"Christine Gets Applause at Theater Debut," *Los Angeles Times,* May 9, 1953.

"Christine Finds World Changes With Her," *Los Angeles Times,* December 2, 1977, in ONE Institute, Subject File "Jorgensen, Christine."

"Christine Changes, and So Have Times," *Los Angeles Times,* December 1, 1977, in ONE Institute, Subject File "Jorgensen, Christine."

"Christine Jorgensen: A Personal Autobiography," Advertisement, *Los Angeles Times,* October 22, 1977.

"Christine Jorgensen Appearing at Engelbert's," *Data-Boy Magazine* (December 5, 1985), in ONE Institute, Subject File "Transsexuals VI."

"Christine Jorgensen Dies at 62," *San Francisco Examiner,* May 4, 1989, in ONE Institute, Subject File "Christine Jorgensen."

"Christine Jorgensen Is Off on a 20-City Tour," *Publishers Weekly,* August 8, 1968, in ONE Institute, Subject File "Christine Jorgensen."

"Christine Jorgensen Looks Back 25 Years," *San Francisco Chronicle,* December 2, 1977, in ONE Institute, Subject File "Transsexuals IV."

"Christine Will Reveal Plans for Future Life," *Los Angeles Times,* May 4, 1953.

"Christine Takes Driver's License Test—and Drives," *New York Journal-American,* February 25, 1953, in VPC/N, Box 1/6.

"Christine's Road Block Ends," *New York World-Telegram and Sun,* February 25, 1953, in VPC/N, Box 1/6.

"Competition for the Stars," Photograph with caption, *Pub-Scrantonian* (Pennsylvania), October 9, 1955, in VPC/N, Box 6/6.

"Court Makes It Official, Today He IS a Woman," n.p., n.d. (ca. November 8, 1955), in VPC/N, Box 4/6.

"Danish Officials Probe Latest Sex Operation," *Los Angeles Times,* April 19, 1954, in ONE Institute, Subject File "Transsexuals VI."

"Doctor in GI Sex Change Case Found," *San Francisco Examiner,* April 19, 1954, in VPC/N, Box 1/6.

"Doctor Tells Doing Two," n.p., n.d., (ca. February 1953), in ONE Institute, Subject File "Jorgensen, Christine."

"Dr. Elmer Belt," Obituary, *San Francisco Chronicle,* May 20, 1980.

"Dr. Willard E. Goodwin, A Life Remembered," Clark Urological Center Newsletter (University of California, Los Angeles, Medical School) 11:1 (Spring 1999): 1-2.

"Dutch Psychiatrist Says 'Tamara' Had Neurotic Desire to Be a Girl," *New York Post,* November 8, 1954, in VPC/N, Box 1/6.

"Ex-GI Now a Bride," *San Francisco News-Call Bulletin,* November 13, 1959, in VPC/N, Box 1/6.

"Ex-GI Who Became Bride Held on Check Charge," *Los Angeles Times,* August 28, 1955, in VPC/N, Box 1/6.

"Ex-GI's Case Called 'Extraordinary'," n.p., December 4, 1952, in VPC/N, Box 1/6.

"Ex-Man Christine's Matrimony Delayed," *Los Angeles Mirror,* March 31, 1959, in VPC/N, Box 1/6.

"Ex-Man Forgets She's a Lady. . .," Photograph with caption, *Los Angeles Mirror,* April 16, 1954, VPC/N, Box 1/6.

"Ex-Paratrooper, Now 'Bride' Through Aid of Surgery, on Honeymoon Tour," n.p., July 28, 1955, in VPC/N, Box 1/6.

"Ex-Soldier Tells of Change to Fair Sex," *Los Angeles Daily News,* December 1, 1952.

"Former GI Transformed Into Lovely Woman in Long Series of Treatments," *Los Angeles Times,* December 1, 1952.

"Former Soldier, Now a 'Bride', Fulfills Destiny at Long Last," *Los Angeles Mirror-News,* July 29, 1955, in VPC/N, Box 1/6.

"GI Who Became 'she' Denies Wedding Plans," *Los Angeles Times,* January 28, 1955, in VPC/N, Box 1/6.

"He (She) Asks Name Change," *Los Angeles Examiner,* October 14, 1955, in ONE Institute, Subject File "Transsexuals VI."

"Honeymoon After Sex Surgery," n.p., July 28, 1955, in VPC/N, Box 1/6.

"If Sex Changed, Do It Before School Age, Says Doctor," *Los Angeles Daily News,* December 4, 1952.

"In Christine's Footsteps," *Time* (March 8, 1954), in ONE Institute, Subject File "Transsexuals VI."

"Inside Report on Homosexuality in America," *People Today* 4:7 (March 26, 1952): 2-10.

"Is Christine Really A Man After All?," n.p., February 15, 1953, in VPC/N, Box 1/6.

"It's Christine," Photograph with caption, *Los Angeles Times,* February 26, 1953.

"Jorgensen Speaks on Transsexual Rights," Photograph with caption, ACLU Open Forum (Southern California American Civil Liberties Union), October 1982, in ONE Institute, Subject File "Jorgensen, Christine."

"Left U.S. as Mister, Comes Home a Miss," *Los Angeles Times,* February 13, 1953, in VPC/N, Box 1/6.

"Man Has Sex-Switch Operation, Flaunts Finery at Sad Cops," *Keyhole* (2nd March Issue, 1956), n.p., in ONE Institute, Subject File "MacLane, Dixie (Earl)."

"Man Who Became Woman Now Bride," n.p., July 28, 1955, in VPC/N, Box 1/6.

"Man Who Changed Sex to Woman Becomes Bride," *Tampa Morning Tribune,* July 29, 1955, in VPC/N, Box 1/6.

"'Man-Woman' Cleared of Masquerading," *Los Angeles Herald and Express,* February 14, 1956, in ONE Institute, Subject File "MacLane, Dixie (Earl)."

"Man-Woman Has Troubles," *Los Angeles Herald and Express,* August 23, 1955, in ONE Institute, Subject File "Transsexuals IV."

"Mr. Is Now Miss by Court Order," *Los Angeles Examiner,* November 9, 1955, in VPC/N, Box 5/6.

"Neat Trick—'Lassie'," *Long Beach Independent,* November 4, 1954, in ONE Institute, Subject File "Transsexuals VI."

"New Role for War Hero," n.p., n.d. (ca. 1954), in VPC/N, Box 1/6.

"New Sex Switches," People (May 5, 1954), n.p., in ONE Institute, Subject File Transsexuals IV.

"Note Desire to Escape All Sex Among Christine-Minded Men," *Long Beach Independent,* April 8, 1955, in ONE Institute, Subject File "Transsexuals VI."

"Office Clerk Cleared of Charge of Masquerading," *Los Angeles Times,* February 15, 1956, in VPC/N, Box 4/6.

"Paper Calls Christine Woman in Name Only," *Los Angeles Times,* April 7, 1953.

"Parents Will Stand by Son Changed to Woman," n.p., November 7, 1954, in VPC/N, Box 1/6.

"Police Seeking Tamara, Either Male or Female," *Los Angeles Mirror-News,* August 19, 1955, in VPC/N, Box 1/6.

"'Ray' Pulls a Christine, So Now, Please, It's 'Rae'," *Los Angeles Mirror,* March 23, 1956, in VPC/N, Box 5/6.

"'Real Me, Not Physical Me, Has Not Changed,'" n.p., December 1, 1952, in VPC/N, Box 1/6.

"Rich Socialite-Father to Become a Woman," *Los Angeles Mirror,* May 4, 1954, VPC/N, Box 5/6.

"S. F. Heir Plans Sex Surgery," *San Francisco Chronicle,* May 5, 1954, in VPC/N, Box 1/6.

"Second Ex-GI Becomes Woman," *Los Angeles Examiner,* February 25, 1954, in VPC/N, Box 1/6.

"Sex-Change 'Individual' Not Guilty," n.p., February 2, 1956, in ONE Institute, Subject "Sex Change Not Rare, U. S. Doctors Claim," *Los Angeles Mirror,* December 2, 1952.

"Sex Change Girl Back Home After Denmark Operations," *Los Angeles Herald and Express,* May 13, 1954, in ONE Institute, Subject File "Transsexuals VI."

"Sex Change Plan Stymied," *San Francisco Examiner,* May 5, 1954, in VPC/N, Box 1/6.

"Sex-Altered Christine to Become Bride," *Los Angeles Times,* May 31, 1959.

"Sex-Change Pioneer Dead of Cancer at 62," *Gallup Independent* (New Mexico), May 4, 1989, in ONE Institute, Subject File "Christine Jorgensen."

"Sex-Surgery Patient Whacks Photographer," *Los Angeles Times,* April 17, 1954, in ONE Institute, Subject File "Transsexuals VI."

"Sex-Switcher Home—She'll Tell All in Book," *Los Angeles Mirror,* May 13, 1954, in ONE Institute Subject File "Transsexuals VI."

"Strip City," Advertisement, n.p., n.d. (ca. 1955), in VPC/N, Box 1/6.

"Tamara Nabbed as Forger," *Los Angeles Herald and Express,* August 27, 1955, in VPC/N, Box 1/6.

"Tamara Rees Courtland. . .," Photograph with caption, *Kittanning Times* (Pennsylvania), September 1, 1953, in VPC/N, Box 1/6.

"Television," Drum (January 1, 1969), reprinted from *Women's Wear Daily,* in GHP, San Francisco, 1950s-1960s, Box 2/4.

"The Great Transformation," *Time* (December 15, 1952), in VPC/N, Box 1/6.

"The Tragedy of a Sex Changeling," *Pageant* 10:4 (October 1954): 114-121.

"The Truth about Christine Jorgensen . . . Mirror," Advertisement, *Los Angeles Times,* April 12, 1953.

"Today in the Mirror . . . The Truth about Christine Jorgensen," Advertisement, *Los Angeles Times,* April 13, 1953.

"Today's Best Bets: The Lid's Off—With Art Linkletter," *Los Angeles Times,* November 9, 1967.

"War II Vet, Father of 2, Woman Now," *Long Beach Independent,* November 11, 1954, in ONE Institute, Subject File Transsexuals VI."

"Well, Is it Dixie Belle or Dixie Bill?," *Los Angeles Mirror,* February 14, 1956, in VPC/N, Box 1/6.

"'Woman Freed From Man's Body' Wants Name Change," *Los Angeles Mirror-News,* November 9, 1955, in VPC/N, Box 5/6.

Authored Sources

Barton, William S., "Total Sex Change Called Impossible," *Los Angeles Times,* February 19, 1953.

Bayer, Ronald, *Homosexuality and American Psychiatry: The Politics of Diagnosis.* (Princeton: Princeton University Press, 1987).

Benjamin, Harry, "Transvestism and Transsexualism," *International Journal of Sexology* 7 (1953): 12-24.

Benjamin, Harry, "Transvestism and Transsexualism: A Symposium," *American Journal of Psychotherapy* 8 (1954): 219-230.

Benjamin, Harry, *The Transsexual Phenomenon.* (New York: Julian Press, 1966).

Bérubé, Allan, *Coming Out Under Fire: The History of Gay Men and Women in World War Two.* (New York: Free Press, 1990).

Boynoff, Sara, "Nature Seldom Errs in Determining Sex," *Los Angeles Daily News,* December 25, 1952.

Boynoff, Sara, "Strange Man-Woman Personality Told," *Los Angeles Daily News,* December 28, 1952, in VPC/N, Box 6/6.

Brevard, Aleshia, *The Woman I Was Not Born To Be: A Transsexual Journey.* (Philadelphia: Temple University Press, 2001).

Brevard, Aleshia Crenshaw, interviewed by Susan Stryker, August 2, 1977, Gay, Lesbian, Bisexual, Transgender Historical Society of Northern California, Oral History Collection #97-040.

Buckley, Peter, "The Christine Jorgensen Story," *Films and Filming* (December 1970), n.p., in ONE Institute, Subject File "Jorgensen, Christine."

Bullough, Vern L., "Virginia Prince (1913—)," in Vern L. Bullough, ed., *Before Stonewall: Activists for Gay and Lesbian Rights in Historical Context.* (Binghamton, NY: The Haworth Press, 2002): 372-375.

Bullough, Vern L., and Bonnie Bullough, *Cross Dressing, Sex and Gender.* (Philadelphia: University of Pennsylvania Press, 1993).

Bullough, Vern L., *Science in the Bedroom: A History of Sex Research.* (New York: Basic Books, 1994).

Capsuto, Steven, *Alternate Channels: The Uncensored Story of Gay and Lesbian Images on Radio and Television.* (New York: Ballantine Books, 2000).

Cauldwell, D. O., "Man Becomes Woman. . .," *Sexology* (March 1953): 494-502, in VPC/N, Box 1/6.

Cauldwell, D. O., "Psychopathia Transexualis," originally published in Sexology 16 (December 1949): 274-280, reprinted in *International Journal of Transgenderism* 5:2 (April—June 2001), available online at http://www.symposion.com/ijt/cauldwell/cauldwell_02.htm.

Cauldwell, D. O., "Transsexualis: Psychological Transsexualism," in *Questions and Answers Involving Sexual Ethics and Sexual Esthetics.* (Girard, Kansas: Haldeman-Julius Publications, 1950): 22-24.

Christopher, Don, "The Paratrooper Who Became a Stripper," *Cabaret 1: 9* (January 1956): 39-42, 47.

Crane, Lowell, "The Hush Hush Romance of Christine Jorgensen and a Vanderbilt Stepson," *Confidential* 2:5 (November 1954): 20-21, 49-50.

Cummings, Katherine, *Katherine's Diary: The Story of a Transsexual*. (Port Melbourne, Victoria: William Heinemann Australia, 1992).

D'Emilio, John, *Sexual Politics, Sexual Communities: The Making of a Homosexual Minority in the United States,* 1940-1970, second ed. (Chicago: University of Chicago Press, 1998).

Davis, Alvin, "Christine Woman in Name Only," *Los Angeles Mirror,* April 16, 1953, in VPC/N, Box 1/6.

Davis, Alvin, "'Christine' Jorgensen Is NOT a Woman," *Los Angeles Mirror,* n.d. (ca. April 1953), in VPC/N, Box 1/6.

Davis, Alvin, "'Christine' Woman in Name Only," *Los Angeles Mirror,* n.d. (ca. April 1953), in VPC/N, Box 1/6.

Davis, Alvin, "Doctor Says Christine Would Have Killed Self," *Los Angeles Mirror,* April 15, 1953, in VPC/N, Box 1/6.

Davis, Alvin, "The Truth about 'Christine' Jorgensen," *New York Post,* April 6, 1953, in HWC, Crossdressing, Finnochio's, etc., Box 1/1.

Devor, Aaron, and Nicholas Matte, "ONE Inc. and Reed Erickson: The Uneasy Collaboration of Gay and Trans Activism, 1964-2003." *GLQ: A Journal of Gay and Lesbian Studies,* 10:2 (2004): 179-209.

Devor, Holly [Aaron], "Reed Erickson (1917-1992): How One Transsexed Man Supported ONE," in Vern L. Bullough, ed., *Before Stonewall: Activists for Gay and Lesbian Rights in Historical Context.* (Binghamton, NY: The Haworth Press, 2002): 383-392.

Dillon, Michael, *Self: A Study in Ethics and Endocrinology.* (London: William Heinemann Medical Books, 1946).

Docter, Richard F., *From Man to Woman: The Transgender Journey of Virginia Prince.* (Northridge, CA: Docter Press, 2004).

Ecker, Beverly, "Christine Jorgensen: Still On Stage; Still Having No Doubts," *Easy Reader, Dining and Entertainment Guide* (Redondo Beach, California), September 8, 1983, in ONE Institute, Subject File "Christine Jorgensen."

Elbe, Lili, *Man into Woman: An Authentic Record of a Change of Sex. The True Story of the Miraculous Transformation of the Danish Painter, Einar Wegener.* Ed. by Neils Hoyer, trans. from the German by H. J. Stenning, intro. Norman Haire (New York: E.P. Dutton and Company, 1933).

Erickson Educational Foundation, Concerning the Erickson Educational Foundation. (Baton Rouge, Louisiana: Erickson Educational Foundation, n.d. [ca. 1972]), in ONE Institute, Subject File "Transsexuals II."

Faderman, Lillian, and Stuart Timmons, *Gay L. A.: A History of Sexual Outlaws, Power Politics, and Lipstick Lesbians.* (New York: Basic Books, 2006).

Feinberg, Leslie, "Christine Jorgensen, a Life of Courage and Dignity," *Workers World,* May 18, 1989, in ONE Institute, Subject File "Jorgensen, Christine."

Ferrero, Leo, "Christine's Theatre Debut Fails to Click," *New York Journal-American,* May 9, 1953, in VPC/N, Box 1/6.

Forchammer, Vernon, "Change N.Y. Vet's Sex From Man to Woman," *Los Angeles Herald and Express,* December 1, 1952, in VPCN, Box 1/6.

Forchammer, Vernon, "Ex-GI, Now Woman, Happy at Change in Sex," *Los Angeles Examiner,* December 1, 1952 in VPC/N, Box 1/6.

Geffner, David, "Wake Him When It's Funny!," *DGA Monthly* 26: 3 (September 2001); available online at http://www.dga.org/news/v26_3/feat_garrymarshall .php3.

Geiger, Jack, "Doctor Tells Amazing Story Of Reverse Sex Operations," *Los Angeles Herald and Express,* December 2, 1952, in VPC/N, Box 1/6.

Goodwin, Willard E., and Ralph R. Landes, "A Chat with Elmer Belt," *Urology* 10:4 (October 1977): 398-402.

Goodwin, Willard E., Gerald D. Leve, and Robert J. Stoller, "Sex Change Treatment: Medical and Social Aspects," Videorecording, UCLA Office of Instructional Development (1975), 60 min.

Hale, Walter, "Will the Baby Be as Batty as Its' Mother?," *Tomcat* 1:3 (1957), n.p.

Hamburger, Christian, "The Desire for Change of Sex as Shown by Personal Letters from 465 Men and Women," *Acta Endrocrinologica* 14:4 (1953): 361-375.

Hamburger, C., G. K. Stürup, and E. Dahl-Iversen, "Transvestism," *Journal of the American Medical Association* 152:5 (May 30, 1953): 391-396.

Hammond, Fay, "Christine's Femininity Charms Interviewer," *Los Angeles Times,* May 9, 1953.

Hirschfeld, Magnus, "Die Intersexuelle Konstitution," *Jahrbuch fuer sexuelle Zwischenstufen* 23 (1923): 3-27.

Hodgkinson, Liz, *Michael Née Laura.* (London: Columbus Books, 1989.)

Hopper, Hedda, "Dick Powell to Direct Wife in Ride Tiger," *Los Angeles Times,* March 15, 1955.

Humphrey, Hal, "Good Old Days Staging Comeback," *Los Angeles Times,* March 3, 1966.

Ingrassia, Michele, "Christine Jorgensen Obituary," Newsday (May 5, 1989); available online at http://www.transhistory.org/TH_NewsClip_Christine1.htmlln.

Jones, Dilys, "S. F. Man Plans Surgery To Become Woman," *San Francisco Examiner,* May 4, 1954, in VPC/N, Box 1/6.

Jorgensen, Christine, *Christine Jorgensen: A Personal Autobiography.* Intro. by Harry Benjamin. (New York: Paul S. Eriksson, 1967). Reprinted, with intro. by Susan Stryker. (San Francisco, Cleis Press, 2000).

Jorgensen, Christine, "Few Brickbats and Many Joys in Her New Life," *Los Angeles Examiner,* May 22, 1953, in VPC/N, Box 1/6.

Jorgensen, Christine, "Letter Tells Sex Shift," *Los Angeles Examiner,* December 2, 1952, in VPC/N, Box 1/6.

Jorgensen, Christine, "The Story of My Life," *American Weekly,* (February 15 and 22, March 1, 8, and 15, 1953), in VPC/N, Box 1/6.

Jorgensen, interviewed by R. Russell, Christine Jorgensen Reveals (New York: J Records, n.d. [ca. 1957]).

Jorgensen, Christine, interviewed by Mike Wallace on *PM,* 1959, audiotape in author's possession.

Keerdoja , Eileen, with Elaine Sciolino and Kim Foltz, "Jorgensen Enjoys Being Christine," *Newsweek* (March 20, 1981), n.p., in ONE Institute, Subject File "Jorgensen, Christine."

Kinsey, Alfred C., Wardell B. Pomeroy, and Clyde E. Martin, *Sexual Behavior in the Human Male.* (Philadelphia: W.B. Saunders, 1948).

Lasezkay, George, "Exclusive Interview Praises Christine," *Daily Trojan* (University of Southern California), May 12, 1953, in VPC/N, Box 1/6.

Legg, W. Dorr, *Homophile Studies in Theory and Practice.* (San Francisco: ONE Institute Press/GLB Publishers, 1994).

Lucas, Don, interviewed by Susan Stryker, June 13, 1997, Gay, Lesbian, Bisexual, Transgender Historical Society of Northern California, Oral History Collection #97-035.

Maraventano, Louis W., "How the Sex Change Is Performed," *Inside Story* (June 1958), n.p., in VPC/N, Box 1/6.

Martin, Joseph, and Henry Lee, "Tamara Would Start a New Life Where Nobody Knows of the Old," n.p., n.d., (ca. 1954), in VPC/N, Box 1/6.

Meyerowitz, Joanne, *How Sex Changed: A History of Transsexuality in the United States.* (Cambridge, MA Harvard University Press, 2002).

Meyerowitz, Joanne, "Sex Change and Popular Press: Historical Notes on Transsexuality in the United States, 1930-1955," *GLQ: A Journal of Lesbian and Gay Studies* 4:2 (1998): 159-187.

Morgan, Patricia, as told to Paul Hoffman, *The Man-Maid Doll.* (Secaucus, New Jersey: Lyle Stuart, n.d.).

Mulligan, Arthur, "Charlotte Home, Battles Photog Like the Charles She Used to Be," *Los Angeles Daily News,* April 17, 1954, in VPC/N, Box 1/6.

Nardi, Peter M., and Nancy E. Stoller, "'Fruits', 'Fags', and 'Dykes': The Portrayal of Gay/Lesbian Identity in 'Nance' Jokes of the '50s and '60s," Unpublished paper, presented at the annual American Sociological Association meetings, Toronto, August 1997.

Nation, Earl F., "Elmer Belt," *Hoja Volante* 205 (May 1999): 1-5.

Osborne, H. Durant, "Blushing Bride Is Daddy, Too," *Los Angeles Mirror-News,* n.d., (ca. July 1955), in VPC/N, Box 1/6.

Ostow, Mortimer, "Transvestism," *Journal of the American Medical Association* 152:16 (August 15, 1953): 1553.

Patton, Jude, "Female-to-Male Transsexual: Transsexual Sexologist," in Bullough, Bonnie, Vern L. Bullough, Marilyn A. Fithian, William E. Hartman, and Randy Sure Klein, eds., *Personal Stories of "How I Got into Sex": Leading Research-*

ers, *Sex Educators, Prostitutes, Sex Toy Designers, Sex Surrogates, Transsexuals, Criminologists, Clergy, and more.* . . . (Amherst, New York: Prometheus Books, 1997): 334-338.

Pondillo, Robert J., "Censorship in a 'Golden Age': Postwar Television and America's First Network Censor—NBC's Stockton Helffrich." Unpublished Ph.D. dissertation, University of Wisconsin-Madison, 2003.

Prince, Virginia, "The Life And Times Of Virginia," *Transvestia* 17:100 (1977).

Prince, Virginia, "My Accidental Career," in Bullough, Bonnie, Vern L. Bullough, Marilyn A. Fithian, William E. Hartman, and Randy Sure Klein, eds., *Personal Stories of "How I Got into Sex": Leading Researchers, Sex Educators, Prostitutes, Sex Toy Designers, Sex Surrogates, Transsexuals, Criminologists, Clergy, and more.* . . . (Amherst, New York: Prometheus Books, 1997): 347-359.

Racht, Leon, "Bewildered Kin Await Return of 'Boy-Girl'," n.p., December 1, 1952, in VPC/N, Box 1/6.

Racht, Leon, "Mother Had No Indication Son Might Be Transformed," *Los Angeles Examiner,* December 1, 1952, in VPC/N, Box 1/6.

Rees, Tamara A., "Male Becomes Female," *Sexology* 26:4 (November 1959): 212-218.

Reese, Tamara, *Reborn: The Factual Life Story of a Transition from Male to Female.* (n.p., 1955).

Roberts, Whitey, Binder: "Nance," Library, The Magic Castle, Hollywood, California.

Romesburg, Don, "Ray Bourbon: A Queer Sort of Biography." Unpublished M.A. Thesis, University of Colorado, 2000.

Sampson, John, "Dear Mum and Dad, Son Wrote, I've Now Become Your Daughter," n.p., n.d. (ca. December 2, 1952), in VPC/N, Box 1/6.

Schaefer, Leah Cahan, and Connie Christine Wheeler, "Harry Benjamin's First Ten Cases (1938-1953): A Clinical Historical Note," *Archives of Sexual Behavior* 24:1 (February 1995): 73-93.

Serlin, David Harley, "Christine Jorgensen and the Cold War Closet," *Radical History Review* 62 (1995): 136-165.

Star, Hedy Jo, *I Changed My Sex!: The Autobiography of Hedy Jo Star formerly Carl Hammonds.* (Chicago: Novel Books, 1963).

Superior Court, Los Angeles, California, *The Matter of MacLane,* C 650125, filed October 3, 1955.

Stryker, Susan, *Queer Pulp: Perverted Passions from the Golden Age of the Paperback.* (San Francisco, Chronicle Books, 2001).

Sullivan, Ann, "Christine Jorgensen Performing Again," *Oregonian* (Portland, Oregon), June 15, 1979, in ONE Institute, Subject File "Jorgensen, Christine."

Thackrey, Ted, Jr., "Dr. Elmer Belt, Internationally Known as Public Health Advocate, Dies at 87," *Los Angeles Times,* May 19, 1980.

Timmons, Stuart, *The Trouble with Harry: Founder of the Modern Gay Movement.* (Boston: Alyson Publications, 1990).

Transvestia 1:1 (1952), in HWC.

Transvestia 1:2 (1952), in HWC.

United Press, "Christine 'Female' But Can Never Be Mother," *Los Angeles Herald and Express,* February 18, 1953, in ONE Institute Subject File "Jorgensen, Christine."

United Press, "Sex Change Fulfills Lifelong Dream of Girl," *Los Angeles Herald and Express,* December 2, 1952, in VPC/N, Box 1/6.

Wheeler, Richard, interviewed by Richard F. Docter, September 16, 1997; in author's possession.

Wheeler, Richard, interviewed by Richard F. Docter, August 30, 2004; in author's possession.

Wheeler, Richard, interviewed by C. Jacob Hale, January 20, 2005; in author's possession.

White, Ben, "Ex-GI Becomes Blonde Beauty: Operations Transform Bronx Youth," *New York Daily News,* December 1, 1952.

Wiedeman, George H., "Transvestism," *Journal of the American Medical Association* 152:12 (July 18, 1953): 1167.

Williams, Dick, "Christine's Act No Wow," *Los Angeles Mirror,* n.d. (ca. May 8, 1953), in VPC/N, Box 1/6.

Winchell, Walter, *Winchell Exclusive: "Things That Happened to Me—and Me to Them."* (Englewood Cliffs, New Jersey: Prentice-Hall, 1975).

Wood, Edward D., Jr. (writer and director), *Glen or Glenda.* A Screen Classics Release, 1953, 67 minutes.

Worden, Frederic G., and James T. Marsh, "Psychological Factors in Men Seeking Sex Transformation: A Preliminary Report," *Journal of the American Medical Association* 157:17 (April 9, 1955): 1292-1298.

Wykla, Franklin J., "Christine Jorgensen 25 Years Later!," *Data-Boy Magazine,* October 20, 1977, in ONE Institute, Subject File "Transsexuals IV."

Chapter 1

Christine, 1988

On February 27, 1988, 150 cross dressers,[1] many of them in shimmering floor-length formals, downed a cocktail or two in the gilded banquet room of Chicago's Ramada O'Hare Hotel awaiting Miss Christine Jorgensen, indisputably the world's most celebrated transsexual.[2] Most of the men in this audience were married and most had been cross dressers for years. In suits and gowns that appeared a bit out of style, these temporary ladies often resembled grandmotherly members of a women's club. Beneath the spaghetti straps and silicone breast forms, they represented an affluent, older, well-functioning and highly educated cross section of Main Street USA. The opportunity to meet Christine Jorgensen and to hear her speak was one of the incentives for coming to Chicago in the winter, but it was not the only reason. They had come to the Windy City for three days of strategic planning,[3] and to develop better outreach programs to help other cross dressers. They were all aware that Miss Jorgensen had been born a male, and that as George Jorgensen Jr. he had served for about a year in the U.S. Army. They also knew she became a transsexual in the early 1950s, and that extensive international publicity accompanied this event

Christine had been recruited to attend this convention by one of her close friends, a much-admired transsexual, Sister Mary Elizabeth.[4] Christine had top billing as the most honored guest; however, she had never previously participated in a convention of this kind, for she preferred to avoid appearances that linked her with cross dressers, female impersonators, or transsexuals. She considered herself to be a woman, not a transsexual. This was a label she despised, although it was her transsexuality that had propelled her to international fame. Now, she was weakened by cancer and extensive chemotherapy.

Becoming a Woman: A Biography of Christine Jorgensen
© 2008 by The Haworth Press, Taylor & Francis Group. All rights reserved.
doi:10.1300/5896_01

1

When Miss Jorgensen arrived at Chicago's frosty O'Hare Airport, she left the aircraft in a wheelchair before being welcomed by two cross dressers with years of experience in support groups. Both of the ladies were about fifty but looked far younger in their carefully selected winter suits, precisely applied makeup, tasteful jewelry, and upswept hairdos.

Upon arriving, Christine quickly established rapport with her new friends. She was exceptionally skilled in making others feel at ease, speaking graciously, using humor, and establishing herself as the kind of woman who flies first class. They gathered her bags and drove to the nearby hotel.

After a quick survey of her suite, Jorgensen invited her two new friends to join her for a drink, which they eagerly accepted. Soon, she was sharing her long-held philosophy concerning the significance of being different. She spoke of the importance of encouraging each individual the freedom to become the person he or she was destined to be. Doing most of the talking, Christine gradually wound down and announced she was going to take a nap. On the following day, she visited with the convention organizers, but mostly kept out of sight. She drank a little, smoked a lot, and made some telephone calls. There was little concerning the convention that was of interest to her, other than the speech she would deliver on Saturday. Miss Jorgensen was a very spontaneous and experienced public speaker; she never considered making notes or writing the text of a speech.

Jorgensen's luncheon talk was built on a personal account of her struggles as a troubled youth and her difficulties in resolving her own transsexual struggles. Her style was intimate, almost confidential, as if to invite her listeners to become her friend, and she used a great deal of humor. She had each of the ladies sitting on the edge of her chair, especially when describing her medical treatment in Denmark at the age of twenty-six, and then telling of her highly publicized return to New York City in 1953. After speaking, she generously signed autographs and chatted with her fans. She would not be a speaker at the evening banquet, but she knew everyone would be nicely dressed for this concluding event.

The banquet began at seven. As the group assembled, she glided into the room in a glittering black pantsuit, three-inch high heels, and several pieces of ornate, oversized jewelry. Everyone who saw her agreed she communicated a very impressive presence. As she moved from one table to the next, she paused to greet the guests and to make eye contact. Christine Jorgensen knew how to make an entrance and she knew how to work a room. One of the first ladies to give her a hug was Alison Laing, a retired chemist, who had been cross dressing for thirty years. "Good evening, Christine. May I bring you a drink?" Laing asked. "Oh, please do. Vodka, with ice and a twist of lemon," Jorgensen answered with a theatrical accent. She then added ". . . but make it a double."[5]

I had met Christine Jorgensen a few years earlier at an AIDS fundraiser in Venice, California; however, at that crowded event there was little opportunity for conversation. Similarly, I had not been introduced to her or spoken with her at this convention. Looking forward to shaking her hand, I had taken my place at the elevated head table, pushed aside a vase of flowers, rearranged my silverware, and unfolded my napkin. As she worked her way to the front of the room, she projected a larger-than-life aura, moving with dignity as she approached each table, then purred in her contralto voice: "Hi ladies. I'm Christine Jorgensen and who are you this evening?"[6] Most of the cross dressers in the audience were thunderstruck by her elegance, her welcoming smile, and her sophistication. She seemed not only at ease, but to be enjoying herself while giving lots of attention to her admiring audience.

Now sixty and fully in charge of the banquet room, Christine appeared to be everything a celebrity transsexual should be: charming, feminine, relaxed, and chatting easily, while commenting on the fingernails and jewelry she observed. Best of all, she was very friendly. In her attention-getting black pantsuit and stunning evening makeup, she appeared to be similar in appearance to some of the other cross dressers, but far more attractive. Despite being seriously ill, she revealed no physical discomfort. She moved easily and gracefully, while greeting these many men-in-dresses whom she neither knew nor understood. Those in attendance that evening recall her exceptional warmth, her brilliant smile, and her charming manner.[7] Few realized she was ill, although there had been newspaper accounts of her treatment for cancer.

The ones who shook hands or hugged Christine that evening had to be brief, for she was working her way toward the head table. Everyone gave her their attention, and the ones in the back of the room stood to get a better look, stretching and straining like kids at a circus.

They were eager to check out the most famous transsexual in the world. For this group, the presence of Christine Jorgensen was something like having Walter Cronkite show up for a meeting of student journalists.

The emcee introduced Christine: "Ladies, shall we give a warm welcome to one of the nicest women you'll ever meet, our special guest of honor, Christine Jorgensen?" All 150 ladies stood, applauding politely and enthusiastically. Then, most of the ladies used both hands to smooth their skirts before regaining their seats.

Observing Christine at close range, I was surprised to see the puffiness of her face and her increased girth compared to the younger, trimmer, healthier appearing lady I had met prior to her chemotherapy. Her jowls seemed especially swollen, and she was noticeably heavier than the slender performer whose long, narrow and feminine face I had seen many times in newspaper and magazine photographs. She wore a large diamond ring on the fourth finger of her left hand. Her makeup was immaculate, with each eye outlined with a very precise, thin, dark brown line, accented with substantial mascara. She wore a touch of rust-colored blush and coral lipstick. It was obvious that she was wearing a short wig, lightly curled in front, auburn in color, with oversize earrings that bounced against her shoulders. She was quite animated and playing to the audience.

Miss Jorgensen transmitted a sense of importance, and she commanded the center of attention in a crowded room, but there was no hint of pretentiousness. In 1988, Christine was as radiant, as dazzling, and yet as tasteful and sophisticated as the lady who stunned reporters in Copenhagen at her first formal press conference in December 1952. At that time, photographs of the glamorous Christine were transmitted by the wire services to the newspapers of the world, providing the story and the before and after pictures of the former American GI who had been medically transformed into a beautiful blonde.

Eager to greet our guest, I approached her to be introduced, and then commented briefly on my role at the convention as a psychologist and gender researcher. As I sat down, Christine took out a cigarette, lit it, and exhaled a considerable cloud of smoke. One person at the table, a former smoker, then politely asked her to put away her cigarettes. "What? Well, of course, I am going to smoke," she insisted, " . . . is there a law against my smoking in here?" No, there was no law, but while the person did not want to be rude to a guest, neither did she intend to enjoy her prime rib dinner seated next to a smoker. Then, Jorgensen and the nonsmoker, issued brief position statements on the rights of smokers. Their arguments were totally in opposition. It was all cordial and ladylike, but there was no doubt that each would stick up for what she believed. The nonsmoker then politely indicated that she would move to the far right end of the speaker's table, well out of the smoke zone. Responding to this opportunity, I explained that I would like nothing more than to sit next to Miss Jorgensen. Stretching the truth, I said I would not be troubled by the smoke.

The prospect of sharing a dinner with our guest and being able to interview her was both unexpected and delightful. I was familiar with the major landmarks of her life story, although I knew few of the details. I was aware that I was sitting next to the woman who had become the world's first celebrity transsexual, and that she had become an icon for what transsexuality means in our culture.[8]

Trying to get a conversation started, I began with questions about transgender theory, but she showed little interest. We then exchanged some small talk about her career in show business as our dinner was served. Over dessert, I decided to pop one of my more important questions: "What do you think are the most likely causes of transsexualism?" Without a moment of hesitation, she responded: "Two main points: hormones and genetics." Hoping to draw her out I asked, "Can you comment a little more on that?" She then explained something she had said in scores of newspaper interviews, reeling off sentence after sentence in a much-scripted manner:

> You've got to remember that we all have both male and female hormones, and each person has different combinations of these, and that's one of the main things that makes us what we are. And so far as genetics is concerned, everyone knows we develop as human beings based on our genetic makeup. What we look like and every part of our body depends on what we got genetically from our parents.

I nodded again, hoping she would continue after having another sip of wine and lighting a cigarette. She was chain smoking. Gazing over the audience, Christine made eye contact with several ladies at the nearby tables, smiling, waving, and wiggling her fingers. She turned to me and asked if any of the men-being-women in the room were transsexuals? I explained that there were a few, but that most of the participants were cross dressers, or in the language of yesteryear, transvestites. That is, men who cross dressed occasionally while living and working as men.[9] Her wine glass was refilled and I lit her cigarette. She seemed relaxed, comfortable, and very pleasant.

My strategy in speaking with Christine was the same that I had used for thirty-five years as a clinical psychologist. I offered some questions and then sat back to listen while unobtrusively making notes. "Had she been much interested," I asked, sounding very academic, "in cross cultural examples of transsexualism, such as men living as women in the Pacific Islands, in Asia or Africa?" This inquiry, however, failed to open her mind or loosen her tongue. She responded, "Of course, there are transsexuals in all cultures, as you know, but I haven't been a student of that. I'm more interested in American history," she explained, "and I'm very interested in the controversy about who killed President Kennedy." I sensed we were on the edge of slipping off the topic of transsexuality so I counter-punched with a difficult question: "I wonder if you have developed any idea about the number of male to female transsexuals who may exist in America," I asked, feeling sure that this could not be answered without considerable discussion.[10] I knew it was difficult to define who is a transsexual. She finished her dessert, took another sip of wine and said: "I'll tell you this. Ninety percent of the transsexuals I have met are not true transsexuals at all. They have not had a lifelong pattern of feeling certain they should have been born female, like I experienced, and Heaven only knows why they have wound up believing they must live as a woman."[11] She showed complete confidence in her conclusion, adding: "At least, the transvestites you see in this room know who they are, while some transsexuals do not." She spoke with great authority, as if I might be one of the scores of news reporters she had set straight since 1952.

Loosening up a bit, Christine then explained the importance of fetishism to the cross dresser, emphasizing that sexual arousal had never been a part of her experience.[12] She stated that most cross dressers lack the facial features, the body shape, and other physical attributes of women, and she then summed up the differences between what she called the true transsexual and the transvestite: ". . . 90 percent of the transvestites look like men who are wearing wigs. They really don't look like women." But she made it clear that she was not putting anyone down, she was simply offering her own view of one major difference between transsexuals and cross dressers.

I was determined to press on with other questions so I mentioned a couple of the major books on transsexualism that had been written over the past twenty years and invited her evaluation. "Harry Benjamin," she emphasized, "knows more about transvestism and transsexualism than any other doctor I know, and he has been a wonderful personal and professional help to me, going back to when I first returned from Copenhagen in 1953." I had never met Dr. Benjamin but I had much respect for his 1966 book, *The Transsexual Phenomenon,* and for his depth of knowledge about the many variations of transgender behavior so I joined in singing his praises. Then I asked: "But how about some of the other major contributors to transgender theory," I inquired. "What do you think of the books by the UCLA psychoanalyst, Robert Stoller?"[13] She paused and asked: "Who?" I explained that researcher and clinician Robert Stoller had become one of the best-known contributors to transgender theory, and that during my years in the Department of Psychiatry at UCLA, I had come to know him and respect him very highly. "Frankly," she said while tenderly fingering her glass of wine, "I've never heard of him." She was again smiling, smoking, and waving to some of the nearby cross dressers, a few of whom had come to the head table to shake her hand and to request an autograph.

Pursuing what I thought was an important question, I asked if she was familiar with the distinction psychologist John Money and transgender organizer Virginia Prince had made by sharpening the difference between the terms, sex and gender? She showed no interest in the question. Christine was a woman with a mind of her own, a capacity not only to have opinions and to express them directly, but also to be dismissive of others. She was a charming person who could sometimes become rude, acerbic, and hostile, especially after several glasses of wine. I later learned from friends and relatives that for the past few years she had been drinking far too much, and that when this occurred, she became downright nasty and noisy. One of her closest friends told me she liked to dismiss advice by saying: "I don't need opinions; I have plenty of my own."[14]

My goal was to keep the conversation rolling along, so I dipped into Christine's past history and asked about the origin of a term that has become a shorthand, superficial explanation of transsexualism:

"How did you happen to invent the definition of "transsexual" as being a woman in a man's body?" Lighting yet another cigarette, she explained that it was not her phrase, but rather, part of a newspaper article and that the phrase just seemed to have stuck. Since then, I've kept my eyes open for the original source of that language, but so far haven't found it. We talked briefly of news reporting, noting that newspaper articles often do not explore a topic like transsexualism in depth or delve into the complex variations of this behavior. It seemed clear that Miss Jorgensen had little interest in transgender research or theory. She was a performer, not a researcher. It was also clear that she used some well practiced-phrases to respond to my questions, causing me to feel much like an untrained cub reporter.

Christine wanted me to understand the sequence of surgical procedures she had undergone in Denmark in 1951 and 1952, beginning with having her ears "pinned back." A year later she underwent castration, and finally, amputation of her penis. She reminded me that upon her return to America she had not yet received a surgically created vagina, although many newspaper reports left readers assuming she had. Her first vaginal surgery, she commented, was in 1954.

Taking a broader view of her own career, she explained that her strategy in meeting with the press was to say as little as possible about her operations. She had learned that a tight-lipped management of her medical history had encouraged the public to form whatever conclusions they wished. Understandably, many people thought that being a woman meant you also had a vagina, or that you might even have female reproductive organs. When interviewed, by the press, Christine often revealed nothing specific about her sexual anatomy.

She was quite open in describing many of her best friends as gay men, while emphasizing that these were not romantic relationships; they were simply close friendships that she treasured. Her strongest relationships, she noted, were with members of her immediate family, although she did not discuss family members in our conversation. As she spoke, I came to see her as a very experienced theatrical performer doing her act, speaking her lines, adding a few dance steps here and there, and above all, playing for laughs and ending it all with hugs and kisses as the band played on. Christine loved the smell of the grease paint and the roar of the crowd. Having people respond to her with kindness and applause meant something profoundly important to her. Earning self-respect, approval, and the admiration of others may have helped to bolster a shaky sense of self-esteem.

We spoke for about two hours, touching upon many topics, and allowing me to gather some impressions of this most famous transsexual pioneer. At the time, I had no plan to write Miss Jorgensen's life story, but I believed I could use her comments for interesting quotations to illuminate college lectures. She grew somewhat less defensive in responding to me as the interview proceeded, especially after I put my pen in my pocket, although her guard was always in place. She was a pro in dealing with the kinds of questions I raised.

I first became professionally interested in Christine's life story following my retirement as a college professor. Early on, during the process of researching her story, I realized that a more complete description of her life required the study of several poorly understood issues. For me, the most interesting unresolved questions were these:

1. What were the major steps in the formation of Christine's transgender identity? Did she cross dress or perceive herself as a girl during her youth? How did her feminine gender identity emerge? What "sex change" information was available to her? Did she have any role models?

2. What motivated Copenhagen's prestigious endocrinologist, Christian Hamburger, to accept the case of a depressed, penniless, American ex-GI who insisted he must be transformed into a woman?

3. Did Christine help to produce the profusion of publicity that announced her transsexualism to the world in 1952, and that transformed her from a debt-ridden twenty-four year old unemployed would-be photographer into a well-to-do celebrity?

4. Did she have the glandular disorder she described to her parents to explain her transsexual change? Was she an intersexed person?

5. While Christine stated that she grew up falling in love with men,[15] and that she had always hoped to be married to a man, what were her actual sexual or romantic relationships?

6. Christine had the social skills to establish enduring friendships, but she also had a long history of disputes with those close to her. Some of these disputes escalated from angry letters to law suits. She displayed a pattern of love and hate in some of her relationships, and of turning to bite the hand that fed her; this was a problem throughout her adult life. What motivated this behavior?

Understanding more of the Jorgensen story is both intriguing and important, for she was an unusually intelligent and gifted pioneer transsexual who shaped the very meaning of this term. She also showed the world that a man can become a woman, even an unusually beautiful and clever woman, who was able to earn a great deal of money in show business.[16] Through her transsexuality, Christine became an accidental icon and poster girl for transsexualism without intending to do so, and her case became the prototype for what our culture first called "sex changes."[17]

After Christine's highly publicized emergence in 1952, transsexualism was never quite the same. Fifteen years later, gender identity clinics would be established in major medical centers to provide surgical assistance for males and females making a change in gender role. Despite this, many people continued to be certain that a reversal of gender role is nothing more than a tragic mistake or an immoral choice.

In our culture, most people believe there are two sexes, male and female, and that these work in harmony with two genders, masculine and feminine, and that sex and gender must be congruent. But Christine's case proved that this is not always true. Many Americans also believe that transsexuality is simply a matter of personal choice. On the other hand, nearly all transsexuals argue that gender identity is the motivational force that drives their desire for gender transformation, and that this has nothing to do with personal choice.[18] This disagreement is not even close to resolution.

As we examine Christine's life, it will be important to remember that despite some important recent discoveries about the impact of fetal hormones upon the brain,[19] not much more is known about the precise causes of transsexualism than was known when George Jorgensen Jr. sailed to Copenhagen in 1950.

At a broader cultural level, we must also acknowledge that a half-century after the "Ex-GI" from the Bronx burst onto the front page of the *New York Daily News* as a glamorous "Blonde Beauty," half of our nation continues to regard both transsexualism and homosexuality as immoral or sinful. The other half looks on in awe, fascinated at times, but always amazed if not confused. Many Americans remain wary of gays and lesbians, and they are almost as unclear about what it means to be a transsexual. As we shall see, Christine Jorgensen was a far more complex personality than was portrayed by her autobiography or her press releases. In some ways she became very effective in coping with life's challenges, while at other times she was prone to depression and reliance upon fantasy solutions. When she lost faith in someone she could attack them as if her life was at stake. For decades she worked to strengthen her own sense of self-worth, and to overcome the residual effects of painful rejection inflicted by her childhood peers. Even as a youngster, Christine was a strong, determined, and inventive person who was fortunate to have grown up in a well-functioning and loving family. The continuity of these highly beneficial family relationships and the personal support she felt from all of the Jorgensens provided the foundation for both her successful transsexual redefinition of herself. It all began in Throggs Neck, a part of the Bronx.

Chapter 2

The Jorgensens

George William Jorgensen Jr. was born May 30, 1926, at the Community Hospital in Manhattan and raised in the Throggs Neck district of the Bronx, a few miles north of his birthplace. He was Florence Jorgensen's second child; there was nothing remarkable about her pregnancy or George's birth. He was fortunate to have loving parents and to grow up in a stable, caring family. The families in this neighborhood were hard-working, ethnically diverse, middle-class folks who knew and cared about their neighbors.[1] Along Dudley Avenue, where George grew up, there were "Italians, Irish, Jews, Germans, and some Scandinavians," one of the former residents told me, "and they all got along wonderfully well." There was a patch of green in front of some of the homes, a hedge here and there, many trees, and often, a small lawn in the back yard. For those who enjoyed fishing and boating, this was a great place to live, for the predictable northeasterly winds and the mild water temperatures during much of the year made Eastchester Bay and Long Island Sound ideal waterways for sailing and fishing. For a Danish family, living near the water was important. More than two dozen Jorgensen relatives lived nearby, forming a cohesive and supportive family.

The first of the Jorgensen family to settle in the Throggs Neck neighborhood was Charles Gustav Jorgensen who came to the United States from Denmark in 1870. The grandfather of George Jr., he arrived here as a single man in search of greater economic opportunity. As a skilled carpenter, he quickly found work, mainly erecting homes and small commercial buildings. Grandfather Jorgensen spent his entire life working in construction and property development. He and his wife, Anna Maria Magdalena Petersen, raised nine children. They lived just four blocks from their son, George Sr. and his wife, Florence.

Becoming a Woman: A Biography of Christine Jorgensen
© 2008 by The Haworth Press, Taylor & Francis Group. All rights reserved.
doi:10.1300/5896_02

George Sr. married Florence Hansen in 1920, and like his father and brother, they moved into a Jorgensen-built house a few miles south of Pelham Bay Park. It was just a fifteen-minute walk from the Westchester Square elevated rail station. Their two children were a daughter, Dorothy ("Dolly"), and a son, George Jr., who, at the age of twenty-six would become Christine Jorgensen. George Sr. had many of the personality characteristics of his immigrant father.[2] In social situations he was reserved and soft-spoken, while in a one-on-one conversation he became more talkative. Highly intelligent, reliable, and hard working, he was a fine craftsman who was dedicated to the well-being of his family and he was also loyal and helpful to the entire Jorgensen clan. George Sr. was a man of many hobbies and talents. He was interested in electronics, photography, woodworking, metal working, boat building, and he was an inveterate fisherman. As children, George Jr. and Dorothy enjoyed spending vacation days with him on Eastchester Bay in the wooden boat he'd built in their basement. "Dolly and George could bait a hook as well as anybody," according to his cousin Robert Andersen.[3] Another of the older friends of the Jorgensens, Vincent Manno,[4] said George Sr. was "like all of the Danes . . . he was most comfortable on the water with a fishing pole in his hands, or in the basement, building something with his woodworking equipment." George and Florence were the kind of people everybody loved having as friends." A close relative explained that the senior Jorgensen "wasn't the sort of man who pushed himself toward prominence in groups, but he was very good in close relationships."[5] George Sr. had served in the Coast Guard before his marriage. A self-contained and reticent gentleman, he smiled easily and was especially loving and patient with children. Often, he'd gather up a gang of the neighborhood kids and take them for a picnic at the zoo or to one of the huge Bronx parks.[6] At that time, children were admitted to the Bronx Zoo for eleven cents.

The construction business produced a comfortable income, especially during the boom years of the 1920s when home sales were at a peak. But with the arrival of the depression in the 1930s, George Sr. was forced to seek work on projects operated by the New Deal's Works Progress Administration. Like most Americans, it was all he could do to earn a living. There was no extra money. He helped to build LaGuardia Airport, and later worked as a carpenter for the City of New York and for the Board of Education. He didn't have to worry about the family budget or the management of money; his wife took care of that.[7]

Florence Hansen Jorgensen was seen by her friends and neighbors as a model wife, mother, and homemaker.[8] A no-nonsense lady who was invariably frugal and who sewed her children's clothing, she was also friendly, warm, and a good listener. Florence maintained a tight rein on all family activities, from meal planning to the budgeting of vacations, and from arranging special dinners at holiday times, to smoothing the ruffled feathers of neighbors or relatives. An excellent cook, she was respectful of community standards. Florence would go out of her way to lend a hand to people in need. She also kept well informed of her children's progress at school, and insisted that Dorothy and George Jr. understood that their parents were in charge. Her home was immaculate and the hedge on the street was always properly trimmed. Her neighbors considered her a strong woman who was not hesitant to express her point of view. She did not favor harsh or physical punishment, but through her posture and the expression on her face her children learned that their mother meant what she said. For her, rules were to be followed without excuses and no back-talk was tolerated. There was plenty of love within this household, but there was also an unspoken respect for the authority of the parents and the grandparents. George and his sister were taught never to bring disgrace upon the family name. It was Mrs. Jorgensen who insisted on regular church attendance, and on tithing, even during the difficult years of the Depression. But while she was very structured and organized, Florence Jorgensen was also a very affectionate mother who cared more about the welfare of her husband and her children than anything else in her life. She also knew how to relax and have a good time. Like most of the women on Dudley Avenue, she smoked and downed a few beers with her husband and their many Scandinavian friends. In the Danish tradition, she was very interested in family history, a hobby she passed on to her daughter who became an outstanding genealogist.

In her 1967 autobiography, Christine noted that there were "26 aunts, uncles, and cousins in our Bronx neighborhood . . ."[9] and she described growing up in a very loving and supportive family: "Dolly and I were surrounded by a closely-knit affectionate family of the sort that gives a child a warm feeling of belonging."[10]

Dorothy was three years older than George. When George was born, his sister began to call him "brother," but at age three she pronounced this "Brud," (rhymes with spud) and the nickname stuck. Within the family, until the era of Christine Jorgensen's emergence, his parents always called him Brud and so did all the relatives. Blonde and pretty, Dolly was a strong student both academically and in her social relationships. However, she suffered some embarrassment over the peculiarities of her younger brother. For example, during elementary school she was aware of the teasing and taunts he suffered, and she hated having the other kids asking questions about him. Why, she had asked her parents, couldn't George just be more boyish like the other young men on Dudley Avenue? The parents offered no explanation, for they didn't know what to say. Some of his classmates probably did consider him to be different, but other than having a somewhat frail upper body, prominent ears, and spindle-like legs, no one seemed able to say exactly how he was different.[11]

Unlike her brother, Dolly had high academic and professional goals. She could throw a baseball, fish, and swing a hammer as well as any of the boys on her block, but she certainly was not a "masculine" girl. Dolly and George loved the long, hot, easy summer days when they'd go fishing with their dad or just hang out at the Askov Hall Beach Club where they were members.[12] This beach club was the center of their teenage social lives.

When her brother became Christine Jorgensen at the age of twenty-six and emerged in the headlines, Dolly began to draw a distinction between "real life," her code word for family relationships, and "fantasy life," which stood for Christine's show business career. She never really approved of Christine's gigs in cabarets.[13] Seeking to insulate her own family from Christine's celebrity, she planned to keep her two daughters in the dark about her famous new sister's transsexual change, but found this impractical. Her oldest child had heard all about this at school, and Dolly wound up telling both children the entire story of Christine's transsexuality while they were in elementary school. For them, "Aunt Chris" was the same no matter what her gender history may have been.

In her younger days, her self-confidence and willingness to speak out was occasionally seen as overconfidence or curtness. This was especially true in the post-war 1940s when young women were not expected to express strong opinions no matter what they might have to offer. But in contrast to what some called her assertiveness, her friends viewed Dolly as a sensitive, well-informed, and conventional person.[14] Dolly has always cared a great deal about how others perceived her. For example, as an adult, she had been invited to attend an overnight church retreat that was also to be attended by the man she had been dating. Dolly sought the advice of relatives concerning the propriety of attending such a retreat, concerned that others might get the wrong idea.[15] Anything that suggested questionable behavior or a lack of respect for the rules of the community was not something Dolly wanted on her record. This sense of rectitude is something to keep in mind as we later explore the personality of Christine Jorgensen. The Jorgensens were a family of high standards and they cared about what the neighbors thought of them. Respectability meant a lot.

Dolly never felt at ease with newspaper people or with Chris's show business friends; she avoided publicity much as did Chris's Copenhagen doctors. As an adult, she was a far more self-contained and aloof person than Christine, but her loyalty to her transsexual sister and to her entire clan was never questioned. While she quietly took some pride in the celebrity and financial successes of Christine Jorgensen as an entertainer, she very seldom attended any of her performances. She made it clear that she did not approve of the cabaret crowd who spent recreational evenings in smoky nightclubs. She imagined such places might smell like a second-rate beer garden. In her view, all of this was "fantasyland."[16]

While her brother was in Denmark, Dolly was the first person he turned to for financial help. In 1953, when he ran out of money she quickly loaned him several hundred dollars, a considerable sum fifty years ago.[17] At other times during Christine's life it was Dolly who was among her closest, most supportive, and most trusted of intimate friends and relatives. This was especially true after their parents died within a span of eighteen months during the late 1960s.

Dolly and Chris maintained a close relationship throughout their lives, although each believed the other was rather difficult to deal with. Reportedly, none of their differences ever resulted in anything close to an estrangement.[18] Dolly had the peacemaking skills she'd seen her mother use in helping to mend fences among neighbors and relatives. However, one close friend of Christine's told me "Dolly never really understood what Christine was all about, and never really accepted her. . ."[19] However, there is a good deal of evidence to the contrary. Dolly may not have appreciated her sister's transsexual celebrity with all this meant for the family, but she did respect Christine. For example, years later, when she compiled an award-winning family genealogy, Dolly invariably identified her former brother as Christine and she always addressed her cards and letters to her as Christine Jorgensen.[20] Her genealogical records show the birth of Christine Jorgensen and never mention George Jr's. birth name. However, when Christine's story made headlines Dolly hated the publicity. In 1953, when a pushy reporter tried to snap her picture and pressed her for information she not only refused to be interviewed, she turned away and would not confirm her name. In many ways, Dolly is similar to both parents: Like her father, she is a strong yet private person who avoids the spotlight but shines in person-to-person conversation. But like her mother she is highly structured, thrifty, somewhat inflexible, and as described by some, a bit standoffish.[21]

Throughout their lives, she and Christine squabbled and sometimes strongly disagreed, but they always found ways to resolve their differences. Similarly, while there have been a few long-standing tensions within the Jorgensen clan, most of the relatives will do almost anything to resolve a family dispute. In dealing with her brother, and later, with Christine, Dolly never abandoned the role of the older mentor-sister.[22] But one of the things that kept them together was Christine's especially close relationships with Dolly's two children. Along with their mother, they did all they could to assist their aunt as her health declined in the 1980s.

Much can be learned about the dynamics of the Jorgensen family from one of Christine's most loyal cousins, Robert Andersen. He is said by family members to portray many of the characteristics of Danes. He is tall, slender, rugged, and reserved, yet smiling and welcoming. He is also a man who holds his cards close to his chest and says little.[23] Robert Andersen is a man of many abilities, having worked as a maritime engineer and faculty member at a maritime academy before changing careers to become a specialist in agricultural management. Years later he worked as a planner/designer in office layout and space utilization for the State of New York, helping to open scores of government offices in the World Trade Center. He did all these things in addition to operating his own dairy and cattle insemination business in upstate New York. Like all of the Jorgensens, he has kept busy. At age eighty-four, he and his wife became award-winning digital photographers.

Robert grew up in a two-story Jorgensen-built house identical to George's, about four blocks away from his cousin. Sitting at their wood plank kitchen table in the 200-year-old farmhouse they have lived in for more than fifty years, the Andersens have clear memories of the youthful George: "He was teased a lot by the other kids, taunted and called names, especially in elementary school, but never by those of us who knew him," said Robert.

Robert Andersen's artistically talented wife, Amelia Weiczkowski Anderson, was one of four sisters from a Polish family in the Bronx. Amelia told me, "George ran around with several of us, all girls, and we just considered him the same as anybody else. He didn't act feminine so far as we noticed. We never teased him."[24] Robert had always been a good friend of George's, and so had Amelia. When they were married in the Presbyterian Church just down the street from George's Dudley Avenue home, they asked him to serve as Robert's best man. George was honored to participate. In their wedding picture, he appears very slight compared to his towering cousin.

Amelia recalled that when George was a teenager, in 1944, and she was dating her future husband she had agreed to accompany George to a De Molay dance. He had been elected chaplain of the youth auxiliary of the Masonic Order, and he was eager to take a date to the dance. However, he had never taken a girl out in his life. Amelia was happy to be asked. "He was a very good dancer," she said, "and he was also an exceptionally good ice skater." Continuing, she said "George dressed and behaved just like any of the boys, and for any sort of a special event he always wore a shirt, a tie, and a suit." She smiled warmly as she described the events of so many years ago: "We liked him and he was popular with those who knew him. But the elementary school teasing did cause him to become a little reserved and uncertain of who to trust. At our wedding he didn't stand out as different," Amelia noted, "but I would say that to some he might have seemed a little 'arty'." By this she meant George's appearance was similar to some of the aspiring theater people they occasionally met. However, "None of us ever had the slightest idea he was struggling with thoughts of a sex change." Nor did any one she knew think of him as being attracted to young men. Concerning George's time in Copenhagen, she said none of the family members realized that

George was undergoing medical treatment in Denmark. The family all thought he was studying photography, a fiction his mother might have encouraged. "This was a solid, church-going family," Amelia said with pride. Even at the peak of her fame, Christine found time to call upon the Andersens and have a meal with them on their farm.

Chapter 3

Elementary and High School

The home George Jorgensen Sr. built for his young family was almost identical to a score of others he'd built using a floor plan that sold well, and that young middle-class families could afford. For many young couples, moving to the Bronx had been an escape from the crowded, smaller, less healthful apartments of Lower Manhattan. As viewed by these New Yorkers, the Bronx had long been perceived as a parklike suburb, and a big step upward in social standing compared to the tenements of the Lower East Side. The house young George Jr. called home has not changed much in the past eighty-five years.[1]

George's early childhood was described in the 1967 autobiography as a lonely, traumatic passage, of a " . . . frail, tow-headed, introverted child . . ."[2] who was learning some tough lessons about gender conformity. For example, there is described a Christmastime when the family was gathered at Grandmother Jorgensen's to open their presents. George had longed to receive " . . . a pretty doll with long, golden hair . . ."[3] but was much disappointed to unwrap his present—a shiny red train. "It must have been at about this stage," George explained, "that I became aware of the differences between my sister, Dolly, and me." These were gender lessons he didn't like, but he paid attention and tried his best to live up to the expectations of his parents. Later, when George attempted to question some of these gender rules through discussion with his mother, she told him that the differences between boys and girls was " . . . one of God's surprises." He replied: "Well . . . I don't like the kind of surprise [that] God made me."[4] Almost twenty years later, he confessed to his Copenhagen doctor that he had always felt he should have been born a girl, and that he had always wanted to be a girl. For George, the elementary school years

Becoming a Woman: A Biography of Christine Jorgensen
© 2008 by The Haworth Press, Taylor & Francis Group. All rights reserved.
doi:10.1300/5896_03

would not be easy. As explained in Christine's autobiography, George had always felt more like a girl than a boy and behaved in ways that other kids regarded as feminine. It didn't help that he was underweight for his height. Looking back, Christine Jorgensen described George during these prepubescent years as "sensitive . . . shy . . . withdrawn and miserable." However, some of the time these personal feelings were masked by a smiling, gregarious, and happy-go-lucky façade, the funnyman and the prankster. No matter how "sissified" he may have felt, the youthful George learned ways to get along with others and invariably stayed out of trouble. Other than his slight body, his cousin, Robert Andersen, told me George was considered "just as normal as anybody else."[5] He came from a hard-working, socially involved, middle-class family, and no matter what his innermost feelings may have been, his actual conduct reflected a respect for the conventionality of the entire Jorgensen family. It's no surprise that his mother is said to have considered Dolly and George "just typical children."

At the age of five-and-a-half, George Jr. began walking to his neighborhood public elementary school. George attended this school from kindergarten through the eighth grade, progressing year by year with classmates he knew very well. He stayed out of trouble but he never showed his considerable ability.

During his elementary school years, George received more than his share of teasing and name-calling. After school, some of the boys would cluster around the candy store, only a block from school, often taunting and challenging him. One of the biggest and toughest of them, Danny Riley seemed to delight in making George cry and run for home. Today, Riley seems somewhat ashamed of the teasing and humiliation he inflicted on the far-smaller George: "It was just something we did in those days . . . teasing and calling names was almost like an after-school game."[6]

There were about a dozen boys of George's age in the neighborhood. They nicknamed George, "Goose," or "Cousin Goose."[7] At least for some, the term has a distinct and unmistakable sexual connotation. For boys of that era and even today, to be "goosed" meant to have another boy simulate the insertion of a finger into the anus by touching the seat of the trousers. For George, this nickname stuck and it was a humiliation and a reminder that he was seen as a sissy. His older, more loyal cousin, Robert Andersen, never heard this taunting, sexually loaded nickname. But on Dudley Avenue, most of the kids called him Goose, including some of the girls.[8] Understandably, George felt excluded from this peer group and his defense was to avoid interacting with these youngsters and to adopt the role of the loner. He preferred to wander over to Hoe Avenue for a visit with his grandmother, and to play catch with Robert Andersen. Curiously, this nickname is not mentioned in the 1967 autobiography.

To be rejected by other boys and labeled a sissy inflicted psychological wounds upon George Jr. that were never entirely healed. Quite possibly, this mistreatment contributed to his childhood aloofness and uncertainty about whom to trust. Feelings of peer rejection may also have contributed to Christine's later anger toward those she believed had offended or mistreated her. In elementary school, to have the reputation of a sissy meant you were a noncompetitor in the rough-and-tumble sports nearly all the boys played after school. Worse, when taunted or pushed around, all the kids assumed a sissy would not retaliate, thereby encouraging more abuse. The boys in the neighborhood teased and ridiculed George about his supposed girlish qualities, and his preference for playing with girls. These friendships with girls were totally beyond the understanding of the preadolescent males on Dudley Avenue.

Ann Hope Fisher, another of George's first cousins who lived around the corner from the Jorgensens, explained that as a youngster "George was a loner, but he and some of the neighborhood boys would operate their model railroads in the basement." Again, this report is partially at variance with Christine's 1967 book describing George as very isolated from other children, especially the boys. It wasn't quite a matter of total social isolation. He maintained an excellent relationship with his cousin, Robert Andersen, and a few of the other neighborhood boys played with him. So, at least close to home, George managed to turn aside from the teasing he experienced at school and to project the image of a socially confident, self-assured, and well-functioning youngster. These friendly relationships, along with the sustained approval of his parents provided a base of self-esteem that was shaky, but the foundation was there.[9]

When Christine Jorsensen looked back on these childhood years, she reported, it was during this time that her feelings of wanting to be a girl grew stronger. These feelings, however, also led to serious social difficulties. In her autobiography, she provides two examples of how her "feminine characteristics" resulted in humiliation and tears. The first incident dealt with a few unhappy days spent as a camper at a boys-only summer camp across the Hudson River in New Jersey. At Camp Sharparoon,[10] she recalls, the organization of the daily program was "militaristic," and the other boys tormented George with taunts about "looking like a girl," and of having feminine mannerisms. It seems these boys noted George's "girlish" characteristics soon after the camping week had begun. His age at that time is not stated, but he seems to have been about seven. He begged his parents to let him return home, which they allowed him to do. In contrast, his sister had been sent to a girls-only camp, and when George visited there with his parents he felt entirely at ease and free of the harassment endured at Camp Sharparoon.[11]

Even greater humiliation was recalled in an incident that occurred when he was in the eighth grade and about to graduate from grade school. From the autobiography, we learn of his hiding a sample of needlework in his school desk. It was comforting for him to fondle this, and to secretly take it out and admire it. But what George didn't know was that his teacher had not only discovered his secret treasure, but she had asked Mrs. Jorgensen to come to her classroom while school was in session for a confrontation in front of the class. Upon summoning George to the front of the room, she presented the needlework and demanded to know if it was his. "Yes," he replied. She then asked Mrs. Jorgensen: ". . . do you think this is anything for a red-blooded boy to have in his desk . . . the next thing we know, George will be bringing his knitting to school."[12] George recalls this as an especially hurtful incident, not only to himself, but also to his mother. Quite obviously, he felt ridiculed and demeaned in front of his classmates. His mother, Christine wrote in 1967 ". . . was always my champion when others laughed at my 'sissified' ways." It was, however, events like this that provided a foundation for building a strong bond of affection between George and both of his parents, a bond that held the family together when they learned of the "sex change" of their son in 1952. Evidence shows that George's parents had ample opportunity to learn how others thought George was "sissified." It's not clear, however, what they may have made of this. Perhaps, like most parents, they simply assumed he would grow out of this "stage" of development.

For her autobiography, Christine probably encouraged the tale of a feminine and trauma-filled childhood, for as an adult she preferred to explain her development as a story of converting tragedy to triumph. More specifically, she characterized her life as progressing from feeling like a girl with the body of a boy, to becoming an adult woman. In contrast, some who knew George in those early years remember him as a slender, underweight lad, but also as outgoing, friendly, athletic, and self-confident. What's more, cousin Robert Andersen explained that as George moved on to high school, he stood out as a young man who was especially able to hold his own in discussions with older teenagers and adults.[13] "I was more the quiet type," Andersen told me, "while George would speak up and even confront adults when he disagreed with them." In personality, George was sometimes as extroverted and socially adept as his mother, while at other times he showed the reserved self-confidence of his tough-fisted father. Although many neighborhood peers saw him as a loner, in some situations, especially among his best friends, he behaved more assertively. Standing up for yourself and saying what you believed needed to be said was an admired quality among the Scandinavians at the Askov Hall Beach Club. Like these strong, independently minded adults he viewed as role models, George never was a pushover, and his resilience and persistence later served him well when he had to make decisions about his transgender future. It took a great deal of personal courage to redefine his identity, and to become a transsexual. As a teenager, George Jorgensen Jr. was not a wimp despite the picture drawn in the 1967 autobiography.

But despite some important personal strengths, as a growing teenager, George also developed a lot of self-negating ideas and beliefs that fostered guilt, shame, and at times, a preference to keep to himself. Very possibly, his early religious training exacerbated these difficulties. One question was especially troubling for George: He had learned at church and from his school friends that homosexual relationships were considered sinful and immoral. In the Jorgensen household, the word was never spoken. Among his neighbors, "homos" or "queers" were thought to be unacceptable, even dangerous people. Hence, a series of romantic attractions to other young men became his greatest teenage conflict. Try as he might to avoid these crushes, George persistently fell in love with other male youths of his age. This conflict would contribute to episodes of depression, low self-esteem, low aspiration for success, and much personal unhappiness.[14] It's a story told over and over by gays in our culture.

Striving to fit in despite these conflicts, George pretended to be a typical heterosexual guy. This is why, as noted earlier, it was so important for him to take his friend, Amelia, to the De Molay dance, and for him to become a member of this group. As a youth with a religious background, he knew his attraction to men was condemned in the Holy Scriptures, and he therefore did all he could to avoid suspicion of being gay.[15] However, the inner tensions he experienced were a serious detriment to his high school career, his self-concept, his mental health, and his relationships with peers. The process of gradually revealing his sexual preference to others and of gaining greater self-acceptance extended over several years.

During these teen years, his father wanted him to develop some practical skills in farming, and to learn to fit in with other young men. He therefore arranged for George to spend many of his summers at the upstate farm of his sister in Albany, New York. As told by Christine, George had been "shipped off with a blanket roll and a few dollars in pocket money" to gain some experience looking after animals and doing farm chores with his favorite cousin, Robert Andersen. The only difficulty was that some of the nearby farm kids looked at the underweight George and concluded that he was "that strange kid from the city."[16] George, we are told, refused to join them at the swimming hole without a one-piece bathing suit that covered his upper body. This was felt to be necessary due to "shyness . . . and my natural modesty."

It was a different story at Askov Hall, the private beach club where George felt safe and tended to be more outgoing. Here, he enjoyed making new friends and socializing with other teenagers. His extroversion and guarded self-confidence were personality characteristics that would benefit him throughout his life, and that contributed to Christine's successful career in show business. The experience of having grown up in a loving, constructive, and emotionally supportive family served to counterbalance the teasing and rejection he experienced as a youngster, although the quest for confirmation of respect from others was a lifelong struggle.

Throughout his school years, George tried to stand tall despite his short stature.[17] He consistently sought to conceal both his growing sense of feminine gender identity and his attraction to young men. He sought to present himself as just as masculine as any of the Jorgensen men. This false public persona came at the price of great internal conflict; he felt "tortured and confused" and like an "outsider" during these developmental years. What is most important is the incompatibility between his private identity as a somewhat feminine-appearing youth, and his generally successful effort to appear otherwise, both within the family and among his friends. Looking back on her childhood, Christine said her sense of wanting to be a woman was growing stronger year by year.[18]

George need not have worried about maintaining the secrecy of wanting to become a woman, for these thoughts were entirely unrecognized by others. Even the idea of a "change of sex" was foreign to most people at that time. More than anything, throughout his years in high school, it was important for him to show his parents and all of the Jorgensens that he was a normal young man.

Christopher Columbus High School was located a ten-minute electric trolley ride from George's home. Like many American high schools of that era, the curriculum was divided into two tracks: an academic track designed for students seeking precollege courses, and a commercial track for those who wanted to become tradesmen, technicians, or office workers.[19] His older sister had selected the academic track and so did George. But he never fully invested himself in school or in the development of a network of friends at Christopher Columbus. Most of the students had no idea who he was, although he always seemed ready with a joke or an amusing remark. Unlike his eight years in elementary school, George was not rejected. Rather, he was ignored. Of course, many of these teenage students probably felt the same way. Throughout his four high school years he showed little interest in social activities, and although he graduated on schedule, his grades were consistently mediocre. The school staff did not think of him as having special promise or even as a strong prospect for college. He revealed little of the high intelligence, talent, or creative flair others would later credit to Christine. He was never in a school play nor did he join any of the clubs. At several important points in his life, George would fall back upon his interest and skill in photography, and as we shall see later, it may even have played a part in the establishment of his relationship with Dr. Christian Hamburger, the leader of the Copenhagen medical team that guided him during his thirty months in Denmark.

The high school experience reminded George that he was often seen by others as a particularly feminine youth, despite his efforts to avoid this. Even his sister chided him about the way he carried his schoolbooks. She told him he held his books against his body as girls do, while boys, she insisted, carried their books at their sides. On another occasion, Dolly discussed George's feminine ways in a college research paper: "she devoted a thesis to the effects of environment on the development of a child . . . I was told I was the subject of this." Dolly had attributed George's feminine interests, in part, "to the fact that I played with girls so much as a child."[20]

During these teenage years, George's strategy was to reveal nothing about his sexual preference, and instead, to present himself as just another somewhat shy, heterosexual young man. Overall, George had effective social skills as a humorous storyteller, listener, and friend, especially of girls. He didn't date girls, but he got along nicely with them. Fortunately for him, there was much less teasing during his teen years, as judged by Robert Andersen who described Christopher Columbus High School as "a place without bullies, and in a time when students were expected to have grown up enough to leave the teasing behind."[21]

But even without the teasing, at the onset of puberty, George's self-esteem and social relationships were later remembered by Chris as more troubled. According to her 1967 account, these difficulties were associated with George's growing gender identity conflict: the sense of having been born a man yet feeling he should have been born a woman. Neither he nor anyone else could fully put into words what he was experiencing; George feared these were not topics to be discussed, even with his parents or his much-loved grandmother. Experiencing much inner turmoil, he was determined to "pass" as a heterosexual male even while secretly experimenting with cross dressing and continuing to feel an unmistakable attraction to other young men.[22] At least once, he secretly shaved his pubic hair, trying to give it as feminine a shape as he could.

George's presentation of himself as a heterosexual youth worked fairly well, and when he became a high school senior he showed much independence by taking a flight to Washington, D.C.[23] He wanted to demonstrate his maturity by taking a plane to the Capitol rather than riding a train, which would have been the less costly choice. It was a daring thing to do, for none of the Jorgensens had ever boarded an airplane. On the morning of his departure in July 1943, George walked to a twenty-one passenger DC-3, climbed the steps of the legendary Douglas tail-dragger, and was surprised to find that the final person to come aboard was Mrs. Eleanor Roosevelt. A few days later he wrote a rambling, poorly spelled letter to Dolly, describing seeing America's former First Lady, and also explaining that while there were lots of places in Washington to visit in the daytime, the evenings were quite long and lonely. Most of his after-dark time had been spent at the Library of Congress because "this was the only place that was open at night."[24] The content and tone of this letter suggests a warm and cordial relationship with his sister, but his handwriting and grammar were terrible. More important, by traveling to the nation's capital as a seventeen year old, George was showing initiative and an eagerness to explore. None of his teenage peers had ever traveled by air. He was proud of himself, and upon returning home he eagerly showed the neighbors his many photographs and pictorial folders illustrating the landmarks of the capital city. Perhaps it was this kind of travel adventure along with the family's Model-A trips that encouraged Jorgensen's lifelong interest in travel, an interest that would later serve Christine Jorgensen as a show business personality. Whenever she began to sag emotionally, the prospect of another trip never failed to perk her up, and when her bookings sagged, Christine's thoughts turned to spending time in far away fantasylands.[25]

Despite George's determination to appear heterosexual, he repeatedly became involved in love affairs with young men followed by intense feelings of shame and guilt, with a promise to himself to abstain from these relationships in the future. But regardless of his vows and promises, throughout these teenage years George experienced at least three "crushes" with male peers. While a reading of the 1967 autobiography would suggest that all of George's romantic escapades were platonic, Jorgensen later described some early childhood sex play with boys, and some youthful erotic adventures with teenage young men. It's unclear what credence should be given such reports.[26]

Although they were concerned about him, the Jorgensens did not treat their son differently than did other middle-class parents in Throggs Neck. They were aware of the well-known developmental struggles of teenagers, and they hoped George's periods of depression and social withdrawal would abate with the passage of time.

Although he experienced much inner conflict and uncertainty about his future, there were some important positive factors, which provided wind to his back. Of the greatest importance was his ability to "pass" as a heterosexual teenager, coupled with the strong family support he had always relied upon, and a conviction that he could stay out of trouble. At base, all of the Jorgensens were socially conventional people. Throughout his teen years, George was a very socially involved person who successfully concealed what appear to have been gay romantic affairs. To accomplish this deception, George seems to have avoided any affiliation with the New York gay subculture or attendance at any of the Halloween "drag" balls.[27] He surely must have known of these events as they were widely publicized. In particular, the Harlem gay Halloween balls drew thousands of cross-dressed men and were extensively reported in the newspapers. As later perceived by Christine, his romantic interludes were best understood as a "woman" falling in love with a man. To complicate all of this, George was also privately cross dressing, an activity often mentioned in transsexual histories.

For any teenager, privacy in a crowded house is usually highly valued, and for George, it was especially important. As a young cross dresser, George had acquired some women's clothing, including lingerie, dresses, and skirts, as he later confided to his doctor in Copenhagen. However, in order to dress as a woman, privacy would have been imperative. Very possibly, it was an attic hideaway that provided this opportunity. Much later in life, Christine also revealed youthful cross-dressing episodes using his sister's clothing: Brenda Lana Smith, who cared for Jorgensen during her final six months, wrote that the prepubescent George had "premiered in front of a Bronx bedroom mirror . . . " dressed in his sister's clothing.[28] He would definitely have needed a private place to wear these outfits. Always "prudish," George never acknowledged any of this to anyone except Dr. Christian Hamburger,[29] in Copenhagen, and Brenda Lana Smith,[30] her housemate.

George developed some habits that were not uncommon among the teenagers of his time, but they took a toll on his health in the long run. By the time he entered high school, at the age of fifteen, he had developed what became a lifelong dependence upon cigarettes, which were then available for a penny each at the local cigar shop not far from his home. Why not smoke? His father, mother, and sister all smoked, and one of the greatest baseball heroes of all time, Ted Williams, was endorsing Camels in sports magazines. Perhaps smoking added a touch of masculine risk taking and a chance to imitate adults, and for George perhaps it also acted like a self-prescribed antidepressant. During his high school years, he was seldom photographed without a cigarette.

Although Christine revealed nothing in her autobiography about her progressive difficulties with the use of alcohol, it seems likely that before high school graduation George had probably done some serious drinking. As we shall describe later, in 1947 he experienced a major episode of binge drinking. As a youth, he'd seen plenty of liquor consumed at the Askov Hall beach club, and lots of beer and mixed drinks flowed at the socials and dinners family and friends had enjoyed. As with most Americans, drinking was simply part of the enjoyment of a social gathering. The Scandinavians of Askov Hall knew how to handle their liquor, but they strictly forbade teenagers to use alcohol. It's not clear what set of circumstances led George to become alcohol dependent, but over several decades, that's what happened. When Christine was forty and about to issue her autobiography, Paul Eriksson, her publisher, did not see indications of unusual alcohol use.[31] He was in a good position to observe, as they traveled extensively together to publicize her book. In her fifties, however, Christine drank more heavily, beginning earlier in the day, and in the evening she would often fall asleep with a drink in her hand.[32]

George's interest in girls was more of envy than of romantic attraction.[33] He admired the girls' skills in attracting dates, their flirting and laughing with the boys, their use of makeup and hair styling, and the elegance of their colorful party dresses that shimmered and rustled as they danced. But according to close relatives who knew him then, he never had a girlfriend despite a long list of girls who were his friends.

The Askov Hall Beach Club was one of many similar organizations that various church groups and ethnic clubs in the Bronx established shortly after the turn of the century. The idea was to have a members-only place for dancing and dinners, card playing, a bit of drinking, and programs that would appeal to both adults and teenagers. There was a sense of being a part of a country club without the expenses of a golf course. In the selection of members, racial, ethnic and religious discrimination were taken for granted and never even mentioned. The club is still there, and the card playing and dances haven't changed much, but the Scandinavians have been replaced by the Irish.[34]

Throughout the humid summers, Florence, Dorothy, and George Jr., spent many days at Askov Hall, swimming and visiting with friends. But Mondays were ruled out because it was Florence's washday, and Sundays were partially off limits because of the importance of church attendance. Askov Hall was a happy place, carefree, with five-cent Cokes and cheap beer, and for the teenagers it was a place to get to know one another. George was not only well known here, he was well liked because he was a clean-cut, intelligent, well-spoken young man.

At Askov Hall, most of the social life was upstairs, but beneath the community room where the adults played cards, dominos, and Chinese checkers, there were dressing rooms for men and women separated by a partition of unfinished pine boards. Danny Riley told how the boys used a pocket knife to enlarge cracks between two boards allowing a peek at the girls in their changing room. It must have seemed incredibly daring. George, according to Riley, joined in this prank until the elders discovered what was going on and installed a more secure divider. Eager to be accepted and respected as one of the guys, he would go along with what the boys considered fun, just as he would sometimes take chances while driving his dad's car. None of this bravado, however, fully erased his concern that he would be viewed as a sissy. Happily, the Askov Hall teenagers knew better than to tease George, for this was a place for family fun, harmony, and goodwill toward all. The girls especially enjoyed George's friendly, ever-joking style.

There were regularly scheduled dances and other youth events at Askov Hall, and George took an active part: "I seldom missed attending the Saturday night socials at Askov Hall, yet I subconsciously feared them," Christine wrote in 1967. According to this account, George was not especially interested in dancing with the girls, but instead, he identified with them: "I was envious when I saw girls in the arms of their escorts, skillfully employing the standard devices of flirtation."[35] George knew how to pretend to be a heterosexual male, but in contrast, his intense feeling of discontent with his own gender identity was something he did not understand. There was no language for these feelings, no role models for his guidance, no books to read at the library, and yet he struggled with an intense conviction that he should have been born a girl.[36]

One of the girls who lived near Askov Hall told of an unusual date that involved George. She had fallen "madly in love with one of the young men at Askov Hall, and finally he asked to take me out, but only under the condition that we would take George along." Although she thought this was strange, she agreed, thinking that George would be something of an odd man or third party on their trip to the movies. Years later, in retrospect, she came to realize that the man she was so madly in love with was far more romantically interested in George than he was in her. "I was shocked to realize that I had been the extra person on this date, and that the two of them were actually interested in each other."[37]

World War II was raging both in Europe and in the Pacific during 1944, and during his senior year in high school, George was notified twice by his local Selective Service Board to report for a physical examination.[38] America was sending trainloads of recent high school graduates to military basic training centers throughout the nation. Several million American men were in uniform and George was a prime candidate for the draft as he had become eighteen at the end of May, 1944. He reported twice for a preinduction physical examination but was rejected each time upon failing to meet the minimum weight. Reportedly, he weighed 110 pounds.[39]

During his senior year at Christopher Columbus High School, George asked his parents for permission to enroll in an intensive night course in photography at the New York Institute of Photography. As always, Florence and George were encouraging and supportive, although the money for tuition came from a loan backed by one of his father's insurance policies. Cash was tight.[40] While the nation's economy had become much stronger with defense spending related to World War II, the Jorgensens were just scraping by. Dorothy was in college.

At the Institute of Photography, George studied lighting, the chemistry of film processing, portrait photography, motion picture filming, and color film development. He learned a lot that he later put to use in Denmark where he worked without pay in a top-quality photography studio, producing a few "cheesecake" prints that he sold. One of the portraits he produced while at the New York Photographic Institute was of himself, depicting an older appearing, sophisticated George Jorgensen, a cigarette in hand. This photo suggests nothing of the underweight and "underdeveloped" Jorgensen; it is a picture of his own idealized view of himself, a mature, worldly, successful, and fully respectable gentleman. But, there is a more realistic picture, probably snapped by one of George's classmates, showing him in a laboratory coat with a towel over his shoulder, looking very much like any of the eighteen-year-olds of that generation.[41] During his final year in high school, George was keeping busy at Christopher Columbus in the daytime, while taking his photography course at night. His parents were delighted that he seemed happier.

George William Jorgensen Jr. graduated from high school on schedule with the midyear class of 1945, and his yearbook picture in "The Anchor," showed a rather thin-faced young man and mentioned his promise as a photographer.[42] Judging from what Christine said later, his grades did not reflect his abilities. Socially, he was able to fit in about as well as most of the other teenagers, many of whom probably felt awkward and uncertain of their future. As mentioned earlier, during his senior year and probably at the urging of his parents, he had joined the De Molay, the youth auxiliary of the Masonic Order. This is a strong indication that he not only was attempting to present himself as a typical young man, but that he intended to continue to do so. It took another five years for his transsexual identity to become fully formed. He was promptly elected chaplain of the fraternal group. The ceremony welcoming the new De Molay members into the Masonic tradition occurred the same month he was graduating from high school. In the formal De Molay group photograph, George does not appear to be different from his peers.[43] Again, he had succeeded in taking the role of an unremarkable heterosexual male. His master plan for avoiding rejection was paying off, except that his gender dysphoric feelings could not be driven from consciousness, and his daily thoughts of becoming a woman had many of the qualities of obsessive thinking. He couldn't get the images of himself as a woman out of his mind. These were not unwanted thoughts, but they were more troubling and intrusive than were his romantic fantasies.

Chapter 4

RKO Pathé and Military Service

In writing about George's later teenage years, the period between graduation from high school and his departure for Denmark, Christine described George as an emotionally conflicted, underachieving, unhappy, gay-oriented young man without a sense of direction.[1] For a little more than five years, George roamed from job to job and place to place, searching for a more satisfying personal and occupational identity. We are left to wonder, concerning these five years, whether George Jorgensen possessed any clear vision of his transsexual future; would he ultimately be living as a man or as a woman? Unlike enrolling in another photography course or taking up a new hobby, the process of becoming a transsexual often begins early in childhood with a conviction that a reversal of gender role is imperative. For most people, making such a change would be unthinkable, but for the transsexual-in-process it is a compelling motive. During his early twenties, he rarely worked more than six months in any job or spent more than a semester in college-level studies. He was not fitting the mold for the only son in a family of hard-working carpenters, builders, and wage earners. His mother encouraged him to apply for various jobs or to try some college courses, for she realized he was a deeply unhappy person. His father was less understanding, often asking when George would go after a real job. His photography was one of the few activities that he showed much interest in, and even this did not lead to paying work. George often became depressed and went to a lot of neighborhood movies.

During these years as a young adult, George began to aggressively seek information about "sex changes." Although he may have seemed to lack a sense of direction, in fact, he was searching for information that would change his life. In a succession of small steps, he con-

Becoming a Woman: A Biography of Christine Jorgensen
© 2008 by The Haworth Press, Taylor & Francis Group. All rights reserved.
doi:10.1300/5896_04

structed a new view of himself, and for the first time, his gender identity began to take on an entirely new configuration. A major difficulty was that there weren't any medically facilitated transsexual role models for him to emulate. But despite periods of depression, throughout this search for identity George demonstrated much initiative and risk taking. During five tumultuous years, Jorgensen evolved from serving as an Army clerk/typist to being a chauffeur, a grocery clerk, a photography student, a library assistant, and finally, to earning a certificate as an X-ray technician. And throughout this period he became increasingly focused on an impossible dream: to become a woman.

By showing the initiative his father valued so greatly, George was becoming a better informed, more persistent, and strongly resilient person. He was gradually finding a sense of direction and redefining what was possible in his future. He was taking great responsibility in this search for his own gender role during a period that seemed, to any outsider, like a succession of failures and false starts. What appeared to others to be a lack of direction was actually a period of experimentation to formulate and consolidate a personal identity. He was not wandering aimlessly from here to there; he was very actively searching, sharing, and examining his transgender feelings. George was a quick study. He had learned the benefits of using a library and before long he would learn the value of self-disclosure: that is, of openly discussing the emotional part of his life with those he trusted most. One step at a time, he began to explore his sexual feelings with close friends, and to verbalize his vague thoughts about becoming a woman. George Jorgensen was discovering the benefits of accepting his own conflicted feelings and also revealing the truth about himself to others. It is little wonder that this process required years of effort. He had grown up in a highly sex-negative culture, and he was very ashamed of his attraction to men. There were plenty of gay youths in the Bronx and in Manhattan, but he did everything he could to avoid being perceived as gay by his family and friends.

For well over a century, there had been a visible gay subculture in New York City with well-established semi-secretive meeting places, bars, restaurants, pool rooms, and baths. Here, homosexuals could gather and meet friends in comparative safety, although police raids were both common and expected. Homosexual conduct was against the law, but arrest and conviction was rare. The uncommon arrest typically resulted in a night in jail and a small fine. But even this slap on the wrist could lead to the loss of one's job. Throughout New York City, various forms of minor police harassment of gay persons was common until the late 1960s.

But despite legal prohibitions and occasional arrests, New York City, like most metropolitan areas, had a long history of tolerating the development of a vital, growing, loosely organized gay community. Beginning in the nineteenth century, along the Bowery of Greenwich Village, bars had been established that catered to homosexual men. These were retreats also favored by female and male prostitutes and minor law breakers. Hence, they were often the target of police action. By the turn of the century, a more fashionable location was preferred along 14th Street between Broadway and 3rd Avenue, known as the Rialto. This was a broad, tree-lined avenue with many hotels and bars that were well established hangouts for the gays of Gotham. *Gay New York: Gender, Urban Culture, and the Makings of the Gay Male World* describes the gay evening "uniform" of the 1920s: A dark suit with a white shirt, a large red bow tie, and a pair of white kid gloves. Cross dressed men, some of them surely transsexuals, blossomed in this permissive environment.[2] Some of the hotels in the 14th Street Rialto district provided rental space for cross dressers to store their dresses, hats, and shoes, along with comfortable rooms to facilitate their transformation into fashionably dressed ladies. Today, feminine cross-dressed gay men are often labeled "drag queens," but nobody actually knew then, or now, what the sexual preference of these gender-role transgressors may have been. Very possibly, there were both gay and heterosexual cross dressers enjoying an evening in the watering holes of the Rialto. Attired in upscale women's suits and flashy dresses, these men sought to appear as beautiful, feathered ladies, with stylish shoes, hats, gloves, and makeup appropriate to the fashion of the day. During the 1930s and until World War II, the Rialto community migrated northward toward Times Square, where gay restaurants and bars were plentiful until the military police helped bring about their closure in the early 1940s. There had long been a gay community in New York City,[3] but there is no record of George Jorgensen ever participating in this.

An important source of pleasure that contributed much to George's life was reading, and books became an important diversion and escape from his "aching isolation." He especially favored self-help books and stories about American history. George also found solace in philosophical works that provided guidance for finding happiness and meaning in life. His many visits to the Throggs Neck public library led to his first part-time job shelving books and assisting with the custodial work. He took every opportunity to read about human sexuality although there was little to be found in this small branch library. At that time, the typical neighborhood library would not have had any books dealing with so-called "sex changes," and while a few newspaper reports concerning transsexuals appeared now and then, they were rare.

In 1948, George joined millions of other Americans in examining the sensational new book, *Sexual Behavior in the Human Male* by Dr. Alfred Kinsey of Indiana University that reported on the sexual behavior of 12,000 men. Kinsey and his associates interviewed these individuals over a period of about ten years.[4] One of his major findings was that same-sex behavior is far more common in American men than had been believed, a conclusion that stirred much controversy, both then and now. Kinsey also reported that nearly all males masturbated, usually beginning in their early teens, and that failure to do so was predictive of future sexual hang-ups. George's local library kept Kinsey's book under lock and key, just as did most medical and university libraries, but occasionally he'd find an opportunity to read a few pages of this research. Kinsey's study said much about variations in male sexual behavior, but it provided no information about transsexuality or cross dressing. Although Kinsey interviewed the members of one cross dressers' support group, he detected fewer than 200 transvestites among the men who gave their sexual histories.[5]

In his library explorations for transsexual material, George's most likely discovery would have been a 1933 English version of the story of Lili Elbe, a Danish artist who had been surgically transformed to become a woman. In his discussion with his friend and confidant, Dr. Joseph Angelo, in 1950, Jorgensen appears to have referred to this case: "Then, we discussed certain historical cases, one of which had occurred as early as 1930."[6] Reference was made to more than a single case although nothing specific was identified. It would also have been possible for him to have discovered a 1946 book by an English physician, Dr. Michael Dillon, describing various female-to-male sex change issues;[7] Dillon later became a transsexual man. If George had found either of these resources or any other transsexual cases, why was this not mentioned in Christine's autobiography? One possibility is that in 1967 Christine was eager to present herself as the courageous explorer, sailing across the transgender sea without a chart or a compass. Acknowledgement of prior transsexual publications would have diminished Christine's estimation of her own importance and detracted from her tale of becoming the first modern transsexual, an achievement we do not intend to diminish. The point is, there were several books and articles in the published literature on transsexualism that Christine almost certainly knew about. In addition to the New York Public Library, Jorgensen used at least one major medical library in Manhattan. These libraries were only a subway ride from her neighborhood.

Going to libraries was one thing, but getting a job was another. During his first post-high school year, George spent a lot of time in his room, saying little, especially about his future plans. He was depressed and withdrawn. His mother really didn't know how to help, but she urged him to do some repair projects around the house. Although this was not something George especially enjoyed, he was fully capable of helping out, for he had learned the basics of home repair from his father. Within a day or two, all of these assignments had been completed. Now, George needed a job, not just a list of home-repair tasks. Other than part-time library employment, he had never held a job and this concerned his parents. He talked of enrolling in a more advanced photography class at the Photographic Institute, but he showed no initiative beyond mentioning the idea. Florence was convinced that he needed to get a full-time job and gain more occupational experience. It was wartime, and with millions of men in the military, jobs were easy to find. She urged him to telephone some bridge-playing friends at Askov Hall, to ask if they could help him find some work connected with photography.[8]

Larry and June Jensen both worked for RKO-Pathé, a cinema production and newsreel company in Manhattan. They had known George for years, and were eager to help him; through their recommendation an interview was soon arranged. Within days, George was offered a job as a footage cutter, working with the weekly news films that were sent to theaters across the nation. The job required some judgment in clipping segments from the newsreels according to subject matter and splicing each batch of footage onto an appropriate reel. The work reminded him of restacking library books according to their catalog number. He learned the job quickly and the techniques of assembling the various segments of film came quickly to him. These reels of motion pictures could then be employed for stock shots and were used either by RKO or anyone willing to pay for their use; in the trade they call it "the footage business." His work didn't require a lot of creativity, but the job matched his photographic interests, and George quickly became a valued employee. He worked hard to avoid any hint of the sissy status that had plagued him in school. He went to work in a suit and a tie and showed a new interest in keeping his shoes shined; these were responsibilities he previously associated exclusively with going to church.

At lunchtime, when the older employees were sharing vivid descriptions of their weekend dating exploits, he learned to join in with fabrications that were sufficiently realistic to avoid letting on that he didn't date. He gave the names of girls he had supposedly taken out, and mentioned the movies he claimed to have attended, all imaginary, but it worked. George not only got along as an employee, he was liked as a friend and as an energetic and responsible co-worker. It was the spring of 1945 and for the first time in his life George felt a daily surge of self-respect, manliness, and a new confidence when he got up each morning. He knew how to do his job and getting paid every month was a new experience. He was always on time for work, and it was a job he and his parents were proud of. George seemed to have made a fine start; he believed this could lead to a real career. In understanding his sense of identity at this time, he seemed determined to live his life as a man. Even his sister Dorothy expressed pride when she told her college friends that her brother was helping to assemble the weekly RKO newsreel pictures. Clearly, he was forming a stronger and more positive sense of masculine identity. He looked forward to his job; nobody was questioning his manhood. But despite his masculine façade, George had significant uncertainty about how to deal with his growing feelings of wanting to be a woman. He felt he wasn't "normal."

> I wondered if my new associates would notice what I had long since known: that I was one who deviated, emotionally, from what had been termed 'normal.' But I was determined to behave like a man, even if I didn't feel like one, and try to hide the pretense behind a brave exterior.[9]

Christine wrote of these years: "Most people aren't aware of the inner turmoil of others [and] it isn't difficult to put on an acceptable front in public."[10] This was all about George's heterosexual masquerade, a false front he used as part of a continuing effort to be the son he felt he ought to be despite the emotional costs of having to conceal his intense transgender feelings. At least superficially, he was a happier, more secure person, and he was proud that his parents admired the way he was handling his new job and establishing new friendships. He seemed to take real pride in his appearance and to speak with self-assurance, and he also had the distinction of being responsible to splice the RKO logotype rooster or "chicken" as the employee preferred to say, onto the beginning of each weekly newsreel. Ironically, it was through motion picture news reports that moviegoers throughout the world would learn, in 1953, of his sex change and see the first pictures of the stunning Christine Jorgensen.

At this point in his life, at about the age of eighteen, we see George Jorgensen doing everything he could to fit the mold of a hardworking, reasonably masculine young man, building self-esteem through his daily good works, making new friends, and showing himself and the rest of the world that he was a success in a man's job. George was struggling to find himself, to learn whether he could function as a man. He was accomplishing all of this in an environment that he found socially and professionally satisfying. It was one of the segments of his life when living as a man brought him greater satisfaction than dreaming of becoming a woman. But this period of personal growth was about to end: The United States government was still drafting young men at the same time that millions of World War II veterans were being discharged.

When a notice to report for a preinduction physical first arrived from George's local selective service board, he was not concerned. Not only had he failed two previous draft physicals, but the war had ended. He was, therefore, greatly surprised to be ordered to take a preinduction physical examination that resulted in his classification as 1-A.[11] It was even more of a surprise to be told that he'd be inducted almost immediately and that he should put his affairs in order. Why, he wondered, would the Army be drafting anybody when they were processing tens of thousands of men out of the Army each month? His question was soon answered. Shortly after induction, he was assigned to a Separation Center at Fort Dix, New Jersey, to help process thousands of Army veterans back into civilian life.

He hated saying good-bye to his new friends at RKO; this first real job had been an important contributor to his adult identity. For George, the RKO assignment had not only helped him find an occupation that was enjoyable and promising, it was a giant step forward in the shaping of his sense of himself as a masculine young man. In his attempts to conceal his gay and feminine feelings, he had almost fooled himself. Now, along with dozens of other young men his own age, he boarded a train for his first day in the military, traveling to Fort Dix, only a couple of hours west of Manhattan.

On his first day as a soldier, he was issued the standard set of GI uniforms, all of which seemed too large. It felt strange to toss aside his comfortable pants and shirt in exchange for these heavier, stiff, drab, work clothes. George felt a sense of solidarity and camaraderie among these new soldiers who were all strangers to him. A quick rapport had developed amid the laughter and barracks banter; his new Army buddies seemed to be in good humor. George was a little surprised that they seemed to like him.

For all of these men, and especially for George, there was something special about putting on the uniform of the United States Army. Buttoning up the khaki Eisenhower jacket filled him with pride for it signified two things: first, he had qualified for membership in a powerful military organization, thereby acquiring a special new identity; second, "I [George] wanted my parents to be proud of me and to be able to say, 'My son is in the service.'"[12] At RKO, he knew he was a man doing a man's job; now, having been sworn in as an Army private and in the uniform of his country, the entire world could see he was not only a man, he was a soldier. At five foot, six inches,[13] he was one of the shorter men, and he certainly weighed less than most of his buddies, but as he learned to deliver a snappy salute he was standing taller and feeling greater pride in himself than he had ever felt before. Even his appetite had improved.

Private George William Jorgensen Jr. was surprised to experience a new sense of well-being, strength, and greater self-confidence as a soldier. Initially, there would be no sixteen-week basic training for him; rather, he was given a hasty on-the-job training program covering the preparation and management of discharge records. He found the procedures easy to learn, and his typing speed and accuracy increased swiftly with a daily schedule of work in the busy processing center. Each day, thousands of former soldiers were tossing aside their uniforms and heading home.

George Jorgensen was helping to speed these veterans home. As he got the hang of his job and made a few friends, he decided that autumn in New Jersey was not bad at all; he actually liked being in the Army. Obedient, bright, friendly, and a fast learner, within weeks George had been promoted to Private First Class. He was also soon assigned his own table and typewriter. Despite his modest military experience, the newest recruits looked up to him for guidance and he found himself teaching others about military paperwork and discharge regulations.

There was nothing fancy about his living quarters in the standard, wooden, two-story, wartime barracks furnished with steel cots, but he was not complaining. The single downstairs lavatory without doors on the toilet stalls seemed a bit primitive, but he soon discovered less austere bathrooms he could use because he was now a part of the permanent company at Fort Dix, not one of the transient soldiers awaiting their discharge papers who barely knew where the mess halls were.

Fort Dix is a huge military base with its own hospital, commercial areas, a guard house, a movie theater (showing RKO newsreels along with feature films), and many recreational facilities including a library that soon became George's favorite hangout. He often spent evenings there after the flag-lowering evening retreat ceremony. Before long, he was helping to shelve the returned books and to check books in and out. He and the sergeant-in-charge shared their opinions about some of the new books that were popular, especially self-help and career-planning books, and sometimes they talked about photography. It felt great to be making new friends. Like his mother, he was a very orderly person, and using the pocket-sized notebook he always carried, he proudly listed his Army address that authenticated his new identity.[14]

Pvt. G. Jorgensen
20th Co. Sep Center
Fort Dix, NJ
Permanent Party
Serial Number: 42259077
Rifle Number: 1799825

George's pride in military service is an example of his strong motivation to please his parents, and to fit into the role of a young man by actually doing one of the things young men are expected to do in time of war: respond to the nation's call. Developing self-esteem and earning the respect of others were among his most important goals in life, and to a great extent, they were the themes that motivated the different phases of Christine's later career. George's gay inclinations had not subsided, but he knew how to keep them concealed, and with the many demands of his military schedule, it also seemed easier to put aside his thoughts of becoming a woman. Although this didn't disturb him as much as it had the year before, there was seldom a day when he didn't think about it.[15]

His fourteen months in the service strengthened his skills in presenting himself as a respectable, self-confident, supposedly heterosexual young man. Although he became aware of other gay military personnel, he never had any sexual relationships with them (we are told). He followed the rules, learned how to do his job well, including a great deal of typing, and stayed out of trouble. It was the same conventional pattern he had followed in high school and at RKO. On weekends, he'd usually take the train into Manhattan and then ride the Bronx-bound Pelham Bay subway home, getting off at the elevated Westchester Square station, then walking along East Tremont Avenue past the Presbyterian Church, and finally turning north on Dudley Avenue, a street he knew so well. Nobody ever called him Goose when he had his uniform on.

George realized how proud his family was to have him arrive at home with his new Pfc. stripe on his sleeves, and he smiled warmly as they embraced him and insisted on taking a picture showing the new chevrons he had sewn on his jacket and his shirt. After the picture taking, they went up the narrow stairway and into the living room. George looked into his own little bedroom and noticed nothing had been changed. His pictures of his sister, Dolly, snapshots of their dog and the family, his posters and keepsakes were all in place. He sat down and began to change into his civilian clothes as his mother prepared supper.

Both of his parents were thrilled to see him looking so healthy and happy, but Florence was concerned that his new self-confidence might peel off as he took off the body armor of a soldier and pulled on his old clothes. She may have prayed that this Army experience would go on for a long time and the result will be a more self-sufficient, confident, and successful George. Like mothers everywhere, she cared deeply for her son.

It seemed like one of the best times of his life, but it was too good to last, for after a few months of busy but undemanding clerical duty at Fort Dix he was assigned to a basic training center at Camp Polk, Louisiana. George's military career had not included skills such as marching, infantry squad tactics, or firing a weapon. This required a short addendum in his notebook, adding to his growing sense of really being one of the guys. At Camp Polk, you had to learn to be an infantryman, not just a clerk/typist. His new address was added to the one he had recorded for Fort Dix.[16]

N. Camp Polk, LA
29th TNG BN Bit 6

After a few weeks in Louisiana, George was worn out by the physical demands of basic training. It was a hot and humid dawn to dusk routine, and he especially disliked the prospect of firing his rifle at the range target that was shaped like a human body. Under no circumstances could he imagine firing a weapon at anyone, and he therefore asked a buddy to load his ammunition and fake his qualifying shots. The sergeant supervising the rifle range pretended not to see what was going on.

The Danish Royal Library, known in Copenhagen as the Black Diamond, contains little pocket notebooks and penciled paragraphs of philosophy and life guidance that George carefully transcribed from psychology and self-help books while he was in Louisiana and at Fort Dix. These had become his guidelines for living and perhaps they became a substitute for the more religious guidance favored by the rest of his family. The selected material often dealt with life as a struggle, achieving peace of mind, having faith in God, meeting challenges, and the search for meaningful contact with other human beings. Many of them had a religious theme. He was searching for meaning in his life and for a more clearly defined sense of himself. More than anything, George had always been in search of self-respect and this was to be a lifelong, elusive, and too often disappointing quest. But now, quite unexpectedly and long before the end of his sixteen weeks of basic training, his unit in Louisiana was disbanded. The Army needed clerk/typists, not riflemen, and he was herded onto a poorly ventilated troop train for the return trip to Fort Dix.

George liked his assignment at Fort Dix. He knew the importance of getting the names and numbers exactly correct when typing discharge documents, to be certain that medical records and other data were properly recorded for the Veteran's Administration, and to see that the required paperwork was in the right place at the right time. George seemed to stand more erect in his uniform and to smile more. His parents told their relatives every one of George's new military adventures. Superficially, everything seemed better for George, but privately, without ever saying a word about his inner feelings, Pfc. Jorgensen retained some serious doubts about his masculinity, and even about his male sex organs. Comparing himself to other men in the barracks, he felt he was different in several important ways, for he had little or no hair on his limbs or his body.

"My walk could scarcely be called a masculine stride." He felt his gestures were effeminate and that his voice had a "feminine quality," but most significant of all, George was convinced that "the sex organs that determined my classification as a 'male' were underdeveloped." He also concluded that both his feelings and his anatomy suggested that he was either "a homosexual or a woman."[17]

George's conviction that his sex organs were "underdeveloped" was one of his firmly held but erroneous beliefs. It was a defensive notion that he never abandoned until years later, in Copenhagen, after the amputation of his testes and penis. This anatomical evaluation of his supposedly deficient sexual anatomy helped to support his longing to become a woman, but it was an underestimate of how his sex organs compared in size to those of other men. We are not told whether George believed his penis was abnormally small, a common male preoccupation, or whether he thought there was something "underdeveloped" about his testicles.[18] Perhaps he was referring to both. What is known is that none of his three preinduction physical examinations, which were very thorough, or his Army discharge physical, or his physical examination in Denmark revealed anything abnormal about his genitals or any other part of his anatomy.[19] George's concerns about his body reveal more about his self-concept, his body image, and his uncertain masculinity than his knowledge of anatomy.

Psychologically, his self-assessment of being "underdeveloped" was George's way of making sense of his powerful gender identity conflict. Increasingly, he felt destined to become a woman, and that he must do so, yet he had only a vague idea of how to accomplish this. Throughout his life he had envied and admired women, while not feeling a sexual attraction. He was certain he should have been born a woman, and his focus on his supposed genital abnormality was consistent with his view of himself as a victim of a prenatal hormonal accident. No evidence of this was required; he simply believed it was true. But his feminine gender identity strivings were kept hidden from others, who consistently responded to him as a far more typical young man than he ever acknowledged to himself. Absolutely no one thought of him as a person who might undergo a "sex change." He made certain of this.

Several years earlier, one of the farm boys George met during his summers in upstate New York with his cousin, Robert Andersen, was a lad identified as Tom Chaney in Christine's autobiography. Tom was four years older than George. The two had shared a close friendship that grew while Tom was in the Navy for several years, and they had maintained their relationship through an exchange of letters, said to be entirely circumspect. None of this correspondence has survived. During Tom's Navy years, George did everything he could to: "push the perplexing thoughts of Tom Chaney into the background . . . and the confusion about my place in the world seemed to be resolving itself slightly. My euphoria was short-lived, however." Even the thought of Tom facing danger while in the military was upsetting. "I remember being overwhelmed by the revelation that, despite earlier denials, I was in love with him."[20]

George was so ashamed of these feelings that he was unable to discuss it even with Grandma Jorgensen, his closest confidant. A strong theme in Christine's 1967 autobiography is the extensive description of several same sex love affairs, coupled with an insistence that George was as sexually pure and inexperienced as a person could be. Sexual behavior is never admitted. Meyerowitz[21] attributed this to the "prudish" side of George, as a youth, and later, to Christine who was also portrayed in her autobiography as virtually sexless. Christine's autobiography reports that this "perfect" love could find fulfillment only in fantasy, should Tom die while in the military.[22] Skipping ahead to the culmination of the Chaney story, two years later, on a weekend at home during George's Fort Dix Army hitch, Tom returned from his military service and surprised George with a phone call:

Hello . . . I'm back . . . I'm in New York at the Commodore Hotel
. . . Come on down and have dinner and then we'll spend the evening on the town.[23]

George's pulse quickened, he felt exceptionally excited, and when
they met later that day at the hotel he hoped for an embrace, but there
was only a handshake.[24] Throughout this reunion which extended
through dinner and into the evening, George struggled with the tension between his passionate love for Tom, and the nonsexual behavior
Tom returned. Even as they reminisced about their summer fun together, George clarified his own thinking about whether any romantic
relationship was possible and concluded it was not. Later that night,
feeling rejected and disappointed, he reread Tom's letters, studied the
keepsakes and photographs they had collected from earlier times,
then slowly, one by one, threw these treasures into the furnace. The
way to forget about Tom, he concluded, was to throw himself head-
long into a job and to prove that he had what it took to be a real man.
He thought he could do that, although he had no prospect of employment. George became depressed, something that would trouble him
for decades in the future.

In 1946, all newly inducted Army personnel were classified as Veterans of World War II, and they were also eligible for the various benefits of the GI Bill and the World War II Victory Medal. George
would rely on these benefits for the next thirty months, bouncing
from job to college and back again. His job had become the work of
finding himself. Until he completed his transsexual change in Denmark at the age of twenty-six, he was always either unemployed or
close to it, but the GI Bill provided benefits that allowed him to travel,
experiment with college, gain additional photography training, and
even take a short course as a medical technician.

During the years between high school and his departure for Denmark, the most difficult and most important goal George experienced
was to clarify his thinking about his feminine gender identity, and
how this might help to dim the fires of the homoerotic attractions he
considered immoral. He really didn't know how to define these feelings, or where to seek help. Meanwhile, at Fort Dix, his buddies typed
out his honorable discharge papers and after just fourteen months he
had become a military veteran. It was December 1946; he turned
twenty in May. George had little idea of how valuable the GI Bill
would be.

Chapter 5

Hollywood, 1947

Taking off his uniform for the last time upon returning home, George moved back into his closetlike room and quickly found that most of his pre-Army clothes were a bit tight. Within days, he applied for his former job assembling stock footage at RKO Pathé, but was told the position was not available.[1] Very possibly, this was due to the return of former employees who had served in the military and who had federally guaranteed rights to return to their prewar jobs. In any case, after again requesting help from his Askov Hall friends, Larry and June Jensen, George was hired by RKO Pathé as a chauffeur in Manhattan, a job he held for about eight months. Many times, he was asked to drive a visiting celebrity to a press conference. He observed how simple it is to hold such a press gathering, especially if you have anything newsworthy to say. Occasionally, he would even be asked to make telephone calls reminding particular reporters of some sort of press event. He found this easy and far more interesting than his assignments as a driver.

George considered himself a photographer, not a chauffeur, and he soon came to hate the work; he felt it was demeaning and that it didn't lead anywhere. During this time, his friend, June Jensen, had left her marriage and moved to Hollywood. George wrote her saying he was determined to "try his luck" in search of a photography job in the movie capital. "Hollywood is big enough for both of us," she assured him, and soon he quit his job and boarded a bus for California. It was August, 1947. He had a lot of ambition but not much money and no contacts within the movie studios. Armed with a camera, his portfolio of pictures, and $500, he was on his way.[2]

Traveling by bus from the Bronx to Los Angeles, George paused for a few highly inspirational and somewhat religious days at the

Becoming a Woman: A Biography of Christine Jorgensen
© 2008 by The Haworth Press, Taylor & Francis Group. All rights reserved.
doi:10.1300/5896_05

Grand Canyon where he stayed at the charming and historic Bright Angel Lodge. While overlooking the canyon, he was deeply moved by the contrast between the smallness of man and what he considered the enormity of this great expanse of "God and Nature." This experience seems to have been similar to the religious emotions he had felt a few years earlier, and he concluded that "a change of view was taking place and I regard it, even now, as a turning point in my life."[3] George was opening himself to new experiences, new feelings, and to the recognition of turning points in his life. He was actively in search of not only a clarification of his gender identity—he was seeking a new life.

Perhaps his motivation for personal growth helped him to reveal more about himself to other people, to stop hiding, and to allow others to see him as both a possible homosexual and as a man who wanted to become a woman. He would soon find an ideal time and place to do this, on the patio of an off-white, stucco-covered Mediterranean-style residence on a tree-shaded avenue in Hollywood. June Jensen had been renting a room in a pleasant house on Irving Avenue, just a few blocks south of the main gate of Paramount Pictures on Melrose Street, and she arranged for George to rent another of the bedrooms. Mrs. Jensen was an experienced film editor and had little difficulty finding work. Within a year she was in another relationship and married soon thereafter. For George, however, it was a less successful story, at least from an occupational perspective.

Rather than setting out immediately to search for a job, George bought paint to spruce up the small patio at the rear of the house. The patio became an evening conversation hideaway for June and George. Here were two New Yorkers in search of new, happier lives, and under the stars on cool evenings, they shared their feelings for hours and spoke without inhibition of their occupational and personal goals, their conflicts, frustrations, and love affairs. Very possibly, the therapeutic benefits of this relationship meant more to George than getting a job, for this was an extremely important period in the reformulation of his gender identity. Night after night, he was coming to grips with what was really on his mind. Between the two of them, there was a great deal of soul searching and self-disclosure going on, punctuated by episodes of tears and laughter. For him, the relaxed, private evenings, the smoking, the glasses of wine, and the sharing of emotional and intimate stories, 3,000 miles from home, all contributed to a much-needed emotional catharsis. These conversations became increasingly intense, uninhibited, personal, and filled with self-revelations, a new experience for George who had kept his homosexual and gender identity thoughts so closely guarded.[4] He experienced a liberating sense of relief after confiding his conflict filled feelings to June.

This new experience of disclosing his feelings did not happen all at once. On one occasion, after being "confronted" by a homosexual film maker who treated George as a fellow homosexual, he was "appalled and disgusted" by this person and upon returning home "I couldn't bring myself to say anything about this unpleasant encounter." On the one hand, he perceived himself as an effeminate male with underdeveloped sexual organs and as a person who had fallen in love with several other men. On the other hand, his prudish and moralistic values resulted in "a fear of homosexual contact that was probably based on the hidden belief that I, too, deviated from what was termed "normal.""[5]

June and George were delighted to welcome June's friend from Denmark, Helen Johnson, who had attended the same elementary school in Denmark. Helen was single and about the same age as June. Again, a woman had become a part of George's life and she would play an even greater role, quite unexpectedly, in the years ahead. With Helen joining in, the evening conversations among the three young people developed into something akin to group psychotherapy with animated sharing of feelings and discussions of personal conflicts, aspirations, and emotions. For the first time, in sessions that went beyond any of his many adolescent talks with Grandma Jorgensen, George told his two friends about his homoerotic feelings and, very importantly, of his desire to live as a woman. For the first time, he had articulated these thoughts to other people despite feelings of shame. Helen became quite direct in her questioning: "There are a lot of effeminate men in the world . . . Maybe you're one of them?" The conversation continued: "You mean a homosexual," he responded. June added that she had been wondering if he was gay, and George then described a recent sexually intense exchange with a young gay director at one of the studios who had propositioned him. George emphasized his "shock and fear" of being "openly classified as a homosexual." George often confounded feelings of romantic attraction to men with opposing feelings of revulsion. He told June and Helen:

> I can't even think of a relationship like that with another man. . .
> Yet I have to admit I'm drawn to some men. I know I notice

them, not as a man, but as a woman might. I just don't know what category to put myself in.[6]

As described in Christine's autobiography, George was shocked and repulsed when he felt this individual was hitting on him. But quite a different outcome is described in a short letter to his parents, wherein he revealed a dinner and theater outing with a "director friend" he had met at one of the studios. This seems to be the person he had mentioned to June and Helen. George wrote:

> 4 June 1947
> Dear All -
> Thanks for your cards. I had a swell birthday.
> Had dinner and went to the theater with a director friend. So you see I am getting to know the right people. The influential one's [sic] anyway. Some of them aren't ideal friends but their [sic] worth knowing for business contacts.
> Thanks again for your thoughtfullness [sic]
> - Love.
> Georg[7]

We have no way of knowing if this relationship was more than a casual friendship, but George's suggestion that this person may have been less than an "ideal" friend clearly suggests an ambivalence in his feelings toward him. As we have seen throughout his life, George repeatedly found himself in relationships with men that produced intense conflict. In confessing his romantic attractions toward men to June and Helen, he was crossing the boundary of secrecy. However, in revealing more of his feelings to his two friends, he also became more forthright about his vision of himself as a woman, something he had never discussed with anyone. On what must have been a very special evening, George expressed his thoughts of becoming a woman for the first time, although he hedged somewhat with the wording:

> Maybe you'll think I'm insane, but did either of you ever look at me and think that I might not be a man at all, but a . . . woman? . . . I have the physical characteristics of a very immature male, but as far back as I can remember, I've always had the feeling . . . the emotions of a girl.[8]

Perhaps without fully realizing it, during these emotion-packed and confidential conversations with two young women, thousands of miles from home, George had gradually discovered a rationale and found the language to express both his homosexual feelings and his feminine gender identity. It was a major conceptual breakthrough for him. As he put it, he was a man, attracted to some other men, but only in the way a woman would be. This made sense to him. As a woman in love with a man, the relationship would be heterosexual, allowing him to live free of the shame he had endured for so long. (Lightning and thunder are uncommon in Hollywood, but this moment of self-discovery deserved some sort of triumphant movie-making sound effect with a musical accompaniment. George lit another cigarette.)

If he could live his life as a woman, he reasoned, this would make him a fully respectable person no matter with whom he fell in love. He would then be a person worthy of the admiration of his parents. Going a step further, he introduced the theory that his homosexual and gender identity problems were based on hormonal abnormalities, and that they could be addressed through medical help, although he had no idea just what that would require. Reflecting on these earlier conversations, Christine later summarized the significance of her new sense of direction: "Not only had my growing desire to seek medical help been reinforced, but I had broken through a heretofore impregnable barrier."[9]

It was no accident that George considered a hormonal explanation for both his sexual turmoil and his gender-identity conflict.[10] The discovery of male and female hormones had taken place about fifteen years earlier and had been prominently featured in news reports. The idea of universal bisexuality was being discussed in both technical journals and newspaper articles.

After these cathartic evening discussions, George was less anxious and less inhibited about revealing his motives to others, and he was eager to find a way to get the medical help he would need to become a woman. At last, he believed he had a new goal that could turn his life around, but he had no job, little money, and far too much time on his hands. He earned a few dollars stacking soup cans and cereal boxes on the shelves of a nearby market, but soon his thoughts were of returning home. He was nearly broke.

Emotionally, he had gained a lot in Hollywood and he now held a new, clearer goal, but this was not a place he could build a career.

He'd been dependent upon the monthly $65 unemployment benefit that ex-GIs were eligible to receive. Then, out of the blue, he learned that his mother had won a $750 share of "a consolation prize" at the Irish Sweepstakes, and she sent her son $250. "I immediately invested my [prize money] . . . in a complete dental repair job, which included an upper plate."[11] Was George paying an early price for his chain smoking? For years, the publicity photographs distributed by Christine Jorgensen would glisten with a row of sparkling white and perfectly formed teeth thanks to "Mom's bet on the Irish Sweepstakes."

Soon, June had remarried and Helen had returned to Denmark, leaving the young Mr. Jorgensen lonely and dejected: "To hell with it, I might as well give up and go home," he concluded. It meant another admission of failure, another uncertain occupational change, another reason for disappointment for his parents, and a feeling of having flopped again. On the other hand, "I couldn't stack grocery shelves for the rest of my life."[12] His Hollywood career had lasted about one year. He planned a trip home by starting with a side trip to San Francisco, and upon arriving there in November 1947, he mailed a beautiful postal card photo of the Golden Gate Bridge to his parents and assured them that he was well. However, an unusual episode was just ahead.

In her 1967 autobiography, Christine omitted many of the details of what was clearly a drunken weekend in San Francisco en route to the Midwest. Although the consequences of this binge are presented in considerable detail in her book, we are not told what actually took place as George prepared to take the train to Minneapolis for a visit with his Aunt Augusta. Also, there is no explanation for why the planned route began with the detour to San Francisco. These mysteries are left for resolution by the readers of her autobiography, but it seems likely that Jorgensen was deeply ashamed of whatever it was that happened in San Francisco, for only a diffuse outline was revealed.

George liked to travel and perhaps he simply wanted to visit the City by the Bay, or perhaps he was hoping to link up with friends, but whatever the motivation, his stop there turned out to be a very alcoholic weekend. For Christine, smoking and drinking were to be lifelong problems, sufficiently serious to affect her health and longevity.

George boarded a Greyhound bus in Hollywood and by the time he arrived in San Francisco at the bus station south of Market Street, he was very ill and disconsolate. He was "really sick . . . . sitting in the bus terminal . . . shivering and burning . . . ."[13] However, the postcard to his parents suggested he was feeling fine. There is no explanation of what happened next, but surely, George had begun a bout of heavy drinking; he wrote he had no memory of the circumstances. The next thing he became aware of, said to be days later, he was looking out of a train window: "I opened my eyes and saw a snow-covered land-scape . . . and asked the conductor where I was." He replied: "Just pulling into Minneapolis."[14] The conductor added: "That must have been some farewell party! The night you came aboard in San Fran-cisco you were loaded! It's a good thing you had a ticket in your hand."[15] Christine then wrote that while she had had a vague notion of hoping to visit her Aunt Augusta in Minneapolis, she had no recol-lection of purchasing a rail ticket. What happened during the "lost weekend" in San Francisco? We shall never know. George was func-tioning so poorly when he boarded the train he had failed to check three of his bags, none of which ever turned up.

George was not well acquainted with his Aunt Augusta, the oldest daughter of his grandfather, Charles Jorgensen (from a premarital af-fair in Denmark), but he thought he could drop in on her as part of his return trip to the Bronx. He planned to surprise her by turning up on her doorstep, so he was surprised to see her waiting for him on the railway platform. Although she produced a telegram giving his arrival date, he had no recollection of having sent this from San Francisco. As the con-ductor said, "That must have been some farewell party!"[16]

Throughout her adult life, Christine erected strong defenses against disclosing personal information that she considered her business alone. The Jorgensens valued their privacy. In any case, the days in Minne-apolis brought George much closer to his aunt, as they shared many stories about how each had dealt with the hardships in their lives. However, though George was exceptionally faithful and attentive to relatives, before going to Copenhagen, he never discussed his sexual or gender feelings with any of them. After a week or so, George was aboard a train back to his home, and he realized that the sharing of his feelings with Aunt Augusta, like his evenings in Hollywood with June and Helen, had been a rewarding and cathartic experience. More than any thing else, Augusta had shown George that life works best when you can show others "enormous and envious personal cour-age."[17] Before Augusta died, he would visit her again, in 1953, this time as a national celebrity newly named Christine Jorgensen.

Chapter 6

The Male Hormone

Home again in the Bronx and feeling like a loser, the newspaper ads for help wanted appeared to offer little of interest, and as an escape, George began attending movies, day after day, sleeping a lot, and smoking more than ever. George was depressed. He seemed physically and emotionally worn out. After about three months, still somewhat low and unhappy, he hit upon the idea of attending Mohawk Valley Community College in Utica, New York, again drawing upon the benefits of the GI Bill. But the required first-year liberal arts courses of science, history, and foreign language held little interest, and academically it seemed very difficult compared to high school. So George packed up, then moved in with four roommates in barracks-like postwar housing in Utica. His greatest joy was riding around town in their Model A, killing time, and accomplishing nothing important except that he was successfully presenting himself as a college guy. He'd do anything to avoid the label of "sissy." And just as he had found among his buddies at Fort Dix, these college students actually seemed to like him.[1]

George invested little effort in his college studies, but on a Sunday morning in the spring of 1948, he experienced a surprisingly emotional part of himself: a sudden and intense reawakening of his religious feelings. Like most of his Danish friends, George had been baptized a Lutheran, but his family attended the nearby Presbyterian Church In Throggs Neck, just down the street from his house. It was with the Utica Presbyterians that George suddenly felt he had found a loving family of fellow churchgoers. Greatly moved by a persuasive sermon that may have both touched and relieved his sexual guilt, he found God to be "an all-loving, all-knowing presence."[2] Surely, George must also have also come to believe that an all-forgiving God

Becoming a Woman: A Biography of Christine Jorgensen
© 2008 by The Haworth Press, Taylor & Francis Group. All rights reserved.
doi:10.1300/5896_06

could understand his homosexual desires and lift the burden of guilt he had carried and concealed for so long. George found much meaning in the Bible quotations he heard that day, quickly linking them to the frustrations of his own life, and he also realized that through a deep religious experience, forgiveness and compassion were possible. "I left the church that day in a state of elation and happiness, and my emotional burdens seemed lighter to me than they ever had before."[3]

God, he discovered, could be a healing force, a powerful ally in the battle for self-esteem, and a penetrating laser illuminating a new and more successful direction in his life. We are not told exactly what led him to this church, but very possibly it was the same feelings of emptiness, guilt, despair, and loneliness that had plagued him for so long. Now, he would begin to attend services on a regular basis, meeting many friendly people, and finding a "serenity" he had never before experienced. Among his new church friends, he seemed happy to be George and he was thinking less about becoming a woman. Just as he had felt a highly cathartic experience upon revealing his feminine identity feelings to June and Helen on the patio in Hollywood, he was again offloading some guilt and shame, putting his faith in the Lord, and searching for an alliance with a power greater than himself. This reawakening of his religious feelings seemed to comfort him, and he felt more like the decent, respectable, and responsible person he wanted to be. At heart, George strongly sought to be just like the other Jorgensen men: hard working, tough, reliable, and respected. With the "hand of God" now so close to him, George found peace in these words: "lo, I am with you always, even unto the end of the world."[4] He felt he was no longer alone. He experienced a "new energy" and his friends noticed more smiles, and less time with his head down, sitting alone in deep thought.

Even better, he felt a new sense of direction through this religious awakening: "My new-found faith helped me to improve my general outlook . . . I had never forgotten the conversation with my friends, June and Helen, or their sound advice to consult a doctor."[5] That is, a doctor who could help him to formulate a plan to become a woman. It didn't happen suddenly, but over several months George had constructed a strongly biological, even a specific medical explanation for his sexual and identity conflicts. If he suffered from a medical difficulty, he reasoned, the best course of action would be to redouble his efforts to find the best possible assistance from physicians. He didn't know exactly who could help him, but he knew that finding the right doctor should be at the top of his agenda.

Soon, bursting with "an unfamiliar energy," he settled on a new vocational goal: "I decided to give up my studies at college and return to my first love, photography."[6] So, just nine months after beginning his college work in Utica, he enrolled in the Progressive School of Photography in New Haven, Connecticut. For George, this didn't feel like quitting, but rather, it was a recommitment to building a career as a photographer. George remained on the lookout for medical assistance to help him manage his ever-present transgender thoughts.

Through a newspaper article concerning hormonal research, George learned of scientific studies based in New Haven, possibly at Yale. As noted earlier, Joanne Meyerowitz reasoned that the doctor identified by a pseudonym in the 1967 autobiography as Dr. Grayson may have been Frank Beach, a renowned physiological psychologist and authority on sex and reproduction.[7] Beach was the author of a several highly regarded books. In Christine's book we are told that George made an appointment, had an interview, yet was not given a medical examination before being referred to a psychiatrist, leaving George profoundly disappointed. As Christine reported in 1967, he had been more explicit about his feminine gender identity feelings with the New Haven doctor than he had ever been before: ". . . even as a child I was 'girlish,' and I've grown up with what I think are the emotions and desires of a woman . . . I'm an underdeveloped male (so, am I therefore) one of nature's mistakes?"[8]

George was gradually giving a more honest and complete accounting of his feelings to medical and mental health professionals, and he was consistently explaining his difficulties as due to some kind of biological problem. Perhaps this is one reason that he had never shown any interest in psychotherapy. Jorgensen's later interview with a New Haven psychiatrist did not lead anywhere, and he felt great disappointment in these "medical men" who had failed to understand his problems or to offer real assistance. He concluded: "I returned to school, trying to convince myself . . . that my photographic work would be fulfilling enough."[9] Was he struggling to put aside his desire to become a woman?

Throughout this period, he also began to spend more time with his former neighborhood buddy, Jim Frankfort. This would evolve into a three-year love affair, ending only when he sailed to Copenhagen in 1950. When George was in a fulfilling gay relationship, he appeared to experience less of a sense of urgency about his hoped-for gender identity transformation. Little detail is provided to explain the "chance" renewal of their friendship, but their relationship was described as nonsexual yet very intense. Jim Frankfort, as he was named in CJ's 1967 autobiography, was George's age but was over six feet tall and with many strongly masculine features. In contrast, Jorgensen felt "pale," even "fragile." They met for lunch, and after an enjoyable conversation, Jim suggested they also meet for dinner, which they did. Jim then urged that at a later date they should meet in New York City, and George agreed. Before the evening had ended, George felt the same feelings of affection and the sexual excitement he had known with Tom Chaney: "I became aware . . . of the warm pleasure and enjoyment . . . [that] began to grow into a nameless dread, a fear that with further contact with him I might lead myself into another emotional vortex."[10] The tension between George's prudish morality and his longing for a loving gay relationship seemed to tear away the defenses he had tried to erect against these feelings. From a psychological perspective, it is difficult to reconcile Jorgensen's repeated stories of falling in love with men accompanied by the disclaimer that nothing of a sexual nature ever occurred.

Feeling much internal tension about the Frankfort relationship, his first thought was to seek medical help, especially "about my effeminate appearance." Even if his mind could be "adjusted" to accept his femininity, what, he wondered, could be done about his "feminine body?" Year after year, Jorgensen had gradually convinced himself that his homosexual attractions were founded on a feminine appearance along with "glandular problems." But interviews with people who knew George during those years do not confirm his description of appearing particularly feminine. On the other hand, while he could pass as a typical male much of the time, homosexual men often hit on him, something he said hurt him but also appealed to him. George had continued to visit public libraries and he was about to read a book that changed his life.

George loved to browse through the stacks of public libraries; they were free, and a great escape. He had worked at the Throggs Neck Public Library and at the Fort Dix library, and occasionally he would discover a book so unique, so mind altering, that it could be marked as a turning point in his life. The finding of a small book, just 243 pages, titled *The Male Hormone,*[11] provided such a moment of epiphany for George. The hormonal story it told consolidated his vision of himself more than anything that had ever occurred before: Without exaggeration, De Kruif's book may have been the decisive contributor in the reshaping of his gender identity, for it focused on the power of the sex hormones to alter behavior and thinking. It also suggested that sex could be altered; at least, it could be in rats.

George studied some basic biology in high school, but he knew little of the human endocrine system. During his lifetime there had been gigantic advances in understanding how the sex hormones influence the formation of the reproductive system. The breakthrough work had taken place during the mid-1930s in the Netherlands, France, and Switzerland, initially with the identification of the female hormones. By 1941, the male sex hormones had also been identified and synthesized. Soon thereafter, science writer Paul De Kruif set out to explain his views concerning the potential medical benefits of testosterone. He wrote his book less than a decade after the drug companies developed ways to mass produce testosterone. De Kruif told the story of how this hormone influenced many other organ systems and supposedly extended longevity. A fifty-four-year-old medical and health writer, he was a contributor to *Readers Digest* and had previously written *Microbe Hunters* and nine other health-related books.

The Male Hormone, published in 1945, was interpreted by George as an explanation for both his homosexual attractions and his feminine gender identity. The hormonal information seemed of overwhelming significance and gave him a new view of himself. The author did not say that testosterone was a causal or curative factor in homosexuality, nor did he attempt to explain what later came to be known as transsexualism, a topic that was not even mentioned by De Kruif. Rather, De Kruif primary goal was to explain how testosterone had been discovered, the creation of a synthetic version, and its importance in sexual development, sexual potency, and longevity. De Kruif had taken testosterone for a year, beginning in his late forties, and he felt sure it was helpful. Throughout the book, the author emphasized the many promising but unproven medical uses of testosterone, and he also advocated it as a near universal treatment for aging and for many chronic illnesses. He concluded:

The news seems incredible [showing] how testosterone sharp-
ens nerve reflexes and upsurges in the mental power of the
brain. What is most significant in the biological sense is that testosterone engineers the human body's building of its own pro-
teins which are the stuff of life itself.[12]

His enthusiasm went well beyond the facts. De Kruif's overly dramatic, simplistic, working-man's prose encouraged the nontechnical
reader to take an interest in health topics such as mental illness, hun-
ger, health insurance, penicillin, blood circulation, and even microbi-
ology. His formula was to weave a storyline based on published scientific work, often erecting a supposed conflict between prestigious,
"powerful doctors" who, he claimed, sought to control the rest of the
medical profession: scientists and inventors versus the establishment
as ignorance versus the emerging wonders of science such as sulfa
drugs and testosterone. The powerful men were his "villains"; the scientists and physicians who were advancing science and medicine
were his "heroes." De Kruif favored framing technical and scientific
challenges as battles, wars, and contests of power. These were ideas
that anybody could quickly grasp, and for De Kruif, the good guys
always won.

De Kruif explained the historic studies of the endocrine glands, beginning with the work of Eugen Steinach in Austria in 1912. Initially,
Steinach worked entirely with animals, but De Kruif brought it to life
with many examples of how his findings might apply to human development. Steinach had transplanted the gonads of male guinea pigs
into females to induce male mating behavior, and he produced female
mating behavior in his male animals by castrating them and trans-
planting ovarian tissue. De Kruif explained that the sex glands were
the critically important determinants of various primary and secondary sex characteristics, and that perhaps they also had many medical
applications, although often his enthusiasm for the therapeutic use of
hormones raced well ahead of hard data. Although the historic work
on hormones was not new when De Kruif's book was written, it was
the first time Jorgensen had ever read about anatomical sex changes.
It was the closest demonstration of sex reversal through hormonal
treatment that he had ever heard of.

George began to speculate about the possible personal implications of this animal research. He raced through De Kruif's book with
passion and found two themes that especially caught his attention.

First, that the testicles of men were described as the major source of testosterone, but that all men also produce small amounts of estrogen, the major female sex hormone; women did just the opposite by producing small amounts of testosterone and far greater amounts of the female hormones. He reasoned that this could be a key factor in producing a glandular imbalance between male and female hormones. Second, Jorgensen realized that such a supposed imbalance might cause the feminine characteristics he so often attributed to himself. Very possibly, this was the origin of Jorgensen's glandular imbalance theory to explain his emerging feminine gender identity. As we shall learn, however, he was not a victim of a glandular disorder.

After reading of the powerful effects of testosterone, George reasoned that hormonal factors might also be related to his romantic attraction to men. In his view, perhaps his body was struggling with too much or too little testosterone. At this moment of discovery, through the serendipity of his love for books, he had stumbled upon something he called his own "salvation." It was this hormonal research that reorganized his view of himself more than anything else.[13] Christine later described it in these words: "the science of body chemistry . . . opened a door on a new and shining vista." When least expected, on a snowy December day in Utica, George had developed a new way of thinking about himself and his future. His view of his own identity and of his sexual struggles began to be restructured. Finally, he could see how the ideas in De Kruif's book offered both an explanation of his own difficulties and a plan of treatment. He now focused on his problems as glandular difficulties having nothing to do with guilt, shame, or morality. In this new view of himself, his difficulties were not due to supposedly improper sexual impulses but to chemicals. In place of self-reproach and low self-esteem, he concluded that his problems could be managed like any other illness. He now believed the "hormonal imbalance" that had caused him such troubling frustrations could be brought under control through proper medical treatment. George had never heard of the "medical model," but without intending to do so, at least for our culture, he placed transsexuality firmly within this frame of reference. It would be medical doctors who would be called upon to help transsexuals, not social workers, ministers, or family counselors.

He left the library with "a deep feeling of gratitude," purchased his own copy of De Kruif's book, and soon returned to the Bronx for a family Christmas. He now believed, for the first time, that there was hope for an entirely new life-plan if only he could find the necessary medical assistance. As never before, he felt like a person with a huge road map spread before him, but without a definite sense of which road he should pursue. His goal was to become a happier person and to rid himself of the long periods of depression, loneliness, gloom, and the negative self-assessments that had long troubled him.

He had an especially good time at home that Christmas. As always, the Christmas tree was in the center of the living room and on Christmas Eve they opened their presents in a very orderly fashion. Perhaps his parents sensed some renewal of energy, some stronger and more adultlike commitment as George trudged off to New Haven and his January graduation from photography school. He had been in New Haven just four months, but he felt he had learned more from De Kruif's book than he had ever learned from classroom studies. He now had a plan and a sense of direction, if not an exact destination.

The year was 1949 and he was twenty-two. By the end of January he had returned to his tiny bedroom in the Dudley Avenue house. He felt more comfortable with himself than ever before. The main questions he kept wondering about were these: Would more testosterone contribute to my masculinity? Would more testosterone change my homosexual feelings? Would I then acquire "a man's desires, attitudes and emotions . . . I felt certain that . . . the answer would be 'no'."[14] Continuing to struggle with what must have seemed a nearly impossible puzzle, he considered the "more drastic measure of trying to become more feminine. Could the transition to womanhood be accomplished through the magic of chemistry? I feared the answer to that question was 'no,' also."[15]

The dilemma that he faced seemed based on a contradiction: On the one hand he wanted to cast off his homosexual feelings: perhaps the use of male hormones could help accomplish that, but on the other hand, he wanted desperately to live as a woman, and he knew that ingesting testosterone would interfere with this goal. George knew he could not deal with these hormonal issues without learning much more about endocrinology, the potential benefits of medical assistance, and the power of female hormones. The fact that some of the scientific literature dealing with hormonal research was published in foreign languages added to the challenge of his library studies, and he must have wondered if the foreign language requirements in college might have been a good idea after all.

And so he did what he had done many times in the past: he increased his hours of study at the library of the New York Academy of Medicine on 103rd Street in Manhattan. From the nearby Westchester station the subway fare was only a nickel, and this library held vast resources touching on exactly the hormonal questions that concerned him the most. He was beginning to zero in on topics like hermaphroditism, although often the medical reports were not clear to him. What was clear was that in Sweden, some early reports of "sex conversion" in humans had been described "but I had no idea of their scientific importance or how they might apply to me."[16] There was no way he could have felt certain about any direct application of these articles to his own situation, but these technical case reports by physicians, most of which dealt with intersex cases, provided him with a greater sense of hope than anything else he'd ever read. He was ecstatic, despite his certainty that these discoveries were, for him, just a beginning. He repeatedly asked himself: Did he suffer from a "hormonal imbalance?" Could hormones cause his testicles to shrink? Could hormones produce breasts? Could hormones make him a woman? Most important of all, he wondered how he could learn more concerning the intersex surgeries associated with "sex changes" in Sweden.

Chapter 7

The Transsexual Decision

Given what he had learned from De Kruif's book, George set the goal of learning much more about human physiology, and especially, how the hormones work. Lacking a background in biology or chemistry, he decided to take one of the few steps he considered open to him to increase his understanding of human physiology; he enrolled during the late spring or early summer of 1949 in the Manhattan Medical and Dental Assistant's School, again, relying on his GI Bill benefits which had been a Godsend for him. At this juncture, George's plan to leave America for Sweden had not been consolidated; he seems to have been in search of training to obtain work as a medical technician.

During the later part of 1949, he received some elementary training in X-ray and laboratory work, but the highlight of this experience was in meeting a classmate, identified as Mrs. Genevieve Angelo, the wife of a physician. She was also a compassionate and understanding source of counseling for the ever-needful George Jorgensen, who had become more open about discussing both his sexual conflicts and his gender identity struggles. He had discovered in Hollywood that not only did he feel emotionally relieved when he verbalized the tensions that had led to so much guilt, but that these self-revelations had been harmless; the women he confided in proved to be understanding and supportive.

Mrs. Angelo, like many other women in George's life, seemed to turn up at just the right time and to have been an excellent confidant. At lunch, with a glass of wine and a cigarette, he gave his new friend an overview of his life story, including his recurrent but conflicted feelings of falling in love with young men and his persistent conviction that he should be living as a woman. As we have noted, George's homosexual tendency bothered him greatly because the expression of these impulses in a gay relationship were in direct conflict with his "prudish" and "moralistic" values. But of greater significance was his certainty that his growing feminine gender identity was hormonally caused and that this might be medically treated. He emphasized to Mrs. Angelo that beyond any other goal, he wanted to live as a woman; this reflected the ever stronger development of his feminine gender identity. He had no interest in taking testosterone to become a more masculine man. Rather, he explained that he wanted to live as a woman. Talking with her about a sex change and mentioning possible steps he might take to accomplish this was quite different than merely ruminating about his possible future. At lunch, he also wondered if somehow God had placed Mrs. Angelo at the school to assist him. As a good listener and a perceptive adult, she "somehow felt that there was something seriously wrong with me, that I was effeminate, 'too dainty,'" and Mrs. Angelo asked him directly if he believed he was "different from other people."[1] Perhaps he offered several examples of the conflicting motives that led him to feel so isolated and defeated, and then he asked her to arrange an appointment with her husband.

As best we can judge, Dr. Joseph Angelo was a forty-something general practitioner in New Jersey who had a busy medical practice, but who was willing to see George the following day and listen at length as he poured out his fears, his sexual longings, and his gender identity frustrations. In many ways, the personal history Angelo acquired covered much the same territory of a psychiatric intake interview. He urged George to speak freely about the topics that had tormented him for years. Angelo was an experienced clinician and he encouraged George to do most of the talking.

It's not certain that Dr. Angelo was the first to prescribe commercially synthesized female hormones for George: what is certain is that when he arrived in Denmark he had estradiol "tablets" prescribed by Angelo in his possession. Concerning these "tablets, George may have invented a cover story to shield Angelo from possible criticism for providing these hormones at a time when this was unusual, but not illegal or even medically inappropriate.[2] The apparent cover story, written in 1967, describes George driving to a distant part of New York City, calling upon a pharmacist, and after asking for some ordinary items from the clerk, "I asked for some high potency estradiol."[3] When told that a prescription was required for these female hormones, we are told that Jorgensen then fabricated a story about needing them in connection with medical research. "Let me have 100 tablets," George claims he said to a pharmacist, with all the confidence he could muster. We may ask: In 1949, in New York City, would a licensed pharmacist supply female hormones to George Jorgensen without a prescription, especially on hearing a vague tale about "medical research"? If this is the true account, he would have first obtained estradiol in April 1949; if Dr. Angelo was the first to provide this medication, it would have occurred seven months later, in November 1949. At the least we are told in the autobiography that Dr. Angelo "permitted me to continue to take the estradiol tablets under his direction, knowing that they would not be harmful."[4]

Whenever it was that he began the daily ingestion of these pills, he felt a calming effect almost immediately and a heightened sense of energy and well-being. These were exactly the emotional changes De Kruif had described as among the many alleged benefits of testosterone. Jorgensen's language in describing the "renewal of energy" and other fast-acting benefits of this medication runs close to what he had read in *The Male Hormone*. Almost certainly, some so-called placebo-effects were also involved in George's near-miraculous emotional and physical changes. Christian Hamburger, in Copenhagen, later concluded that the dosage was insufficient to produce any major physical changes beyond slight swelling of the breasts.[5] As Christine said in 1967 "I hoped [the hormones] would not be a destructive force but would help to make me a whole person."[6] It was during this period that George first "wondered if surgery could complete the process [of correcting his body chemistry], [and] remove what I considered a malformation . . . and give me the freedom to find my proper place in the world."[7] Without making a direct statement, George had finally introduced the prospect of amputation of his male sex organs, and thereafter, living in his "proper" place in the world as a woman. Now, he had a clearly defined plan of action; a decision had been made.

There were many discussions with Dr. Angelo who listened patiently and also played the role of the devil's advocate by asking many tough questions about the possible personal costs of trying to undergo a "sex change." For the most part, George parried these questions by explaining that his sexual and gender conflicts were so intense that he simply had to take action, and he alluded to the possibility of suicide should he be blocked from finding assistance in his quest to become a woman. Angelo may have been stalling for time, assuming that George was experiencing a young-adult identity crisis, perhaps struggling to find himself through building a new vocation and developing greater self-acceptance. George would have none of this; he was intensely motivated to proceed with a change of sex as quickly as possible, although he didn't know what options were open to him.

In her 1967 book, Christine gives us little factual information about what she said to Angelo, or his responses, although she believed this relationship was critically important in her decision to seek medical help abroad. In contrast to this lack of detail, many pages of her autobiography are devoted to the description of her erotic attraction to various men. Possibly, young George Jorgensen possessed a better understanding of his gay feelings than of his desire to become a woman. For him, transsexuality was a goal for which he had no role model, no treatment plan, nor did he have a language to express his gender identity conflict, other than the very vague term, "sex change."

Two subthemes were operating in November and December of 1949. First, George was very much in love with Jim Frankfort, who had renewed their romantic affair earlier in New Haven: "my emotional attachment to Jim Frankfort had become increasingly painful to me and once and for all, I wanted to release myself from its strange hold and the possibility of repeating a similar experience in the future."[8]

More simply, he wanted to terminate their relationship. George was very ashamed of his homosexual yearnings. Second, he received a letter from "Dr. Grayson" [possibly psychologist Frank Beach] explaining this: "I understand something like the course of treatment you requested [i.e., "sex change"] was done at one time in Sweden."[9] Apparently, Dr. Angelo had also mentioned something about "sex change" operations having been done in Europe, and George's own research at the library of the New York Academy of Medicine led to the same conclusion. All of this led to targeting Sweden as the most likely source of medical help.[10] There must have been a combination of high confidence mixed with uncertainty when the financially impoverished lad from Throggs Neck decided that "somehow" his destiny lay overseas, although he knew not where or with whom. We are told: "it was shortly before Christmas in 1949, that I made the decision to go first to Denmark, where I had relatives, and then to Stockholm, where I hoped I would find doctors who would be willing to handle my case."[11]

The decision to go overseas was one of the major landmarks in George's transsexual quest, and he was prepared to take whatever risks were involved, including the risk of total failure, for he lacked even the name of any prospective physician in Sweden or anywhere else. Feeling relieved and excited after making this decision, George graduated from a one-semester course at the medical technician's school, and then worked as a clerk at this school for four months. He was able to save four or five hundred dollars toward his Scandinavian exploration. It was November, 1949, and he served as an usher at the wedding of his sister.

Just before Christmas, George purchased a one-way ticket to Copenhagen aboard the Swedish-American liner, *Stockholm*, explaining to his family that he was just taking a "tourist jaunt." His sister, Dolly, reported that she had understood his trip to be no more than a vacation. On May 1, 1950, George watched the Statue of Liberty fade from view as he began a thirty-month adventure. Even he could not envision what lay ahead. After all the good-bye kisses and hugs, he must have felt unsure, not only of where he was headed, but of what would happen when he arrived. There had been a large farewell party for him aboard the ship, but now, underway at last, he felt alone and uncertain of his future. With time on his hands, George considered the ebb and flow of his own identity struggles.

He was very conflicted by his homoerotic feelings and by his quest to become a woman. But even more difficult was the challenge of finding a physician who would make possible the "sex change" he so strongly desired. At this point, George felt like an applicant for medical intervention that he did not understand, to be provided by some hoped-for doctor at some unknown location, possibly in Sweden. It was all very vague, but the dream of becoming a woman kept driving him ahead. He explored the ship, even the engine room and the bridge, but what mattered more was a new romantic attraction to a gay young man his own age. He had just ended a long relationship with Jim Frankfort, and now, he had fallen in love again, and this Atlantic journey had become more exciting than he had expected.

Chapter 8

Copenhagen and Christian Hamburger

Built in 1948, the *Stockholm* had the slender lines of a yacht with a sharply cut bow and a gleaming white hull. Elegant with hardwood paneling, etched glass, and marble trim, she carried 548 passengers; she was the queen of the Swedish American Line. But she was not fast compared to the best of the huge liners that would be built in the following decade. George Jorgensen's voyage from New York City to Copenhagen required ten days. She had a distinguished career, but there was tragedy in her logs as well. Maritime historians recall the collision between the *Stockholm* and the *Andrea Doria* in the fog just twenty miles off Nantucket on July 25, 1956. The collision occurred at 11:10 p. m. during the final hours of the *Andrea Doria's* crossing, with almost 1,700 passengers and crew on board. An hour earlier, the *Stockholm's* radar recognized the approaching luxury liner running westward at twenty-one knots, close to her top speed. Each captain ultimately blamed the other for the accident, but what is not in dispute is that the *Stockholm* turned to her starboard as the ships approached each other, slicing thirty feet into the heart of the *Andrea Doria* and opening her from top to bottom across all decks. The rescue ships were the *Ile de France* and the *Cape Ann;* all but forty-seven passengers from the *Andrea Doria* survived. One person following the news reports closely was Christine Jorgensen, who had crossed the Atlantic on both vessels.

Travel had always been a liberating experience for George Jorgensen, and now, just weeks before his twenty-fourth birthday and with a few hundred dollars in his pocket, his destination was Sweden. But first, he'd stop in Copenhagen to visit Mrs. Helen Johnson and some Danish relatives.[1] George had written ahead to Helen, the young lady he had met in Hollywood three years earlier, who was waiting for him

doi:10.1300/5896_08

to clear customs. She and her husband had one child, and they graciously welcomed George to stay with them for several weeks. As always, George's social skills paid off as he soon became a welcome member of their little household. His friendly, warm, interpersonal style was to be an important asset throughout his life, and Helen's help proved to be of vital importance just when a bit of assistance was needed. It was Helen who led him to Dr. Christian Hamburger.

At the end of May, Helen and her husband invited George to join them for an auto jaunt through eastern Europe. It was a great trip, and the final one he'd take as a man. Photographs from that happy summertime excursion show George wearing a somewhat baggy suit, but always neatly attired with a coat and tie.[2] They returned in mid-July, and Helen then urged George to visit her own doctor to clarify whether Danish physicians might be able to help him achieve the sex change he sought. From news reports, she believed hormone experts were available in Denmark, and she showed George a recent newspaper article about the research of Christian Hamburger. Within a few days, George had visited her physician and this doctor referred him to Dr. Hamburger. This was a most fortuitous series of events, for of all the physicians and medical researchers in Scandinavia no endocrinologist was more likely to have an understanding of George's inner turmoil or to give time toward understanding what he sought. Even more important, Hamburger quickly realized George could become an excellent research subject.

Christian Hamburger was one of three children born into a prominent, wealthy Danish family. His father was a highly successful Copenhagen physician and his mother was a homemaker who encouraged her children to set high goals and to work hard on their academic assignments. His grandfather had been an important Danish composer. As a major part of his medical studies, Hamburger conducted research for three years in the endocrinology laboratories of the University Institute for General Pathology in Copenhagen. In 1933 he completed the equivalent of both an MD and a PhD degree and his extensive doctoral research was published as a contribution to the emerging field of endocrinology. He was especially interested in the gonadotropic hormones. These are glandular secretions transported in the bloodstream that carry messages to the gonads or the ovaries, and to the adrenal cortex. He sought better ways to assess these substances and to measure their interactions.

In both training and temperament, Hamburger was a skillful and creative scientist who has been remembered internationally as one of the pioneers in his field. In 1934, at the age of thirty, he became head of the newly established Hormone Department of Statens Seruminstitut, a part of the Royal Hospital in Copenhagen. Approachable but shy, kind, and very much a family man, Hamburger had many interests and abilities. He managed to direct multiple research projects, to edit a major scientific journal, and to participate actively in the life of his family, while enjoying oil painting, photography, and sculpting. He was a great lover of dogs. Despite his training as a physician, one thing he did not enjoy was looking after patients who were ill. For him, scientific inquiry would always be his highest priority.

In late July 1950, Jorgensen visited the imposing office and laboratories of Dr. Hamburger at the massive, white, Statens Serum Institute, a part of the Royal Hospital complex, close to the waterfront on the south side of Copenhagen. He was told that Dr. Hamburger was on vacation, but his plea for an appointment must have been impressive, as a laboratory assistant telephoned Hamburger at home and obtained permission for George to go there the next day. As planned, the following afternoon, George rode his bicycle through the center of Copenhagen, swinging northward to the Charlotten suburb, a wooded area of impressive larger homes including the Hamburger's residence. According to Jesper, the youngest son of Christian, the family was away at a summer house, except for his father, who had remained at home for a day or two to paint a ceiling; he was still wearing his work clothes when Jorgensen arrived.[3]

A handsome and welcoming man, Hamburger put his paint brush aside and invited the slender American visitor to sit down, have a cup of tea, and explain what he was seeking. Jorgensen told him the truth, emphasizing his sexual conflicts and his ever-strengthening conviction that he must live his life as a woman.[4] George described growing up as part of a hard-working family of Danes, of his tormented early childhood in the Bronx, of his Army service, his church membership and his moral beliefs. He said he felt hopeless after consulting with many American doctors who offered few helpful suggestions. He was sincere, passionate, and close to tears as he insisted that he urgently wanted medical assistance, and that he didn't believe his life was worth living unless help could be found. He discussed his many episodes of depression, self-disgust, guilt, and his thoughts of suicide.

Hamburger listened patiently, asking only a few questions, and he gradually sorted out the major themes of Jorgensen's story. In response to George's questions, Hamburger explained that he did not believe George was simply a homosexual, but rather, that the central issue was his desire to live his life as a woman. Relieved that the doctor had understood what was most important to him, George pressed for information about the medical steps that might be taken to achieve a "sex change." Responding, Hamburger explained what could be expected from the prescription of female hormones, making the point that changing one's appearance is one thing, while actually changing sex is not possible.

Although George was requesting help, he didn't know exactly what he should be asking for, or where such help might lead. He lacked the language to fully express his transsexual feelings. What he did understand was that his life of depression, low self-esteem, and isolation and guilt was a life he wanted to leave forever. He pressed Hamburger with a key question: If he could become a research "guinea pig," taking female hormones as part of a long-term project in Hamburger's laboratory, might this lead to some form of "treatment" whereby he could live his life as a woman? Speaking slowly in English, Dr. Hamburger explained that such a drastic and unusual goal might be a possibility, and that he would be willing to consider this, but no promises could be made. Additional evaluation and consultation were called for, he explained. Dr. Hamburger suggested they take a break, and he then provided some Danish hospitality, serving pastries and tea,[5] as the conversation turned less clinical.[6]

After a cigarette, George began talking in more detail of his family in the Bronx, the construction work of his father and his uncle William, and his father's earlier hobby as an amateur radio operator. He proceeded to tell about helping his dad build a boat, fishing in Eastchester Bay, of his Presbyterian Church membership, and his affiliation with Askov Hall. He spoke of his neighborhood roots in Throggs Neck, his American wanderings from coast to coast, and the schools he had attended, and finally, of his long-standing interest in photography. He then learned that this was also one of Dr. Hamburger's passionate interests, and that prior to World War II he had built a darkroom in his home. Perhaps they talked about various lenses, filters, and lighting; George may have told him of his training in the processing of color negatives. The two photographers probably became even more comfortable with each other during this long summer evening, and in July, in Copenhagen, there was lots of sun remaining.

Hamburger had never been involved in a case of "sex conversion," but as an endocrinologist and full-time researcher, he was probably aware of some of the early medical reports describing efforts to alter the anatomy of hermaphrodites. Beyond these examples, he may have known of the much publicized case of Lili Elbe a Danish artist who received several transsexual surgeries in Dresden, Germany, and he may have known of earlier transgender cases.[7]

Listening to George's history, Hamburger realized that there was nothing life threatening about what he was struggling with, even if his goal was to become a woman. Rather, as Hamburger assessed George's situation, he concluded he had been dealing with very troubling identity problems of long duration, and there was no doubt that he was filled with conflict, unhappiness, and depression. Perhaps, he suggested, George would be a good candidate for psychotherapy, but his recommendation was immediately rejected. That approach had never appealed to George; most of the psychiatrists he had met didn't seem to comprehend the help he was seeking. In addition, he had no way to pay for long-term psychotherapy. Listening carefully, Hamburger concluded that none of the symptoms George described seemed especially remarkable. He correctly assumed that Jorgensen was not an intersex person, something he would soon confirm with a thorough medical examination and health history. Hamburger also felt he needed to be cautious. In seeking to become a woman, Jorgensen was asking for a great deal more than anyone could deliver, especially within a short time frame.

Christian Hamburger loved his laboratory and his scientific work. Independently wealthy, he was not concerned about how the Jorgensen case might impact his job or his reputation. But what, he asked himself, was the best course of action? He knew he could maintain full control of Jorgensen's use of female hormones and be informed daily of how George was reacting to the program, and therefore, he may have reasoned that this was a unique case of a physically healthy, highly motivated young man who urgently was seeking the female hormones Hamburger could provide. Then, he reasoned, many months ahead, perhaps there would be body-altering surgery. During this time, George would serve as a research subject. Hamburger believed George's case could help him to trace both short-term and long-term effects of estrogen in a healthy male, and the interaction of this regimen with other hormones, a line of research that was his specialty. This may have been one of Hamburger's strongest motives for assisting George, but there were also some highly personal reasons that led Hamburger to accept George as a research subject.

The prescription of female hormones to assist severely distressed homosexuals in Denmark had a long history, and the entire topic was controversial. On the one hand, in 1950, laws affecting homosexuals in Denmark were far more liberal than the punitive and criminal statutes widely seen in America. On the other hand, however, there remained many citizens of Denmark who looked down on gays and discriminated against them. As in America, such individuals perceived homosexuality to be a matter of personal choice and as something that could be stopped through will power. They viewed being gay or lesbian as a moral question. In contrast, many socially liberal Scandinavians did not blame gays or lesbians for their sexual preference. Such preferences were considered both by the medical profession and some within the general population as a variation of sexual development having little or nothing to do with personal choice. It was not seen as an illness, but as a variation of normal sexual behavior, probably rooted in biology. In Denmark, in unusual cases, when a homosexual was very distressed and sought medical assistance it was considered professionally appropriate to make an effort to help such a person. The Danish government had established procedures in 1929 for the approval of such intervention. In severely distressed individuals, and in some persons who had committed sex crimes, one kind of assistance was the administration of female hormones. In exceptional cases, castration could also be approved. The logic behind this was that these hormones, with or without castration, would reduce sexual motivation, thereby reducing the probability of unwanted sexual conduct. However, even when a person was pleading for castration, permission from the Ministry of Justice was required. Hamburger knew all of this.

Perhaps while he and Jorgensen talked, their unspoken lines of reasoning diverged. George, the near-penniless applicant, was pleading to become a woman. He considered this the best solution for both his gender identity and sexual conflicts. Hamburger, in contrast, was thinking of a very gradual process of hormonal treatment that he believed would reduce George's sexual tensions, and provide a calming effect. Many months later he would reexamine the question of any additional feminization procedures. In the mind of the doctor, there was no reason to look beyond hormonal intervention to help a very unhappy, sexually conflicted lad with an intense feminine gender identity. The question of whether he would ever live as a woman would have to be postponed. George was a realist. He knew he had no power in this most important discussion of his life. Hamburger was in charge, and he was formulating a plan and a proposal. George took the role of the good listener and he liked what he heard.

For Hamburger, the idea of producing a "sex change" was secondary to the goal of making George a happier and more functional young adult. Jorgensen's thoughts of suicide and his persistent problems with depression needed to be attacked head on. In Hamburger's thinking the idea of a "sex change" should be put aside. He again urged George to consider psychotherapy, but this alternative was quickly rejected. Hamburger reasoned that for the months ahead a step-by-step program could be commenced, beginning with estrogen hormones along with daily observation of Jorgensen's biological and psychological functioning. If this did not help George it could be stopped without any permanent harm. If they were to proceed, the process would be limited to what amounted to "chemical castration," not surgery.

Perhaps Hamburger drew upon his clinical training to silently estimate the potential benefits of working with Jorgensen and the possible hazards, or even the harm that might be done should he prove to be a poor candidate for long-term use of female hormones. He did not have to remind himself of the teachings of his mentors: That first, the physician does no harm. It raises the question: Why would a prestigious researcher and physician, the head of a major research laboratory at the Royal Hospital, accept any risk in trying to assist this youth, no matter how passionate his pleas? Why did Hamburger agree to become involved? He was not much interested in clinical practice, he didn't enjoy dealing with illness, and he had never previously met George Jorgensen. It appears most likely that Hamburger's primary motivation in taking Jorgensen on as a patient was scientific: he wanted Jorgensen to help him to study the reciprocal relationships among secretions of the pituitary, the gonads, and the adrenal cortex. Jorgensen appeared to be an ideal experimental subject. He was highly motivated to take estrogenic hormones over an extended time, and he was willing to cooperate in the collection of twenty-four-hour urine samples, collecting and submitting 100 percent of his urinary output. Furthermore, he was willing to cooperate over a span of many months. An analysis of this urine would contribute to the understanding of the complex relationships basic to the regulation of hormones. Just a year after starting to work with Jorgensen, Hamburger published a technical report on the effects of estrogen on the pituitary and the adrenal cortex that was clearly based on data provided by George Jorgensen. The summary of this 1951 article begins:

> A young man of 24 (Case No. 1) served as experimental subject for several experiments with oestrogenic substances. The patient was suffering from homosexual tendencies, and the oestrogens were given partially therapeutically, i. e., in order to suppress the sexual libido, and partially experimentally.[8]

In short, Hamburger showed that intramuscular injections of estrogenic hormones suppressed the production of other sex hormones. The findings were one of the first demonstrations of these hormonal changes with a human subject. But were there additional reasons that motivated Hamburger to become involved?

Perhaps Hamburger felt a special compassion for homosexuals because his sister was a lesbian. Despite Denmark's comparatively liberal national policies, Hamburger surely knew from his sister's experience how discrimination against gays and lesbians could be profoundly troubling for a homosexual. He could offer no medical intervention to help his sister, but he believed there might be some steps he could take to help George Jorgensen, and he was willing to try.

Another reason that may have played a part in Hamburger's willingness to assist Jorgensen was the fact that the doctor's second wife, the mother of Jesper, was Jewish. The very real threat of extermination of Jews by the Nazis was a national trauma Hamburger would never forget. Like many Danes, Hamburger felt gratitude toward the nations that had ended the occupation of Denmark by the Nazi forces, and George Jorgensen was not only an American, he was a former GI.

Before returning to finish painting his ceiling, he and George reviewed the outline of his medical plan, shook hands, and arranged to meet at the Institute during the first week of August. The doctor also asked George to stop taking the estrogen pills that had been prescribed by Dr. Joseph Angelo in New Jersey, and he agreed to do so.

As learned later, they had not produced much breast development or any other observable bodily changes. He accompanied George to the door and bid him good-bye. George hopped on his bicycle, smoking and smiling, as he rode out of the wooded suburb and across the dark gray cobblestone streets of old Copenhagen to the home of his friend, Helen Johnson. At last, there was a plan.

In brief, Hamburger's primary goal was to use George as an experimental subject, and at the same time, to help him feel less anxious and depressed. By providing female hormones, Hamburger hoped to reduce sexual tensions and to assist him to feel more positive about himself. Hopefully, this would facilitate more effective functioning in many dimensions of his life. He would approach this cautiously, getting to know Jorgensen very well from daily visits, and taking no medical risks. He would begin with modest injections of estrogen, increasing the dosage week by week. Months later, if all went favorably, he would withdraw the hormones to assess the consequences and later, begin them again. Twenty-four hour samples of urine would be collected and George's happiness and social adjustment would be carefully monitored. They could stop the regimen at any time. In the back of Hamburger's mind were some medical assumptions that led him to agree to help Jorgensen. Based on what he wrote in 1951 and 1953, here is what guided his thinking:[9]

1. When they first met, according to Jorgensen, Hamburger did not describe him as homosexual. However, in both the 1951 and 1953 technical reports he left no doubt that this was his impression. However, according to Alvin Davis of the *New York Post,* Hamburger told him in 1953 that he no longer believed Jorgensen had been a homosexual.
2. Hamburger believed that homosexuality was founded upon a biological condition that, for George, was unlikely to be changed through psychotherapy.
3. He knew little of what we label transsexualism, but his assumption was that Jorgensen experienced a very strong feminine gender identity of long standing, and that this was a key issue separate from his homosexual conflicts.
4. He knew of a few intersex cases of "sex changes" where the outcome had been favorable, although he had no personal experience with such cases.

5. As a physician and an endocrinologist, he believed that a long-term approach combining the administration of female hormones with continuing assessment of George's physical and mental status was unlikely to harm him. Possible benefits of this treatment regimen could be assessed over several months. Initially, there would be no surgery.

6. He would consult with other medical personnel as the case developed and prior to making decisions involving possible surgery.

By developing a medical plan to assist George, Hamburger had done something profoundly significant that went beyond simply giving him hope for his future: Hamburger had shown a respect and acceptance of George's uniqueness, including both his sexual conflicts and his desire to become a woman. No professional, no friend, and no family member had ever demonstrated this before. By joining forces with a man who would become a father figure and who was also a physician and a scientist, Jorgensen came to feel like a more legitimate, authentic, and respectable person for the first time in his life.

Chapter 9

Medical Intervention

George's response to taking female hormones was favorable at once: He began to gain weight, to be happier, to be more positive about his future, to look for a job, and to feel that some sort of plan might unfold allowing him to live as a woman.[1] He reported to Hamburger's laboratory daily. He began to let his hair grow and learned to style it in an androgynous fashion beneath a beret or a scarf. George had never developed much of a beard, but he sought electrolysis, and soon, what little beard he had was gone. The daily doses of estrogen began to soften his facial skin. With little restraint, he started to wear more colorful clothing, quite unlike the masculine styles men wore along the twisting pathways inside the defensive moats of the old city.

He also needed a place to live, so he rented a bedroom in the fourth-floor apartment of Miss Elsa Sabroe, "a middle aged woman," who was unmarried and eager to have an American help her to improve her English. The rent was $15 a month. George explained his long-term "sex change" plan to her and she was entirely accepting. The two spent many hours taking turns using her sewing machine, and the highly motivated George gradually acquired some practical sewing skills. With her supervision, he created a small wardrobe of skirts, blouses, and a feminine modification of his suits. But Miss Sabroe became more than a sewing instructor or someone to chalk the hemlines of George's new skirts. She was a highly valued confidant, stepping into the role of Grandmother Jorgensen and June Jensen, listening and responding with support to George's daily experiences. In public, he created a bit of confusion due to his ever-more androgynous appearance. Some people said he looked funny or peculiar, but he was pleased with his longer hair, a little gain in weight, and the

Becoming a Woman: A Biography of Christine Jorgensen
© 2008 by The Haworth Press, Taylor & Francis Group. All rights reserved.
doi:10.1300/5896_09

smoothness of his facial skin as the estrogens began to have their effects. Most of all, he was a happier person.

Beyond his daily hormone injections, what else may have contributed toward the turnaround in George's feelings and mood? Very possibly, he had confidence that his dream of becoming a woman was within reach, and, in addition, it is likely that George had begun to experiment with presenting himself as a woman. Perhaps he was trying on his new feminine outfits in the safety of the apartment, and learning to use makeup and to style his hair in a feminine fashion. But beyond his appearance, the more important development would have been the progressive strengthening of his identity as a woman.

As the months passed, George gradually became a far more feminine person according to the younger Hamburger, who observed him from time to time at his father's laboratory. Male transsexuals typically describe acquiring and wearing women's clothing, often as children or during the teen years, and of presenting themselves in public as women long before proceeding with genital surgery. They describe this urge to change their gender role as something they cannot overcome, and as an expression of themselves that is highly rewarding. This social presentation as a woman is at the heart of the process of strengthening a feminine identity and surrendering the male identity. For some it is a secretive, guilt-ridden experience, and for others it is something that feels so comfortable that, as some say, they are just "being themselves." But for nearly all transsexuals, the journey to reverse their gender role involves practice over many years. Christine Jorgensen denied having engaged in such practice, although there is evidence to the contrary. In 1953, based on the history George had given him, Hamburger described the teenage George:

> [George had been] highly interested in girl's clothes, and himself wanted to be dressed as a girl . . . [Later, George had] . . . yielded to his pronounced transvestic tendencies. He acquired a complete set of women's clothes and secretly put them on. This relieved the psychic pressure he invariably felt in men's clothes.[2]

Continuing, Hamburger wrote that he considered George to be "severely depressed" and that he was concerned about his suicidal thoughts. George's physical measurements were recorded as unremarkable although Hamburger said he was shorter, narrower in the waist, and weighed less than the average male of his age. No health problems were noted when he was examined by Dr. Hamburger both in 1950 and throughout his thirty months in Denmark. Here is what was found in his initial medical examination:

Height	170 centimeters	(5' 6 1/3")
Weight	55 kilograms	(121 pounds)
Blood Pressure	120/75 Hg	(normal range)

"He was of the asthenic type with a feminine habitus. There were fairly pronounced fat deposits in the hip region. There was a pigmentation of the nipples . . . ."[3] There was little hair on his arms or legs, he showed "medium muscle strength," and his voice was "natural." When flaccid, his penis measured three and one-half inches in length; "the testes were somewhat under average size but of normal consistency." The prostate was normal. Two hormonal analyses were carried out (August 2 and 10, 1952) using twenty-four-hour urine samples. Hamburger considered the results "normal" but noted that two of the results were not within the expected range, concluding:

> These figures [for the two analyses] are normal for a man of the patient's age, with the exception of a rather high estrogen level in specimen no. 2 and a rather low androgen level in specimen no. 1. It must be admitted, however, that the technical variation in these biological assays is so great that the figures do not allow of any definite conclusion.

Perhaps the two somewhat abnormal hormonal findings, regardless of the possible unreliability of the measures, along with Hamburger's judgment that George's testes were "somewhat under average size" reinforced Jorgensen's readiness to characterize himself as an intersex person. George probably was told of Hamburger's uncertain hormonal findings in 1950, about two years prior to the letter he would write home explaining all of this to his parents. As described by Hamburger, George's attire was more unusual than his physical dimensions: "The impression he made through his eccentric choice of men's clothing was odd; the colors were too varied for a man, and his clothes were evidentially 'always in the way'."

Sexually, he seemed "passive," and was said to have a "low libido" and was "obviously embarrassed by having been frequently taken for a homosexual." He did not show any "neurotic complaints" and did not seek psychotherapy. Although Hamburger discussed the possibility of providing male hormones, this approach "was firmly refused" by Jorgensen. After his study of *The Male Hormone*, George was aware of the many alleged powers of testosterone, but he ruled out taking male hormones because his goal was to become a woman, not a more virile man. Following Hamburger's consideration of all options "it was decided to provoke hormonal castration by means of estrogenic substances," and this regimen was sustained over ten months. This produced "marked atrophy of the testes . . . together with swelling of the breasts."[4] The "swelling" Hamburger described was all of the breast development Christine achieved through the age of twenty-seven. After returning to the United States, Chris explained to reporters that she found it essential to use "falsies" comprised of padding or foam rubber bra inserts to enhance the appearance of breasts. Based on a photograph taken decades later, it seems certain that Christine received breast implants.[5] On a more psychological level, Hamburger reported several important changes produced by estrogen: "the sexual libido and erections disappeared . . . and this was also true of the mental pressure that he had previously experienced. The patient was now in a state of mental balance, psychically at ease . . . ."[6]

Jorgensen had consistently requested castration, and following interviews with psychiatrist Georg Stürup, permission from the Ministry of Justice was received. Regulations concerning castration and sterilization had been in place since 1929. Initially, the Ministry had turned down Hamburger's application, but after an attorney experienced in these matters was retained, along with Stürup's help, the approval was granted. No estrogen was administered for four months prior to surgical castration on September 24, 1951, sixteen months after his arrival in Denmark. Hamburger, as planned, had proceeded cautiously.

Described by Chris as a "charming, genial, and highly amusing man,"[7] Stürup was a prominent psychiatrist in Denmark, and a physician with extensive experience in the medical management of men who had committed sex crimes. Stürup, who was very knowledgeable concerning the requirements of the Ministry of Justice for approval of castration, asked George to write a letter explaining his motivation for this irreversible operation. The letter was delivered promptly, but reveals little about the psychological life of the author. In his letter, George began by trying to "reconstruct my emotions" as a child, and focusing upon his homosexuality:

> I cannot now recall at just what time I realized that I was different from most other people. Also, I cannot say just when I knew this difference to be of a homosexual nature. I can say, however, that it seemed I have always known the difference . . . or at least from such a time as sexual differences are usually awakened in a child.[8]

It was unusual for George to characterize himself as homosexual; this may be attributable to his awareness that homosexuality was one of the few conditions for which the Ministry of Justice would allow castration. Another reason may be that he assumed this letter would never become public. In any case, George proceeded to explain that the Jorgensens did not openly discuss sexual matters such as homosexuality: "I knew from the 'hushed up' attitude of conversation on such a condition that it was wrong or at least of an unusual and abnormal nature. Consequently I began to build a wall around myself . . . This wall I kept solidly around myself . . . until I was 23 years of age."

In his letter, George went on to tell Stürup that after reading *The Male Hormone:* "I became more convinced that this was the answer to my problem. With this chemical change I could live as, and really be a woman and in this way eliminate the terrible suppression of my real emotions, likes and feelings."[9]

As presented, his letter emphasized intense homosexual urges while partially ignoring his history of strong gender dysphoric feelings. Most likely, this was because the latter was not a justification for castration. Continuing his letter, George described his strategy of total secrecy and sexual abstinence: "[I had] . . . known of the danger and heartbreak that would overcome both my self [sic] and those dearest to me if I should let anyone come to mean too much to me." Jorgensen wrote that his sexual conflicts interfered with scholastic achievement and that "I constantly need new things to keep me from thinking about myself."

George said he was very sensitive to feeling that others perceived him as "a freak" and that "Only another person such as myself can fully understand what it does to me inside." He explained that during his work at RKO in New York City he had become more self-critical and "cold inside" while feeling "very anxious." These emotions, George explained, contributed to his plan to try to find work in Hollywood. Throughout this period "I continued my celebate [sic] life although opportunities arose where I could have lived with a man." He then explained his conviction that respect for the rules of society and a willingness "to fit in" are essential to getting along with others. At base, George Jorgensen, and later Christine both worked diligently to measure up to the moral expectations of middle class America, and to be seen as conventional and worthy persons, entirely free of any stigmatizing characteristics, especially, homosexuality.

The action he decided to take, he told Stürup, was to book a passage to Denmark "six months in advance." But months prior to leaving New York, he fell in love with a young man identified as Jack. As in several previous love affairs "There was at no time any physical or sexual contact between us, for Jack is a normal man and I firmly believe he [sic] even at that time [did] not know of my true feelings for him." This, he wrote, had been an intense romantic attachment: "I grew to love Jack in a way that I had never loved anyone before." But he vowed never to reveal the depth of his love to Jack, for as strange as it may seem, Jorgensen appears to have been a very homophobic person at that time. On the one hand, he often attracted gay men to him and he was also attracted to them. On the other hand, his religious and family values dictated that these feelings were unacceptable and immoral.[10]

Later in his letter written for Stürup, he explained his appreciation for Hamburger's assistance at a time "when I so desperately needed help." He said his estrogen treatments had led to a gain in weight and "[I] . . . never felt better in my life. The future looks so bright and I have reasons to want to live and enjoy life." Some of his joy reflected changes in his body which he appears to have exaggerated: "As a physical examination will disclose, I have changed greatly." Throwing all of his cards on the table, he ended his letter with a plea for Stürup's support of the castration application:

> Without this chance for the future I know that I cannot go on living a good constructive life. For to return now to my old way of life would destroy all my hopes and ambitions as well as my body. This operation is not only helping me but may, perhaps, open a whole new field of investigation for similar cases such as

mine. If you could really realize how desperately we of my race [kind] need help. Please accept this paper with apologies for I fully realize that with these words you shall judge the whole future of my life.

G. Jorgensen.

The application for castration was approved and the removal of George's gonads was accomplished in a thirty-minute surgical procedure at a county hospital on September 24, 1951. His cost was thirty dollars. Hamburger's go-slow plan had taken a major surgical turn in the road, and George was happier than ever.

One of the witnesses to the daily changes seen in George was the youngest son of Christian Hamburger, Jesper Hamburger,[11] (now a Copenhagen dentist). He was eleven when he first observed the "feminine appearing" George Jorgensen at his father's laboratory. Jesper recalls George's unusual appearance, including long blonde hair, and the bright, attention-getting clothing. As with many citizens of Copenhagen, Christian Hamburger rode his bicycle to work on a thirteen-mile round trip from home to the hospital and back. Young Jesper left home at about 4 p. m. and rode to meet his father at his laboratory, and then the two cycled home together, starting near the waterfront, proceeding across the crowded, flat streets of central Copenhagen and northward, to the forested, more upscale suburban area where they lived. These bicycle trips were one of the few times that Jesper could be sure of spending an hour with his busy father, who, after a family dinner, devoted almost every evening to the editing of a major endocrinological journal.

At the laboratory, Jesper and George became friends, chatting daily, although Jesper did not understand George's "confusing" feminine appearance. He asked his father about this. Dr. Hamburger explained little but reassured him that his "powers of observation were accurate," and that George's appearance was, indeed, unusual. He said little more about the matter. The laboratory technicians were also wondering what George's future would be as he progressively surrendered many of his masculine characteristics. One thing was clear: George was upbeat, smiling, fully cooperative, and happier than ever. He never missed an appointment or failed to deliver his urine samples.

During an interview, in a beautiful new Scandinavian home in a suburb north of Copenhagen, the tall, slender, affable, and generous

Jesper Hamburger appeared to have many of his father's qualities, including a considerable empathy for others in need and a willingness to help. Jesper is a very charitable man with an admirable sense of personal and social responsibility. He explained how he had learned of a group of impoverished refugee children with serious dental difficulties. After making an assessment of what was needed, he volunteered to take on half the clinical work, *gratis,* if the local dental association would take responsibility for the other half. For bureaucratic reasons they declined to do so. Therefore, he provided free dental services to all of the children himself. Speaking with me in the living room of his home he described the George Jorgensen he had known forty-three years earlier:

> I'd see him or her in the lab some evenings. He'd always pronounce my name Jazz-per, instead of Jesper, and as the months passed, George started to look more and more like a young woman . . . everyone in the lab was talking about this and wondering what it would lead to.[12]

He described his father's personality as very warm and cordial, but noted Dr. Hamburger was far more comfortable with test tubes and equipment on a laboratory bench than in dealing with patients who were ill. He did not enjoy doing clinical work, and following medical school he became a full-time researcher, seldom returning to work with patients. He expressed much pride in the scientific distinction his father had achieved for his endocrinological studies. The case of Christine Jorgensen, Jesper told me, "was just a minor detour in his scientific career. He paid little or no attention to it after the publicity died down." He added: "Danish doctors don't seek a lot of publicity, you know." With or without public notice, it is certain that Hamburger gained considerable professional stature and recognition for his exceptional leadership in the Jorgensen case, and that he was proud of his pioneering work. He has seldom been credited with being the inventor of the modern protocol for transsexualism, but he was. From a historical perspective, we are fortunate to have Jesper's recollections and the carefully documented publications of his father describing the Jorgensen case, as no other medical records are known to have survived. According to Hamburger's eldest son, Henrik, his father directed that his Christine Jorgensen records were to be destroyed upon his death, and his son did so.[13] Christian Hamburger died in 1992.

The daily routine of coming to the Institute and either ingesting female hormones orally or receiving an injection provided some structure in George's daily schedule. In letters to Joseph Angelo written during the fall of 1950, he explained how much better he felt, and he believed this must be due to "suppressing or canceling out the effects of the male hormones."[14] He was feeling, "alive and confident" especially when he went to the highly regarded photographic studio of Jens Junker-Jensen in the heart of the city to ask for a job. A paying job was not available, but he was provided a place to work on his color photography, and later, to edit his motion picture about Denmark.[15]

As happened so often throughout Jorgensen's life, he and Junker-Jensen became good friends, and George helped to train some of the employees in color photography techniques. Later, while working at this studio, he earned some income by selling glamour photographs to European magazines. Jorgensen showed much initiative in his photographic efforts and Junker-Jensen and his wife and children came to enjoy being with Christine. They forgot entirely about the George they had once known. During 1952, while spending much time with the Jensens, Christine had almost become a member of a Danish family not unlike her own family in the Bronx.

George enjoyed living in the sunny fourth-floor apartment of Elsa Sabroe. She was a wonderful listener, and she was open-minded about sexual topics. She was also an excellent cook. Her middle-class apartment on the north side of Copenhagen was at Naestvedgrade 21 IV (fourth floor).[16] Something of a mother-son relationship had developed, for they liked each other very much, and both felt comfortable sharing the joys and frustrations of their lives. George had learned the value of being candid with those close to him concerning both his sexual feelings and his ever-stronger desire to live as a woman. George's entire income was based on the ten dollars a week his mother sent him, along with a supply of photographic film.

Unable to find a job, George first requested a loan from his sister who sent $400. Later, he made the same request of his old friend at RKO Pathé, Larry Jenson,[17] who promptly sent a similar amount. Jorgensen had a Copenhagen bank account so it was easy to deposit a U.S. check or money order and exchange this for Danish kroners. George hated to ask for money, but he knew he needed a helping hand to carry out his plan to become a woman, and he felt he had to accomplish this no matter what the cost. And how could he have predicted that before the end of 1952, the Hearst Newspapers would provide him with a check for $25,000 in exchange for the exclusive rights to publish his life story?[18] Adjusted for today's monetary values, this amounted to roughly $150,000. During the following year, the impecunious George Jorgensen was to receive more money than any of the Jorgensens had ever been paid for anything. His worn-out winter jacket and rag-tag tennis shoes would be exchanged for a floor-length fur coat, nylons, and fashionable high heels. All of this was only eighteen months away. Once Christine had money in her bank account, the first thing she did was to repay the loans to her sister and to Larry Jenson. Frugality and the repayment of loans was a Jorgensen tradition.

Jens Junker-Jensen and his wife, Edna, took a special interest in George, often inviting him to dinner and taking him to their summer home for a few days of vacation when the weather was nice. They had two children, a boy and a girl. George and the children became friends, and they swam and dove together in the lake near the summer place. The children took snapshots during the long days of the spring and summer, then developed the negatives and printed the pictures with George's supervision. Like his father, he was a good teacher of darkroom techniques and showed much patience with the youngsters.

The head of the Junker-Jensen family was highly regarded as one of the premier commercial photographers in Copenhagen. He knew the officers of city government, the managers of Copenhagen's most fashionable hotels, and many of the newspaper people who relied on him for special photographic assignments. But his specialty was portrait work for the more affluent citizens. They wanted pictures that showed their children at different ages, and group shots of an entire family. George visited Jensen's studio almost daily, threading his bicycle through the traffic while heading south to the studio and parking it on the sidewalk. Nobody locked a bicycle in those days. Then, late in the afternoon, he'd cycle about two miles south toward the imposing white building complex that was the Royal Hospital to keep his medical appointments. Sometimes he returned in the evening to enlarge prints, and from time to time he had an opportunity to share with the Jensens his life aspirations and longing for a feminine gender role. Like Miss Sabroe, Edna Jensen was a patient and understanding listener and an excellent seamstress who assisted with Jorgensen's sewing projects. Even better, as they gained confidence in each other she became one of his most valued confidants. There was nothing they couldn't discuss, from politics to the Danish laws concerning homosexuality and how they differed from the American statutes. Both of the Jensens were protective of George's personal revelations; they were also supportive of his struggle to become a woman. Learning of this goal helped the Jensens to understand why George had been allowing his blonde hair to grow unusually long, something unheard of for men at that time, and why George seemed eager to wear combinations of colorful clothing that most men would reject. Both of the Jensens were artists at heart and they admired their young friend's courage in striving to build a new and more fulfilling identity.

As the days lengthened with the unfolding of spring, Edna Jensen became fully informed of George's hormone regimen. She had come to relate to him as if he were a member of her immediate family. She seemed to take the same role that other women had occupied earlier in George's young life, listening to him discuss his feelings and fears, hearing of his aspirations and frustrations, and helping him learn to cook. She gave him some Danish recipes, showed him a few tricks in hair styling, and demonstrated how she used an eye liner to accentuate her eyes. The hormones George had been taking daily had produced a very slight swelling of the breasts which pleased him greatly, and along with his unusual clothing and long hair, visitors to the Jensen studio who saw George sometimes wondered if they were seeing a man or a woman. But Danes tend to be reticent, and few ever spoke of his appearance. Meanwhile, George grew even closer to the Jensen family and he shared with them all he knew about his doctor's medical plan. But in his future there was much he could not predict. He was not certain that approval would be given for the surgical changes he was pleading for. He felt certain, however, that the time would come when he would live as a woman and be accepted as a woman, and he was certain he could make this dream come true. The Jensens wanted nothing more than to help George develop into the person he felt he was destined to become and their evening conversations became ever more personal. These emotional sessions were a highly rewarding release for him, for he could reveal himself to the Jensens more fully than he had ever spoken to his own parents. While George had grown up in a very supportive and loving family, the topics most important to him, homosexuality and sex transformation, were never mentioned. Nobody in his Bronx neighborhood even used these words, and more than a few admitted they didn't fully understand what they meant. George felt privileged to have the Jensens as a vicarious family for he missed the good times at home. He had delightful memories of the fishing trips, the Saturday night dances at Askov Hall, and, of ice skating with his neighborhood friends in winter.

Both his parents and the Jensens placed the highest of values on strong, helpful family relationships, and while Jensen sometimes questioned him about his chain smoking and his drinking, they knew that in Denmark most people smoked and beer was plentiful at many social gatherings. The same was true on Dudley Avenue, where his parents lived. Back in the Bronx, when relatives asked George Sr. or Florence about George, their standard answer was that he was doing just fine in Copenhagen, studying photography. The last thing any of them ever considered was that George might be involved in a thirty-month sex change program or that he would soon be writing to inform them that they had a new daughter.

Chapter 10

A New Name, a New Gender

During May 1952, Christine's great-aunt, Tine, came to Copenhagen from New York to visit her Danish relatives. Since most of her friends and relatives in Copenhagen had already learned the background of Chris's gender transformation and shown support and understanding, Christine planned to be just as forthcoming with Aunt Tine. Chris described it this way in 1967: "I dressed myself in my new feminine clothing . . . I felt nervous and uneasy . . . [After slipping into a] . . . green skirt, pale-brown jacket and brown suede shoes . . . I looked at myself in the mirror . . . and I liked what I saw."[1]

Later the same day, Edna Junker-Jensen took Christine to a beauty shop and arranged for her to have her first permanent wave, a manicure, a facial, and hair styling. In addition to these happy days, Christine had begun to film her travelogue about Denmark. She had never previously photographed a motion picture and knew little about how such a product might be marketed. The color film was being sent by her mother. Photographs show her filming with a large, heavy, professional sixteen-millimeter camera.

When Aunt Tine was about to return to America, George asked her to deliver a letter to his parents explaining his gender change. He wanted her to hand deliver it and to help the Jorgensens understand that everything was progressing well in Copenhagen. Christine had been telling her parents that her Denmark experience was simply an extended vacation, and although George had confided his progress with hormones and castration to Dr. Joseph Angelo, his parents and the Angelos were not in communication at this time. It would seem likely that one way or another his parents might have regarded the two years in Denmark as more than an extended vacation or a photographic field trip, but perhaps not. George was very close to both of

doi:10.1300/5896_10

his parents and his sister, and it is unclear whether they were entirely in the dark about his medical care. Very likely, however, they did not know of his surgical castration in the fall of 1951, something George's father later found very upsetting.

In an exceptionally important letter to his parents written June 8, 1952,[2] George attempted to present three main points (1) to reassure them that he was healthy, happier than ever, and also more productive; (2) to emphasize that he had received marvelous medical treatment for a "glandular problem;" and (3) most important, that he was now living as their daughter and with the name of Chris. For the Jorgensens, it must have been a bombshell.

At the outset, Chris wrote that she was now "much happier" than ever; gone were the days of depression and gloom. She then explained the "glandular" problem that required female hormones to help deal with this difficulty, and also to produce a reversal of gender. She said her "problem" was entirely biological and that she had long suffered from a glandular imbalance, but that a wonderful scientist/physician had worked a virtual "miracle" to correct this difficulty. The facts are stretched to tell Mom and Dad that at the time of adolescence, when her secondary sexual characteristics developed, Christine had mysteriously developed vaguely described female characteristics. This allusion to some supposed intersex anatomy was a favorite rationalization for Chris, but there was never any evidence to support this. Nor was there any evidence of a so-called glandular imbalance. There had been a thorough physical examination both prior to induction into the Army and again when she was discharged. Later, Dr. Hamburger's examination also resulted in the same nonpathological findings. Anatomically and hormonally, George Jorgensen was an unremarkable male despite Christine's biological theory.

In fairness to Chris, she did not have the language or a causal theory to explain her transsexuality so she used an explanation that made sense to her, focusing on a supposed glandular difficulty. Nor did she have a role model or guidance to help her conceptualize her gender-identity feelings. To her, it seemed logical that since she was being cared for daily by doctors, and receiving both hormones and surgery, that at the core of her difficulties there must be a biological cause. What made the most sense to her was a theory of "glandular imbalance," and she stuck to her guns. To her parents, Chris presented herself as a tragic and courageous figure struggling with a hormonal difficulty that was tearing her life apart, and begging for understanding.

She told her parents that De Kruif's, *The Male Hormone,* was at the heart of her hormonal and glandular theories of herself. Through "tests and an operation," she explained, she'd been greatly helped. The punch line was this: "Nature made a mistake, which I have corrected, and I am now your daughter." The letter contains no explanation about why her supposed glandular problem compelled her to live as a woman. Furthermore, while mentioning an operation the preceding September, no clarification was provided about George's castration, although she promised more details in forthcoming letters.

Chris relied upon the studio photographs taken by Junker-Jensen along with at least one of her own self-portraits to show her parents that their former son had become a beautiful woman. The photographs, all excellent pictures, told Chris's story even more powerfully than her letter. It is clear from both the pictures and her written words that Chris was proud to have achieved the gender changes that were so obliquely alluded to in her letter. She begged for understanding, and, her parents, while they had many questions, were quick to communicate their unqualified love. The glue that held the Jorgensen family together was resistant to dissolution.

The carefully prepared plan for Aunt Tine to carry the letter to the Jorgensens in the Bronx did not work out quite as expected. In a 1984 interview,[3] Chris explained that it was her sister, Dolly, and Dolly's husband, who first visited Aunt Tine, read the letter, and subsequently interpreted it to Mr. and Mrs. Jorgensen. For all of the Jorgensens, the letter was confusing and devastating. They could not believe a son could be transformed into a daughter.

The news was more upsetting to George Sr. than to Florence, but they were both suffering and confused. The following day they did something that could have been predicted within the closely knit network of Jorgensens: They summoned all their relatives to their second-floor living room and presented all of the facts, including the letter and the pictures. Everyone was shocked; they had never heard of anything like this. Looking at George's letter, it was clear that somehow a medical problem was at the heart of the matter. The entire group was astounded. The living room George Sr. and his brother had built thirty-three years before was filled with smoke and wonderment. The aunts and uncles passed around the photographs of Christine, sampled the pastries, smoked their cigarettes, and drank lots of coffee. They must have noticed George's tiny, closet-like room adjoining the living room with his pictures and posters still on the walls. Everything was there, awaiting his return. His Army uniform was still hanging in the closet. Was the George they knew from infancy never coming back? George Sr. wondered aloud if he had been too tough on George when they talked of his taking more initiative to get employment or to enroll in college. Over coffee, the family members posed many questions, but neither George nor Florence could add much beyond the letter and the pictures. They kept passing the photographs around and there was a good deal of head shaking. Their understanding of what had taken place focused on the same theme provided in the letter: A "glandular problem" had required transformation from the George they had known to a new daughter, a very attractive daughter. But the good news was that Chris was now healthy and happy. "Thank the Lord for that," said Florence.

George Jorgensen and the rest of the men were not big talkers. Most of them were two-fisted, no-nonsense construction workers, not gender theorists or child development specialists. These men built houses. They certainly knew nothing of so-called sex changes. They were stunned by the seriousness and mystery of this development, and especially by the idea of castration. The George they had known was the only son of Florence and George Sr. and no one had ever thought, not for a moment, that George had been the victim of any kind of glandular difficulty. He had seldom been ill. All of the women, however, followed Dolly's lead in expressing gratitude to the Lord that George had come through his long medical program in good health, and that he (or she) was happy and stronger than ever. Very likely, none of them used the pronoun, "she" during that evening. George Sr. and the other men were smoking their pipes or cigarettes and they were all uncomfortable. Even Florence, who seldom smoked, lit up, and so did Dolly, who was also a light smoker. The questions poured forth along with some tears. George Sr. was especially concerned when others brought up the topic of castration. He cringed. The entire story seemed beyond belief. He was not sure he understood what it meant for a human being to be castrated.

A practical question was raised: Since they lived in a very friendly neighborhood, should they all be sworn to silence or should the facts and the pictures be revealed to their close friends? Arguments for and against disclosure were heard, and finally Florence ended the discussion by saying she intended to hold a meeting with the families who had known George. A week later she did so, assembling her friends in the living room of a family that lived across the street from Askov Hall. A member of that family who had been present shared with me the proceedings of the meeting.[4] According to later newspaper reports, it consisted of a group of twenty-two people. Their response was much the same as Mrs. Jorgensen had experienced with her relatives. Again, the focus was on "glandular" problems. No mention of sexual matters was heard at either meeting. Even when interviewed in the present, most of Christine's relatives emphasize that, in their view, she did not have a history of homosexuality.

Meanwhile, in Copenhagen, none of these New York developments deflected George from the main goal he had for the summer: He wanted a new passport with a new name and identifying him as a female. For George, a new passport would signify far more than a change of name. It would be Chris's government issued certification for an entirely new identity.

The summer of 1952 was an exciting and rewarding season for Chris, sewing new outfits of stylish clothing including matching gloves, and photographing herself in a series of tasteful, feminine pictures. Rather than hang the new clothing in the closet and wait for her passport, Chris did a considerable amount of practicing the feminine role. Perhaps this occurred both at home and in her neighborhood. She was definitely demonstrating her feminine skills in May of 1952, but she was uneasy about being in public without identification that showed her to be a woman. She wanted proper documentation of her gender change, and she wanted it in the form of a United States passport.

George Jorgensen attributed great significance to the issuance of a new passport with a woman's name and photograph and showing her to be a female. Today, one of the biggest identity-changing steps for transsexuals is a court-ordered change of name. In some states, such an order can include the specification that sex (or gender) should also be changed on public records. This action is as close as most transsexuals can get toward obtaining a legal confirmation of a change in gender status. For George, having a new passport would mean that his old one would be discarded, just as he had abandoned his well-worn masculine clothing. There was the matter of simply having identification that matched Christine's changed appearance, which would facilitate reentry to the United States, but most important of all was her own sense of feminine identity. Chris wanted formal recognition of her changed gender status. However, she may or may not have known that the only feminine identification on the passport would be the photograph George would submit to the State Department. Examining the picture and the first name, anyone could make their own judgment whether they were viewing the passport of a man or a woman. For Chris, the passport would be the culmination of a two-year transformation process. She believed a woman's passport would authorize her to appear as a woman. It would also accord her the status of a woman in society. Later, she wrote:

> Both my doctors and I realized that it would be necessary for me to contact the American Embassy in Denmark and make arrangements to have my passport changed to that of a woman. I was still dressed as George, with my long hair tucked under a beret, when I kept the appointment Mrs. Eugenie Anderson, American Ambassador to Denmark.[5]

With very few exceptions, George was careful never to claim that his new passport would designate him a female, although in 1959 she clearly alluded to having such a passport when she applied for a marriage license. However, in 1952, and for twenty-five years thereafter, an examination of any U.S. passport would have revealed that no sex identification was shown, nor did the words man or woman appear.[6] Prior to 1977, only the photograph and the first name provided a basis for sex identification on U.S. passports. George's new passport application was submitted in the name of Chris Jorgensen, possibly an androgynous choice just in case of difficulty with the issuance of a new passport. Had they refused to attach the new photograph of the feminine Chris, it would still have been possible for an androgynous photo to have been used along with the new name. According to the account given in her 1967 autobiography, George, appearing in his male persona, explained his change of gender to the U.S. ambassador who assured him that there would be no problem. At this point, Christian Hamburger was asked to write a letter explaining whether Chris was a male or a female. He wrote a letter, but made no reference to the sex of the applicant. Later, he noted that so far as he knew, none of the other doctors had written anything to the Consulate concerning

Chris's application, although in 1967 Chris implied that other letters had been written.

Apparently, Hamburger's letter was sufficient evidence to encourage the issuance of a passport, and according to Jorgensen's account, the required application was forwarded for approval by the main passport office in Washington. This was accomplished and the documentation was returned to the U.S. Consulate in Copenhagen. In an effort to examine the original application, a Freedom of Information Act request was submitted to the State Department, but the relevant application documents were not found. It would be of interest to know whether Chris had submitted her photograph as an attractive twenty-six-year-old woman prior to sending the application to Washington. In any case, the attractive and totally feminine-appearing photograph of Chris was ultimately attached to the passport, signed "Chris Jorgensen," with the date of issuance shown as July 23, 1952. A copy of this passport is among the Jorgensen collection at the Danish Royal Library.

When Christine returned to the United States in early 1953, there were scattered news reports alleging that Ambassador Eugenie Anderson had failed to properly screen the Jorgensen application.[7] The implication was that she had let Chris Jorgensen pull the wool over her eyes, but these charges seem unwarranted since Jorgensen had provided her with all of the facts of the case. Chris's new passport faithfully showed what she actually looked like. With or without her new passport, she seems to have had no difficulty in learning to "pass" as Christine. There is no record of George William Jorgensen Jr. ever appearing again.

In May 1952, Christine dressed in one of her colorful new summer outfits, applied her makeup, and went for a stroll in Tivoli Gardens. This is Copenhagen's famous downtown entertainment park just off Hans Christian Andersen Boulevard. There, along the verdant walkways, the flowers of springtime and the bountiful fountains, she found it easy to strike up a conversation with four U.S. airmen who invited her for drinks at one of the many outdoor restaurants. As travelers often do, they spoke of their hometowns, the experiences they were having overseas, and of the many exceptionally beautiful landmarks of Denmark. Smoking and drinking a little, they all relaxed, and as fellow Americans, a pleasant rapport was soon established. One of these servicemen, Sergeant Bill Calhoun,[8] age twenty-four, from

Everman, Texas, showed a special interest in her, and said he'd like to return to Copenhagen and see her again when he could get a longer leave from his post at Bentwaters Air Base in England. Delighted with his attention and his desire to date her, Christine supplied her telephone number, gave him a photograph, and urged him to stay in touch. Soon thereafter, she met him to bid good-bye when he returned to England. They promised to write each other.

When they next met in Copenhagen, Sergeant Calhoun had a one-week pass and he and Christine accepted an invitation from the Junker-Jensens to join their family for a day at their summer vacation home. Once there, Calhoun took several color pictures of Christine showing off her new spring and summer dresses with the fullness of her long skirts helping to accentuate her trim waist. During the next week, there was ample time for them to become better acquainted, although how far this went was later seen differently by Calhoun and Jorgensen. In reviewing their time together, we should keep in mind that Christine's genital surgery was still months away. Perhaps, like many preoperative transsexuals, she had learned to keep her most private parts tucked tightly within undergarments. In any case, Calhoun believed without question, that she was a woman.

After Christine's highly publicized return to the United States, Calhoun, recently married to an English girl, was identified as a "former boyfriend." He described to reporters his highly favorable recollections of his dates with her in Copenhagen. According to news reports, his relationship with Chris became public when one of his Air Force buddies saw her autograph on a picture she'd given him that was displayed near his bunk. He said he had "kissed her more than once" while never suspecting she had been a man, and that Christine had been a "serious girl friend." In another article he was quoted as saying: "She's got a personality that's hard to beat, the best looks, best clothes, best features, and best figure of any girl I ever met." Calhoun and Chris may have been more intimately involved than she wanted to admit, and later, she strongly played down what she said was her "pleasant" time with him. The following year, Calhoun is reported to have told the press: "I want people to know there was no romance between Christine and me. I kissed her a number of times, but what man wouldn't?" In a letter to Christine written after she became a celebrity,[9] Calhoun may have asked her for money in exchange for remaining silent about their relationship. Apparently, Chris did not respond.

There are some inconsistencies in Christine's 1967 description of when certain things happened during the late spring of 1952. For example, Calhoun said he had first met her in May, that she was "dressed like a woman" and that he had spoken to her because she "looked like an American girl." But Christine, in her autobiography and elsewhere, said she had never dressed as a woman in public until her new passport was issued on July 25, 1952. Based on the Calhoun story, it seems very likely that Christine had been working on the development of her feminine appearance and going out in public at least as early as May, 1952. Almost certainly, with her shining blonde hair and a little breast swelling set off by a stylish sweater, lipstick, earrings, and a full circle skirt, she may have looked far more like Christine than George during a good part of 1952. Jorgensen persistently explained the entire Calhoun matter as nothing more than a girl having a casual drink with a lonely serviceman. The Calhoun relationship fits the pattern of all of her romantic episodes as she was silent about how sexually intimate they may have become.

Aunt Augusta from Minneapolis, with whom Chris had stayed for several days in 1947, arrived in Copenhagen during August, 1952. She brought Chris a much appreciated package of clothing sent by her parents and her sister including "dresses, suits, shoes, gloves and handbags." In the most practical ways, the Jorgensen family was doing all it could to show support for its new daughter.

A few months later, while making her travel film during the fall of 1952, Christine had several dating opportunities and noted that she was seldom without a dinner date. At one filming site in July, a prominent newspaper reporter volunteered to help carry her photographic equipment, and after doing so, asked her to join him for dinner. Judging from her description of this highly important journalist, it may well have been Henrik Rechendorff, who later said he was the first to break the Jorgensen story in Copenhagen's largest newspaper, *Berlinske Tidende,* sometime prior to December 1, 1952.[10]

Photographs from that period show Chris looking youthful, energetic, fashionably dressed, and very pretty as a young lady. On another occasion, a wealthy gentleman invited Christine and her friend, Helen Johnson, to be house guests in his expensive home for a weekend. The invitation was accepted. Chris later emphasized that nothing romantic had occurred. Despite these dating opportunities, Chris presents herself throughout her autobiography as a totally celibate and circumspect person. When interviewed by Teit Ritzau in 1984 she said very proudly: "I never took a man into my house,"[11] nor, she said, had she ever moved into a man's home. Some of the sexual passion George felt during his teenage years may have been reduced by long-term use of estrogen. Supporting this view, Christian Hamburger described George in 1953 as experiencing "low libido." Based on her own emphatic statements, she was never romantically involved with women, although many women had close, long-term friendships with her. Chris's strongest friendships and the most enduring romantic relationships were usually with heterosexual men.[12]

Throughout 1952, as Chris gained confidence in her social role as a woman, she lobbied Christian Hamburger concerning the amputation of her penis. Hamburger did not initiate this proposal, but in dealing with her persistent requests he did what he always did when faced with a medical decision: He requested consultation from several trusted senior colleagues at the Royal Hospital, including the psychiatrist, Georg Stürup, who had supported George's castration application more than a year earlier. At this time, Hamburger and his team had been assisting Christine for about twenty-seven months. They decided to proceed with the requested amputation and a date was set for late November 1952. Hamburger was assured by the senior surgeons at the Royal Hospital that the operation was not unique or dangerous. However, there was the issue of Jorgensen's psychiatric status, and whether genital surgery could do him more harm than good. Therefore, Hamburger asked Dr. Stürup to consult with other psychiatrists concerning both George's emotional stability and his probable response to the surgery. He did so, and reported that he saw no objection to the proposed amputation.

Much had been accomplished during the autumn of 1952. Most important, she now looked like a young woman and she had been living entirely as Christine for about six months. Her passport named her Chris Jorgensen and portrayed her unmistakably feminine picture. Her parents had been told of her change of gender. Now, Hamburger seemed to reason that in view of Chris's obvious reversal of gender identity and gender role, there was more to be gained than lost by going ahead with the penectomy. The highly experienced, somewhat crusty, but well-liked Dr. Ehrling Dahl-Iverson would lead the surgical team. Jorgensen's genital surgery was not an unusual challenge: The penis was amputated, the urethra was repositioned, and labia-like cosmetic finishing touches were stitched in place. They were finished before lunch. Within a few weeks, all of the scars would be covered by a thick growth of pubic hair. Dahl-Iverson did not think of it as a morning of surgery that would change the world, but in some ways it did. Chris healed rapidly while spending about three weeks in the hospital. Her patient card on file at the reception desk of the Royal Hospital read:[13]

> Miss Chris Jorgensen
> p. t. Rigshospitalet
> Pavillion IIc East

About ten days later, on December 1, as the Jorgensen sex-change story was being headlined around the world, the biggest newspaper in Denmark, *Berlinske Tidende,* ignored it entirely. Ironically, on that day they featured photographs and accounts of Dahl-Iversen's huge sixtieth birthday party at the Royal Hospital. They reported the Jorgensen story using wire service reports on December 2. Although Christine Jorgensen had become the focus of one of the major news stories of the decade, the editors of *Berlinske Tidende* elected not to track down her doctors or to call upon Miss Jorgensen for an exclusive interview.

Chapter 11

Ex-GI Becomes Blonde Beauty

Two million New Yorkers unfolded their afternoon *Daily News* on December 1, 1952, and were astounded to read a headline some considered outrageous and others found preposterous: "EX-GI Becomes Blonde Beauty" followed by a subhead: "Operations Transform Bronx Youth.[1] The wire services had transmitted the story around the world the night before and for some readers the claim of sexual transformation must have seemed unbelievable; others probably found it exciting, mysterious, or intriguing. Several articles were provided together with pictures of George Jorgensen next to photos of the surprisingly attractive, distinctly feminine Christine. These headlines shouted the story of Christine Jorgensen, a twenty-six-year-old former Army Private First Class who had spent thirty months in Denmark where hormonal treatments and surgery had transformed George Jorgensen into a woman. Beneath the front page headline was a half-page close-up profile of Christine's unmistakably feminine face with her hair in a neat bun, not unlike some of the librarians she had worked with in the Bronx. This was probably the first studio picture of Christine; a signed photograph, it was most likely taken in Copenhagen during the late spring of 1952 by Eveing R. Olsen; as best we can judge, it was included with Jorgensen's June letter to her parents outlining her transsexuality. This dating is significant for two reasons: First, the picture almost certainly was taken prior to the award of Christine's passport although we cannot be certain of this, and second, it was not taken by the well known photographer, Jens Junker-Jensen, who was soon to become a close friend of Christine's. A carefully posed picture, this widely published photograph helped to establish Jorgensen's convincing appearance as a woman. Beside the front page picture of Christine was an Army snapshot showing Pfc.

Becoming a Woman: A Biography of Christine Jorgensen
© 2008 by The Haworth Press, Taylor & Francis Group. All rights reserved.
doi:10.1300/5896_11

George Jorgensen Jr. in his military uniform with an overseas cap, wearing a buttoned shirt with a tie. The picture revealed nothing of the woman somehow submerged within this youthful GI clerk/typist. The front page pictures and headlines summarized the main point of this amazing sex change, all attributed to the " . . . wizardry of medical science." A man had been converted into a woman.

Many of the readers must have wondered if an actual change of sex was technically possible. Could the anatomy of a male be changed to female? Did Christine now have the organs necessary to have a baby? What had the doctors and the hormones done to George Jorgensen in Denmark, and did this mean anyone could now elect to change his or her sex? And what did all of this tell about advances in medicine; if you could change your sexual organs, could you also replace the heart or the lungs? Could a female become a male?

These questions stimulated a curiosity about Christine that propelled the story into one of the major news topics of the year. People wanted to know all of the details, and before long, other news sources would offer highly critical appraisals of Christine. The ministers and the psychiatrists would have lots to say, and at least one New York newspaper would soon declare the entire story a fraud.[2] One thing soon became clear: In a biological male it is possible to remove the external sex organs and to administer female hormones, thereby helping to create the bodily appearance of a woman, but it is not possible to surgically transform a male into an anatomical female. Across the land, several physicians who knew nothing of the case beyond what they had read in their newspapers proclaimed that Christine was not an intersex person born with confusing sexual and reproductive organs. All of these debates and half-informed medical observations led to other troublesome questions, such as whether a new woman like Christine Jorgensen would be eligible to be married. Was she a female if she looked like a woman and lived her life as a woman? Would her birth certificate be changed from male to female? The very idea of sex transformations left many readers amazed, curious, and sometimes upset and rejecting, for the Christine case was not free of strong religious complications based on the Holy Scriptures. In some churches, Christine was denounced from the pulpit along with biblical commentary to support her condemnation. Some New Yorkers wondered what the connection might be between Christine's story and the short-skirted, flamboyant drag queens they'd seen soliciting along Forty-Second Street at Times Square. Was all of this about sex, or perhaps, about homosexuality? Christine, as pictured on page three of the December one *Daily News* in a "new look" business suit with a handbag and gloves, didn't appear like any drag queen they'd ever seen.[3] But more than anything else, the public was thirsty for additional information. This was a big story despite considerable competition for front-page space. General Eisenhower had just been elected President of the United States. The Korean War raged. What was the average citizen supposed to know about changing one's sex? Their first impressions came from an article written by the *Daily News* reporter, Ben White.

Ben White was one of the journeyman feature writers for the *New York Daily News*. He had covered beats all over the city for decades before writing the Jorgensen story, but he had never covered a story quite like this. Experienced newsmen would later say it turned out to be the biggest scoop he ever wrote. It was totally different from stories about scandals and corruption that White had often described in his colorful, punchy articles. He wrote in an easy-to-read style with graphic language, and he always tried to capture a human angle. White knew his way through the New York court system and around the dark brown linoleum corridors of City Hall. He knew the workings of the many bureaus and departments of city government, and he was quickly recognized at the precinct booking desks in all five boroughs. He recognized a story that "had legs" and he knew this story was especially newsworthy, exotic, and somewhat sexy. Man-becomes-woman, he realized, is not much different from the hackneyed definition of news: Man bites dog. It was a perfect scoop for the *Daily News,* a paper that thrived on competition and knew the importance of being first on the streets with a big story like this. This kind of reporting is what made the News the hottest-selling paper in the city, far ahead of all of its rivals both in circulation and advertising revenue. White was eager to work on any story that was racy, violent, sexual, or rancid with corruption. Nasty divorces were his specialty. He recognized immediately that Christine's story was made for the *Daily News,* and he made the most of it.

According to Christine's account, Ben White first called at the Jorgensen's Bronx home on a Sunday in late November while Mr. and Mrs. Jorgensen were visiting their daughter, Dolly, and her family on Long Island. Ironically, Helen Johnson, Chris's friend from

Copenhagen was staying at the Dudley Avenue house when White arrived. She gave him Dolly's telephone number and he called and arranged to meet the Jorgensens at their home the following day.[4] The overnight delay following White's telephone call provided the Jorgensens time to discuss with Dolly what they should reveal to White, and it raises an important question: Did the Jorgensens telephone Christine, then in the Royal Hospital in Copenhagen, to ask her how they should handle this press inquiry? A related question is whether Chris had written to instruct them to tell the truth should a reporter start asking questions. She knew an earlier account of her case had appeared in a Copenhagen newspaper, and this may have motivated her to provide guidance to the Jorgensens. In any case, Florence and George must have regarded White's interview request as of exceptional importance, and while international telephone calls were very uncommon for middle-class Bronx families, something as pressing as the inquiry from White might well have resulted in a call to Copenhagen. Whether Christine guided them is not clear. However, it seems likely that the parents had been directed to cooperate with the press, and to provide the June 8 letter and the photographs that Chris had sent them. In any case, when they met with White the following day, that's what they did. Dolly's role as an advisor to her parents has never been described, but later she proved to be adamantly opposed to any cooperation with the press concerning Christine, even refusing to confirm her own name. Dolly never gave interviews to newsmen and went out of her way to avoid discussions about her famous sister, even with her friends. Perhaps she encouraged her parents to avoid Ben White entirely, hoping to avoid any publicity. At the least, the Jorgensens were not caught off guard by Mr. White, and Christine's account of how these very self-sufficient people were suddenly frightened and supposedly intimidated by a newspaper man seems unlikely. These sturdy people were not easily intimidated, certainly not by Ben White of the *Daily News*. George Jorgensen Sr. ran construction crews and built buildings, and Florence was a very strong-willed woman with a mind of her own. These were people who would not have hesitated to tell Mr. White to "get lost" or to wave him off virtually without comment had they wished to protect Christine's privacy.

According to Chris's autobiography, when they met the following day, White showed them a letter said to have been written by a Copenhagen laboratory technician and giving a summary of Christine's medical procedures. White was careful to withhold the signature from the Jorgensens. As we shall describe shortly, he may have had good reason to hide the name of the letter writer as it seems to have been from a Copenhagen-based special correspondent for his newspaper.

Once the June letter from George and the photographs were given to White, he must have been delighted because he had acquired three kinds of back-up for his story: he had Christine's written account based on her June 8 letter, he had the parents' story of their response to the news that a "sex change" had taken place, and he had been given the very important photographs illustrating the Jorgensens "new daughter." All of this had been accomplished during a single visit to the Jorgensen's residence. We have no way to prove what went on at the time of White's visit, but it's clear that Florence and George made extensive statements to White about Christine's case and provided him with a gold mine of photographs and letters. Today, no one within the family, not even Dolly, can explain why her parents had been so cooperative.

Christine needed money, and she was also highly motivated to get publicity for her film about Denmark. She hoped to get the travel movie booked into theaters through an agency that had shown some interest.[5] She knew publicity could lead to income. Even more important, she had become more proud of herself as Christine than she had been as George, and as her men's clothes were tossed aside she also peeled away years of humiliation and guilt. Feeling like a newborn person, Chris may have sought to reveal her story because, as Christine, she was now certain she deserved the approval and respect of others. After years of shame, she felt like a more respectable person and she was eager to step onto the stage of life, elegantly groomed, a transformed personality with a lovely smile and a shining new identity.

In New York, White had acquired plenty of factual material for his scoop, but he knew no details of Christine's restructured sense of self-acceptance and her quest for achieving respectability. None of this really mattered to him. For White, the important thing was that he had been assigned one of the biggest news stories of the mid-century, a blockbuster, and there was no time to waste. White was a competitor, and he knew the impossibility of keeping secret something of this importance. He sat down to type the lead paragraph, starting off with the main facts as he understood them. He'd worked the same way in hundreds of crime and corruption stories; the supporting information could be clarified later. Working amid the clattering typewriters of the crowded city room, White rolled his first half-page into an old Royal he'd used for years, and wrote the lead: "A Bronx youth, who served two years in the Army during the war and was honorably discharged, has been transformed by the wizardry of medical science into a happy, beautiful young woman . . . ."[6]

The rest of the story flowed easily for this senior feature writer who loved his job, his co-workers, and the city he knew so well. He hand-carried his article to an editor and made it clear that the story deserved a big play. He knew he may have exaggerated or misstated factual material while explaining the main thread of the story, but in New York, nobody knew any more of the facts than he did. The *Daily News* played it as big as it could, and it did it at once. The copy was approved, the photographs were prepared, and about twenty-four hours before the *Daily News* hit the streets all of this, including the pictures, was being carried worldwide by several wire services.

Using the journalistic standards of today, White's failure to check his information with primary sources, especially Christine and her doctors, would be looked upon as bush league news work, but the standards in place fifty years ago allowed more elbow room, at least at the *Daily News*. White could have picked up his telephone and confirmed that Christine Jorgensen was still a patient at the prestigious, massive Royal Hospital in Copenhagen, recovering from the second of two surgeries, but he didn't want to risk being scooped by the smaller but highly competitive *New York Post* or any other newspaper. He felt he had to move ahead with what he had, and as a result, his first story contained numerous errors, none of which bothered either the *News'* editors or later, the readers who sipped their coffee while scanning the headlines, wide-eyed, and somewhat confused, about Miss Jorgensen's transformation.

White told his readers that Christine had established herself in a successful career in Denmark, which was totally incorrect. Actually, she was living on $40 a month, she had no career, and she owed relatives and friends hundreds, if not thousands of dollars. She had never held a job in Denmark. He dramatized the medical management of Christine's case by saying she had received almost two thousand injections, which was far off target. But the readers didn't care whether the count was 100 or 2,000; the point was that a man had been transformed into a woman and the pictures seemed to prove it. Whatever the facts might be, New Yorkers had no reason to find fault with White's narrative. He told his readers that Jorgensen had received six sex-changing operations (actually, there were two), that George had served in the Army for two years during World War II (in fact, he served for forteen months *after* the war ended), that he was working as a photographer in Denmark (actually, as an unpaid amateur film-maker), and that all past Army records had been officially changed (there is no evidence that any military records were changed).[7]

A second article ran in the *Daily News* and was carried by the wire services that December morning without a byline.[8] The headline read: "Letter Informing Parents." This was based on the letter of June 8, 1952, George had written home, telling for the first time his transsexual story, which at that time, remained incomplete. Characterized by the newspaper as a "sensitive and affectionate" letter, it also misinformed the Jorgensens and anybody else who studied it concerning the justification for the change of sex. As noted previously, in his letter to his parents, Jorgensen's explanation for his gender transformation focused narrowly on the thesis that a glandular disturbance had somehow induced female physical development at the onset of adolescence. This was news to his parents and not based in fact, but it made perfectly good sense to George, who had been greatly impressed by the book, *The Male Hormone*. Not only did the Jorgensen clan and their neighbors study this letter and the pictures that accompanied it, outlining George's glandular explanation for his change of sex, but the entire world received this biological explanation which supposedly corrected a "horrible illness." That was George's code word for homosexuality. While White and his colleagues were composing these stories for the New York audience, they were aware that unlike their many reports of mayhem and mischief in Manhattan, the Associated Press, the United Press, Reuters, and the International News Service would soon be transmitting their articles and pictures to every major newspaper in the world.

The *Daily News* was the right newspaper to seize and exploit the story of a former GI who had been transformed into a "blonde beauty" and who became the world's first celebrity transsexual. When this newspaper was established decades earlier by the owners of the *Chicago Tribune,* a far more conservative and journalistically more staid publication, the founding editors wanted to make it a lively, snappy tabloid with lots of pictures and stories that played into the curiosity of their working-class readers. The *Daily News* told its reporters to let the *New York Times* take responsibility for being the newspaper of record. It wanted to become New York's "pictorial newspaper." its readers not only found Christine's sex transformation to be fascinating and puzzling, but they wanted to know the details of the surgery, and what the hormones did to the body. How was her sex changed, they asked? Would the hormone injections hurt? The readers wanted to know about the doctors who had transformed George into Christine, what their motivation was, and whether there might be a flood of new sex change cases from around the world. The thought was both exciting and scary. Of even greater interest was the unspoken question that was not part of the initial flurry of news reports: Did the Christine case have something to do with homosexuality? The *Daily News* would do all it could to respond to these questions.

During the 1930s, the *Daily News* scored an advantage over its competition, including both the *New York Times* and the Hearst papers, by joining four other U. S. newspapers to establish the Associated Press wire service. Each of five well-established newspapers invested $150,000 to share a privileged status with this new photographic service that provided pictures transmitted internationally over dedicated telephone lines. Christine's story was the kind of unique, pictorial, somewhat titillating news report that helped build the circulation and profitability of the *Daily News,* and the editors of the *News* must have loved the content of the Jorgensen story. The photographs helped to give it the "punch" they wanted. They didn't hesitate to use a full front page for their December 1, 1952, "scoop." At the time of the initial Jorgensen article, the weekday circulation of the *Daily News* was about two and one-half million, while the more staid *New York Times* was barely one-half million.

Many major newspapers responded immediately following the December 1 article with their own follow-up stories, based either on wire service summaries and more pictures, or more rarely, from actual interviews with Christine who remained a patient in Copenhagen's Royal Hospital.[9] For example, a *Los Angeles Times* article from the Associated Press described a reporter gaining entrance to her room armed with nothing more than a large bouquet of flowers. No pictures were allowed and neither would Chris tolerate any "silly questions" about her reproductive organs. However, it's clear that her claim to do everything possible to avoid publicity was not true, despite what she told her doctors.

Ben White realized Christine's sex conversion would become a huge story, but as he smoked and typed in the noisy city room of the *News,* nobody predicted the full impact of the Jorgensen articles. This story would ultimately become one of the biggest news events ever broken by the *Daily News,* and it seemed to have taken on a life of its own. Because this story was so remarkable, so different and almost beyond belief, the public kept asking for more about Christine. They wanted to know about her choice of clothing, her hair style and makeup, her romantic interests, her private life, her financial affairs, her future plans, and how she had managed to become such a beautiful woman.

In her autobiography, Christine said she first learned of the *Daily News'* sensational headlines and pictures when a woman identified as Thyre Christensen brought a wire service teletype to her hospital room during the morning of December 1. Recovering from surgery but resting comfortably, she quickly reviewed the teletype printouts based on the *Daily News'* articles and then scanned the photographs and the follow-up stories quoting her parents. Chris said later that her immediate response to this "shocking news" was to telephone her doctors to explain that she was not responsible for this supposedly unwanted publicity.[10] Although Christine sought publicity and needed money, her doctors strongly objected to having the story of this "sex conversion" featured in news accounts. She knew that Danish doctors don't approve of newspaper publicity concerning their patients, so she assured them that she had not been the source. This was partially true but quite misleading.

Although Chris was probably not the immediate source of the "tip" to the *Daily News,* it is likely that the main responsibility for allowing the story to become public rests on her shoulders. There is compelling evidence that her transsexual story was published in at least one Copenhagen newspaper during the fall of 1952, and that she had revealed her entire case history to at least one newspaper reporter at about the same time, swearing him to secrecy. But on December 1, upon learning of the *Daily News'* headlines, her first thought was damage control. She telephoned her doctors to inform them of the publicity barrage and to deny responsibility. They advised her to say nothing to the press. After agreeing to do so, she did the opposite, providing interviews to several newspaper people who had easily gained entrance to her room. Chris was not in the least adverse to publicity. One of the first reporters to visit her that morning was Paul Ifversen, the reporter and friend to whom she had earlier confided her transsexual history. He appears to have been a key player in giving Christine's story to the *New York Daily News*.

Re-reading the wire service articles she had been given, she noted that one story mentioned that the Jorgensens had initially discussed Chris's transformation with many relatives and later, in a second neighborhood meeting, with twenty-two close friends. All who attended those meetings learned of how George had become Christine, and they learned the contents of the June 8 letter. In addition, all of these people had been shown the photographs that illustrated her convincing feminine appearance, set off by long, softly curled blonde hair, and the suit and gloves she had sewn with her landlady and confidant, Elsa Sabroe. Therefore, Chris reasoned, the story was no secret among the relatives and friends of the Jorgensens across the sea in the Bronx. She was also aware that when the story first appeared her doctors could not have known exactly how the "tip" was forwarded to the *Daily News*. Christine emphasized to her doctors that she had not gone to the newspapers, which was true. The scenario is somewhat complex, but we believe the facts justify the following explanation of how the Jorgensen story found its way to the City Room of the *New York Daily News*.

Chapter 12

Behind the Headlines

For most of the world, the *Daily News'* articles on December 1, 1952, were the first account of Christine's sex conversion. However, reporter Henrik Rechendorff said he had discovered the story earlier, and he had written a brief article for Denmark's largest daily, the huge, conservative-leaning *Berlingske Tidende.* Rechendorff, then forty-one, was a prominent reporter in Denmark, and he also served as the host of the Danish radio version of our *Meet the Press.* He met with reporters of the *Los Angeles Times* while he was visiting America as a guest of the U. S. Department of State in August, 1954, and he described his role in the Jorgensen story to a *Los Angeles Times* reporter.[1] When interviewed, the Danish reporter said his initial article provided only a few column inches explaining George's transformation to Christine. He explained to the *Times* that he did not think the story was especially newsworthy. Rechendorff told the *Times* that after his Copenhagen article had appeared, he alerted an American reporter in Paris to the Jorgensen story, noting that he believed it could become a bigger story in the United States, but nothing is known to have developed from that communication. Rechendorff's statements concerning his role in "breaking" the story seem highly credible in view of his exceptional prominence as a respected journalist. What he failed to clarify, however, is how Christine's metamorphis was subsequently published by the *Daily News.*

The story begins with a courtroom episode that took place in the fall of 1952. This highly significant event was something Christine Jorgensen never revealed. She had good reason to remain silent and to invent alternative explanations for the *Daily News'* "scoop." Rechendorff told the *Los Angeles Times* he first learned of Jorgensen's sex change from her participation in a Copenhagen civil court proceeding

Becoming a Woman: A Biography of Christine Jorgensen
© 2008 by The Haworth Press, Taylor & Francis Group. All rights reserved.
doi:10.1300/5896_12

concerning a small unpaid debt during the latter part of 1952. Later, two newspaper articles also described the court scene.[2,3] These articles confirm Rechendorff's account by telling us it was not George who appeared in court, but Christine Jorgensen. Rechendorff reported this as a "sex change" story. The debt matter had been resolved and therefore the judge dismissed the case. It's very important, however, that prior to this court appearance, Christine had given her entire story to a newspaper reporter, swearing him to secrecy.

According to Copenhagen newsman Paul Ifversen,[4] in September 1952 Christine was filming a large crowd in the King's Garden that had assembled to cheer a visiting actor, Danny Kaye. Christine's friend, journalist Ifversen, was assisting her with various motion picture equipment.[5] Judging from other observations Ifversen reported about Chris's changing appearance during 1952, they had apparently been acquainted prior to this event. In any case, Ifversen wrote that Christine discussed the operations she'd been undergoing and she obtained Ifversen's promise to keep this a secret. Significantly, Ifversen was a Copenhagen special correspondent for the *New York Daily News*. Christine's court appearance followed by Rechendorff's brief news report probably caused Ifversen to conclude that this public disclosure released him from his promise of secrecy. Given his relationship with the *Daily News,* he was in a perfect position to forward the story to his employer in New York. Christine could later claim that she had nothing to do with these press reports, but such a claim overlooks both her news-making appearance in court as Christine and also her description of her medical treatments to Ifversen. At that time in her life, Christine needed money and publicity more than privacy.

But if this scenario is accurate, why did the *Daily News* articles fail to reveal this history? One explanation would be the *News* concluded it didn't need to rely upon the more indirect Copenhagen account once the statements and photographs from her parents were obtained by reporter Ben White. He had obtained Jorgensen's June 8 letter to her parents, the pictures contrasting George and Christine, and the names of her doctors. While Ben White's documentation directly from the Jorgensens may have trumped the Ifversen account, the New York editors would not have known about Christine Jorgensen without the initiative of their Denmark representative, Paul Ifversen. In assessing the strength of this explanation, it is significant that Christine almost certainly gave Ifversen her full story, because reporter

White had most of the facts prior to speaking with her relatives in New York. Furthermore, Christine appears to have known Ifversen as a friend as well as a journalist. For example, Ifversen was one of the first people to call on her at the Royal Hospital on the morning of December 1.[6]

There is no record of any journalist pressing Jorgensen for a full account of her possible complicity in the December 1 publicity. This omission is difficult to understand. It appears that many reporters accepted the explanation first provided by Ben White, that a Danish "laboratory technician" had leaked the story. This account was also given in Christine's life story articles in the *American Weekly*. But at a 1960's event, historian Vern Bullough asked Christine if she had been involved as the source of the original *Daily News* story: She responded: "Yes, but let's leave it at that."[7] Perhaps there were two reasons she sought to conceal her involvement with the press: First, she knew her doctors did not want any publicity about her case, and second, she wanted to avoid any implication that she was improperly exploiting her transformation story to generate publicity or income, accusations that came up repeatedly.

Over many years, Christine invented several cover stories about the December 1 news coverage: first, as noted, there was the 1952 tale implicating a supposed laboratory technician. Second, in her autobiography she attributed the *Daily News* "scoop" to a "tip" from a disloyal friend of the Jorgensens in the Bronx, who supposedly sold the story for $200; she never named this person. Third, decades later she told one of her closest friend's, Stanton Bahr, that a "distant relative" gave the story to the Daily News.[8] I believe all of these were false attributions designed to deflect attention from her role in giving the entire story to Paul Ifversen. But in fairness, when Christine appeared in a Copenhagen court room in 1952 she may have had no idea of the publicity implication of her responding, as Christine, to a summons for George Jorgensen. However, it is more difficult to understand why she would have given the details of her case to reporter Ifversen if her goal was complete secrecy. Perhaps she had become proud of her new identity and wanted people to know about her story. The quest for admiration and respect was one of her most persistent motives.

An account supporting this theory comes from a Danish feature writer, Thorkild Behrens, who wrote an article for *Scope's* May, 1953 edition. This writer may have drawn upon the December 2 *New York*

Daily News article by Ifversen, as some of the language of Behrens' piece is quite similar to what Ifversen wrote. Behrens, managing editor of *Ekstrabladet,* said to be one of Denmark's biggest newspapers, stated he first met Christine when she called upon him at his office during the summer of 1952 concerning publicity for her travel film.

> Six months after her sex conversion operation [that is, George's castration in September, 1951], George Jorgensen was summoned to court to pay a small debt. When she appeared, as Christine, in the Copenhagen Hall of Justice they had expected George Jorgensen . . . that is how the story broke.[9]

At the least, the Behrens account is consistent with the idea that the public disclosure of the Jorgensen case originated with her day in court. He seems to have been in error, however, concerning the date of the court appearance, as Ifversen reported this as about three months prior to December 1, not during the spring of 1952. It seems very unlikely that Jorgensen would have appeared in court dressed as Christine prior to receiving her new passport in July, 1952. As noted earlier, she regarded the passport as her official name change and as governmental recognition of her right to become Chris Jorgensen.

In Copenhagen, as the initial Jorgensen story spread worldwide, several news reporters attempted to interview Christine at the Royal Hospital, and she spoke with most of them. Photographers, however, were banned. Christine was not keeping as silent as the doctors had urged. One of the most persistent reporters was an energetic, experienced and capable young man, whose paper, *Politiken,* was affiliated with the International News Service, a Hearst Corporation company. He was a highly experienced and persistent reporter, and after December 1, he managed to gain access to Christine's room at least once a day throughout her stay at the Royal Hospital. He soon informed her he would be bringing a lucrative proposal from the Hearst newspapers for an exclusive series of stories. Christine telephoned her good friend, photographer Jens Junker-Jensen, asking his advice, and he urged her to be cooperative while signing nothing until he could join her to read the written proposal.

Within twenty-four hours, the reporter was back with the proposed contract.[10] Chris's initial impression was highly positive. The terms were clear: Christine was asked to agree to an exclusive arrangement for publication of her life story to appear in eleven Hearst papers, along with elaborate photographic spreads, all to be part of a five-part series for the *American Weekly,* the Sunday supplement that ran in all the Hearst papers. Hearst's initial proposed fee would be $20,000, far more money than any member of the Jorgensen family or any of their Bronx neighbors had ever earned in a year. The more she thought this over, the stronger she was motivated to sign the contract. Basically, Junker-Jensen agreed, but he urged two changes: First, he wanted a separate agreement with Hearst awarding him all of the photography assignments for the articles, and second, he suggested Chris ask for a fee of $30,000. Presented with this counterproposal, an agreement was quickly reached on both issues. They compromised on a fee of $25,000. Everyone was happy. All of this had happened so quickly Chris barely realized that within a single month she had completed her surgery, and that she had been transformed from a penniless and unknown American tourist to an affluent, famous, and beautiful young lady with an international reputation. Very soon, she would leave the hospital.

As remarkable at it may seem, the *Berlingske Tidende* did not print any of the December 1 Jorgensen wire service articles. Waiting a day, they published a short account of the Jorgensen story on page seven of their December 2, 1952, edition, using the wire service reports from the *Daily News.* It was accompanied by the two photographs provided by the United Press, one of George in his Army uniform, and the second, a profile of Christine's face. The newspaper did not interview Jorgensen who was in the hospital only minutes away, nor did it quote anybody else who was connected with the case. This newspaper is described by some of its readers as not only politically conservative, but as unlikely to carry the more sensational news such as the Jorgensen story. The editors also ignored a major press conference Christine held on December 11, not even mentioning that it had occurred, perhaps because it had been arranged by their competitors. The only follow-up article dealing with Christine that they printed throughout December was based on a wire service account of a supposed film contract Jorgensen was said to have signed. The proposed contract did not yield any movie work.

On December 10, Chris was about to leave the hospital. Christine was still feeling the effects of her surgery but she had been given permission to return home. On December 11, to avoid newsmen, she took a taxi to an out-of-the-way hotel in the northern part of the city and registered using a false name. The Hearst contract required exclusive rights to the story of her life, and therefore she wanted to stay clear of the press except for a large press conference had arranged for that afternoon.

Someone close to Christine, probably Elsa Sabroe, arrived at the hotel to deliver a striking new outfit Jorgensen would wear at the press conference. It consisted of a white silk blouse, a dark business suit with matching overcoat, gloves, stockings, shoes, and a hat with a full veil.[11] This was the sophisticated and glamorous image of Christine that the world would see. It was an image that Elsa Sabroe had never known. For all practical purposes, Christine had moved out of her apartment and would never live there again. The fact that millions of people were reading of her "amazing sex change" all over the world propelled her into a career trajectory no one could have predicted, especially her Danish doctors or her Bronx neighbors. Chris showered and dressed for the big meeting with the press. She knew a lot of pictures would be taken, and she was determined to look her best. The black hat and veil seemed to go perfectly with her long coat. Soon, she was off to make news.

On the afternoon of December 11, 1952, Christine Jorgensen did something no other transsexual had ever done before and few have ever done since. Dressed in her new suit and with all the right accessories and jewelry, she took a taxi to a downtown hotel to meet a group of reporters and to show the world what a transsexual looked like. It was imperative to make a strong, positive first impression. This was her opportunity to present herself to the world as she wanted the world to see her. It's a safe bet that she held tightly to Verner Forchhammer's[12] arm as they entered the crowded room, with flashbulbs popping, notebooks ready, and every eye upon her.

All of the reporters were favorably impressed, and the photographs showed a glamorous young blonde who looked more like a movie starlet than a transsexual woman who had just checked out of the Royal Hospital.[13] According to a United Press article, Christine met with fifty reporters and photographers in downtown Copenhagen within hours of leaving the hospital, a virtuoso performance for anyone. Perhaps the reason for rushing this was Forchhammer's interest in controlling the release of news reports and pictures, at least as fully as he could. Chris smiled and posed for pictures before making some brief remarks, none of which revealed anything of medical or personal importance.

The Copenhagen press corps did not ask Chris why none of her doctors had joined her at this press conference, or why the session had not been held at the Royal Hospital. Perhaps they were aware that in 1952 physicians like Hamburger and Stürup considered meetings with the press inappropriate, if not unethical. For these doctors, all trained in Europe, the proper way to report a case would be through a technical account published in a medical journal. These doctors would never participate in a question-and-answer session beside a celebrity patient. However, Hamburger and his associates need not have worried about what Christine would say, as history shows she revealed virtually nothing of significance about her medical treatment or exactly what her "transformation" had entailed.

Although members of the press attempted to question her closely concerning her ability to have a baby, both at this session and earlier in the hospital, they were too discreet to ask if she had a vagina. This was a word no real newspaper would print for more than a decade. Christine projected an image of propriety, elegance, good taste, and refinement. Her words and manner of expression were carefully chosen. One way or another, she invariably attempted to explain to the press that she possessed a body that was partially male and in part, female. This was a tactic that worked nicely because it gave the reporters a vague explanation without actually dealing with facts they could prove or disprove. Christine had won the battle of first impressions by appearing to be a woman in every possible way, and by refraining from giving out the details of her story. This was to become her standard strategy for meeting the press, including a strong emphasis on her supposed intersex status. It was a strategy that usually worked.

Chris wore a black suit with a matching full-length coat over a white blouse, black stockings and high-heeled shoes, and gloves. Her blonde hair was complemented by tasteful makeup, and a hat and veil covered her entire face. Some described her as "radiant" or "dazzling." Wire services carried the story and photographs worldwide, and the Hearst people were pleased that this additional publicity would contribute to public interest in their forthcoming exclusive story of Christine's life.

Upon returning to her hotel room, Chris received a call from the Jensens who urged her to spend a few days with them pending the arrival of her parents. The next day she packed her new outfits and checked out of the hotel with the help of Jens and Edna Jensen, and then rode with them to their spacious postwar home in the suburbs. Living with the Jensens provided a safe place, free of newspeople. It also gave her some breathing room and a few days to collect her thoughts and do some planning for the Christmas days just ahead.

On December 15, Chris presented a preview of her travel film, *Denmark,* in a trial run to 500 Danes who are said to have "applauded."[14] Other reports indicated the film was considered too long, and the Tourist Bureau managers said they were not interested in using it. She announced that the proceeds from the first showing of her film would go to a charitable organization. Chris hated to cut segments from her documentary, but it was far too long. A few weeks later she was urged to cut it to twenty-five minutes.

George and Florence Jorgensen prepared to fly to Copenhagen. The Jorgensens were looking forward to meeting some of their Danish relatives. A messenger delivered a $500 dollar check from the Hearst Corporation; this was part of the deal negogiated in Copenhagen With so much going on, they hardly mentioned Christine until George Sr. sat down to read his newspaper and found her story still making headlines. By now, he had become used to seeing his own name in print and of reading quotations from Florence or other relatives; even the corner druggist had been interviewed about his memories of the former GI. Although newsmen had pestered their daughter, Dolly, for an interview they found her entirely unresponsive. Dolly was aware that a few of her close relatives strongly resented the publicity Christine had generated. Throughout her life she kept her distance from reporters.

For Christine, relaxing with the Jensens at their home and spending time with the children had been much more enjoyable than being in a hospital or a hotel. Edna Jensen, along with Miss Sabroe, had become a close confidant and she had given many hours assisting Chris in her feminine transition. This included everything from working on her makeup and hair styling, to how to walk on cobblestones in high heels. The Jensens were comfortable having their friend either at the studio or at home. No one ever asked about her "confusing" gender status once she began presenting herself as Christine. This didn't happen suddenly, and the Jensens realized that over many months there had been a change in Chris's sense of identity. Taken as a whole,

Chris found her gender transition to be easier than she had expected. It felt completely natural to her and was nothing like putting on an act or wearing a costume.

The Jorgensens arrived, and in what had to be an emotionally charged first meeting with their new daughter, both Florence and George Sr. warmly embraced Chris, shared some tears, provided strong reassurance that they would always be part of the same loving family, and then drove to the home of Christine's cousin where they would stay. Not only was the family reunited, but it was Christmas week in Copenhagen. The streets were sparkling with light and Tivoli was glistening in a fresh coat of snow. Chris had been nervous about meeting her parents for the first time, especially concerning how her father might react, but everything went beautifully as they hugged and kissed each other, and then exchanged gifts. The Jorgensens had always been a close and loving family and for them, the joy of this Christmas reunion was very special.

Her parents spent about seven weeks in Denmark, visiting with relatives, sightseeing, and taking time to get acquainted with their new daughter. Once the articles for the *American Weekly* series had been completed, Chris took her parents to Norway for a skiing vacation. There, in a telephone conversation with Irmis Johnson, she learned that the Hearst people wanted her to return to New York City just prior to the issuance of the first article in her *Life Story* series. She was told the departure date would be February 12.

Christine's departure was a press event orchestrated by the Hearst representatives that included wire service photographers and cameramen from several newsreel companies. Pictures of Christine in her fur coat would appear in newspapers all over the world. Even if Christine had sought a private, quiet return to New York, the Hearst organization had other ideas. They wanted publicity and so did she. Throughout her life, she showed skill both in making news, and, for the most part, in dealing with the press. Episodes of unpleasantness with reporters were uncommon once she got the hang of dealing with hostile questions. And so, it was no surprise that the reporters and photographers who were on hand at Copenhagen's Kastrup Airport on the night of February 11 photographed Christine elegantly dressed in her new suit and fur coat, pretending to board a four engine SAS DC-6B for a transatlantic flight.[15] Hearst rushed these posed photographs to America, providing ample advance notice to the American press of her arrival time, thus ensuring a large contingent of photographers and reporters when she arrived in New York.

Just prior to leaving, Chris hosted a cocktail party to thank her many friends for the good times she had enjoyed in Copenhagen. She then gathered her two battered suitcases and a few cardboard boxes and left Kastrup Airport on Feburary 12. But this was more than a flight home; it was the preface to an entirely new life, a life that she could not possibly envision. It would also become a life with stresses and strains within her closely knit family circle. Her future also was to include the power to earn money beyond her most exuberant dreams.

Chapter 13

Return to New York

The morning of Thursday, February 12, 1953, was clear and chilly at New York's Idlewild International Airport as Christine Jorgensen took a deep breath, then descended the aluminum stairs from a Scandinavian Airlines System Douglas Cloudmaster. She watched her footing on each step. Newsreel films show her descending gracefully, disproving one news report that claimed she was unsteady in high heels. Then, smiling and waving, she responded to the pleas of newsreel photographers by ascending the stairs and reentering the aircraft, then exiting a second time so the news cameramen could get the footage they needed. She knew what they wanted and she gave it to them.

A curious and enthusiastic welcoming crowd of about 350 people were waiting for her at what is now John F. Kennedy International Airport, pressing forward to get a closer look and calling out their greetings. Most of the reporters were in a press room down the hall from the customs area. The flight from Denmark had taken all night but Chris looked radiant, elegant, and, as several news reports noted, "surprisingly beautiful." Several of the Hearst public relations people along with a New York police sergeant escorted her inside the crowded terminal, and kept her separate from the reporters for a few minutes as she smoked a cigarette and, reportedly, downed a Bloody Mary before making her way into the crowded, smoky, press room.[1]

Chris was surprised by the glare of the newsreel lights, the number of microphones, and the noise of the shouting reporters. In Copenhagen, the European press had seemed far less rowdy. Her nutria fur coat, reaching within a foot of the ground, was fully buttoned up and she wore a matching fur cap with a colorful scarf. Over her arm she carried a mink stole with a coat hanger still in place, and in her gloved

doi:10.1300/5896_13

hand she held a packet of documents including her prized passport, the official testimony of her new identity as Chris Jorgensen.

One photograph that appeared in many newspapers and later in *Time Magazine,* showed Christine in the press room, smiling broadly and waving to the crowd with her right arm. To her side and slightly behind were a dozen photographers, three of whom were lying down or kneeling on the floor.[2] It was a disorderly and leaderless meeting as the reporters shouted their questions and fired their flashbulbs while all of the newsreel and television cameras were rolling. Chris did not appear to have the assistance of any press representative although several Hearst publicity people were present. She did just fine without assistance, limiting herself to a very few words of greeting. This was one of the first impressions of Christine Jorgensen for millions of Americans who got their news at their neighborhood motion picture theater.

Christine was twenty-six, and just two months earlier her greatest challenge was to pay her bills from an income of only $40 a month. At the time of her December surgery she could not have anticipated this reception. She was attractively dressed for the event, with appropriate makeup, dark hosiery and high heels, gloves, a hat and veil. Christine appeared confident, sophisticated, and very much in command of the situation, although she must have been anxious as she realized the importance of this grand entrance upon the world stage. Surely, she must have known that many of the reporters were looking for a critical angle to spice up their article. Perhaps the layers of fur, the hat and veil, the scarf and black stockings all served as protective armor against the unpredictable New York press corps. But whatever she may have used as props, they worked very well. Her image was of a very respectable lady.

Olga Curtis of the *San Francisco Examiner* was one of the reporters who met Chris that morning; she filed her story with the International News Service, and it appeared in most of the eleven Hearst papers the following day: "Christine is not only a female; she's a darn good looking female." And later, "Christine wore an expert job of makeup—thick pancake, bright true red lipstick that set-off very good teeth when she smiled, and dark mascara and eye brow pencil to accent her greenish-blue eyes . . . she talked easily in a deep husky voice, with a slightly Continental lilt to her words."[3] The *New York Journal American* reporter was a bit less generous: "she lit a cigarette like a girl, husked 'Hello' and tossed off a Bloody Mary like a guy, then opened her fur coat. Jane Russell has nothing to worry about." With a final barb it was noted that "she teetered precariously on spiked heels."[4]

However, that somewhat nasty profile was totally opposite to how moviegoers saw her as she walked confidently to the many microphones to address the press. Many of the reporters noted that Chris's voice was a bit lower than expected for a woman, perhaps in the contralto range, and when describing the way it sounded, the term "husky" would appear in articles for decades. As with many male-to-female transsexuals, her voice was one of the few physical characteristics that suggested she was not born a female. The voice of many male-to-female transsexuals tends to draw unwanted attention, especially on the telephone.

But newspaper readers could not hear her voice, and they formed their impression of Miss Jorgensen based on what they saw and read. Blonde and splendidly attired, she certainly looked like a woman, in fact, like an unusually attractive woman. And to some who had seen her that week in the RKO Pathé newsreel reports, descending from the aircraft, Christine appeared to have the spectacular beauty of a movie star or a model. Building upon her own sense of feminine taste, style, and graciousness, Christine made one of the most memorable entrances New York had seen in a long time. This former GI from the Bronx had been transformed into a dazzling blonde, and for most Americans, this was the image of Christine Jorgensen that was burned into their consciousness. It was an impression that amazed and intrigued many, titillated some, and for others left them questioning if the surgeons had lost their minds, gone too far, and violated "God's plan" for George Jorgensen. The morality of her sex change became an issue that the most devoted religious believers would never fully resolve, even today.

A reporter called out: "Miss Jorgensen . . . are you happy to be back in America?" She replied: "Of course I'm glad to be back . . . what American wouldn't be? But honestly, I think this is all too much."[5] She scolded the noisy reporters: "I am not just a story . . . I'm a human being, after all." Her well-spoken remarks did not sound much like the comments of an underconfident, shy, George Jorgensen who had shipped out thirty months earlier aboard the *Stockholm*. But Chris's transformed appearance was no more remarkable than the evolution of her of identity and her entire personality. Relatives and friends who knew George as a youngster put it this way: "Christine was a totally different person compared to George. She was outgoing, very friendly, very family oriented and very generous."[6]

She smiled and waved for several more pictures, then after a few brief comments she was escorted by Hearst assistants to a waiting car and driven to a "$52-a-day suite in Manhattan's Carlyle Hotel."[7] She knew all of this was very expensive, but the Hearst Corporation was paying the bill.

In Manhattan, within an hour, Christine changed into more comfortable attire and left the hotel by a side door. She was driven to a reunion with sister Dolly and her two-year-old baby girl. For the first time, Chris really relaxed, kicked off her shoes, and felt she was home, safe, and finally with loved ones again. She was very relieved that Dolly seemed comfortable to meet the transformed Christine. Although she and Dolly had been close, her sister was a person whose likes and dislikes were sometimes hard to understand.

Christine's parents had remained in Copenhagen, possibly to avoid complicating the publicity opportunities of Chris's grand arrival. They returned two days later without fanfare, happy to be back on Dudley Avenue.

The articles in the New York papers and in most other major newspapers described Christine as an attractive, stylish, blonde woman. A few commented on her somewhat large hands and some said her voice was too low compared to other women.[8] Two weeks later, *Time* ran a summary of the Idlewild press reception based largely on what the *Daily News* had published while adding a few hostile comments that had been previously published, including the Jane Russell remark.[9] This was an accurate observation, for at this time, she had very little breast development. For many years Chris relied on "falsies" to enhance her feminine profile. From time to time she denied this, while in other interviews she stated that she had always used breast forms.[10]

Few American newspapers maintained representatives in Copenhagen, relying instead upon wire service reports and photographs. The five Jorgensen articles published in the *Los Angeles Times* during December 1953 provide a typical example of how the larger metropolitan newspapers handled the story. On December 1, 1952, every newspaper in the nation with access to wire service articles told of the "ex-GI transformed into a blonde beauty," as first headlined in the *New York Daily News*. Some papers, including the *Los Angeles Times*, re-wrote the *Daily News* article but while the headlines and the content changed a little, much of the initial presentation of the story was very similar nationwide. The following is a summary of the headlines revealing how the *Los Angeles Times* handled the story:

DECEMBER 1: FORMER GI TRANSFORMED INTO LOVELY WOMAN IN LONG SERIES OF TREATMENTS.[11]

DECEMBER 2: MAY WRITE BOOK, SAYS MAN CHANGED TO WOMAN (ASSOCIATED PRESS).[12]

DECEMBER 3: SEX CHANGE ISN'T TOO RARE, DOCTORS ASSERT.[13]

DECEMBER 7: MAN TURNED-WOMAN DELUGED BY SHOW OFFERS.[14]

DECEMBER 11: MAN CHANGED TO WOMAN SHUNS HOLLY-WOOD CAREER.[15]

Newspapers everywhere scrambled for stories with a local Jorgensen tie-in to augment the wire service articles, and one of them, in Los Angeles, was different than most. It is a good example of what was being sought to satisfy a curious public throughout America. On the day Christine returned to New York, Joe Vaccarelli, who claimed to be one of her old Bronx neighbors, contacted the city editor of the *Los Angeles Mirror*, an afternoon tabloid owned by the *Los Angeles Times* organization, and offered to describe George Jorgensen as a youth.[16] The *Mirror* quickly dispatched a reporter and a photographer. Mr. Vaccarelli explained that several years earlier, he had lived next door to Christine's cousin in the Bronx, and that he'd known George Jorgensen Jr., for seven years. Vaccerelli said, "Nobody thought there was anything wrong with him. Nobody knew he had plans for anything like this." George visited his cousin several times a month and Vaccarelli said he'd met him often. "He was a quiet guy, never the life of the party, but never a wallflower either." "He always had a date . . . but he didn't have any special girlfriend that I remember." Regarding the dating, Mr. Vaccarelli was definitely in error. George had many friends who were girls, but they were not his dates.

None of Chris's family members or other neighborhood friends from the early days ever heard of Joe Vaccarelli, and Chris dismissed the account as "a fabrication." However, much of his description of the youthful George seems on target.

Almost immediately upon her return to New York, Christine decided to rent an apartment on Long Island not far from where her sister Dolly and her husband were living. Chris soon bought a spacious corner lot in Massapequa and arranged for her father to supervise the construction of a 3,000-square-foot, two-story home that she'd occupy along with her parents for the next fifteen years. She liked to call this a ranch house and to pretend she was living in the country.

From a financial standpoint, having a new home was made easier with the funds received from the Hearst organization for her exclusive life story. Meanwhile, her parents sold their home, and over a construction period of about six months, George Jorgensen Sr. supervised the building of their new house. Her father acquired the spacious workshop he'd always wanted, and her mother got a sparkling new kitchen with all the latest appliances. Christine's living quarters consisted of an upstairs suite including a bedroom, bath, and one other room that was used for an office or as a guest bedroom. She also enjoyed a solarium and garden room at the rear of the ground floor. The entrance to this room, a back door, was used far more than the front entry. Living with her parents worked nicely because Mr. and Mrs. Jorgensen kept the home fires burning while their new daughter was earning money by entertaining people throughout the United States, Cuba, Australia, the Far East, and in Europe.

For several weeks, the extensive publicity in newspapers, magazines, and newsreel reports kept Christine busy while her new house was being built. But there was a continuing flurry of newspaper and magazine articles challenging her sex and gender status, with some proclaiming that she was nothing more than a publicity-seeking female impersonator. In Denmark, Christian Hamburger and his associates were preparing an article describing her case that would soon appear in the *Journal of the American Medical Association.* But for the American public, the five-part life-story articles were especially important in helping to portray the Jorgensen narrative as a courageous and successful battle against biological difficulties. The first article in the series appeared just three days after Chris arrived home.[17]

The editors of the Hearst newspaper chain had been quick to respond to the proposal for an exclusive series of Jorgensen articles sent to them by their reporter in Copenhagen, Verner Forchhammer. In New York, the Hearst editors had quickly recognized the news value of the Jorgensen story; it was the kind of sensational news that captured national headlines and held the attention of their blue-collar readers. The Hearst company was publishing eleven daily newspapers across America, and a half-dozen highly successful magazines. Within days of signing this agreement they dispatched Irmis Johnson, an experienced Hearst feature writer, to Copenhagen to work with Christine on the series.

Johnson and Chris worked together for over a month to produce the five-part life history that included a carefully developed account of her medical procedures in Denmark. The series is especially significant because it emphasized Jorgensens theory of transsexuality: for her, it was all a matter of a glandular imbalance producing a vaguely identified intersex condition. It was an interpretation that made sense to many people. Before long, Chris was calling her new friend "Irmy" and they were attending parties together. Junker-Jensen did the photography for the five articles in the series that showed Christine in a variety of newly purchased glamorous suits, dresses, and gowns. One of his photographs showed her at a fancy dinner event escorted by an unnamed gentleman. The series appeared in the Hearst Sunday supplement, the *American Weekly,* for five consecutive weeks beginning February 15, 1953. The Hearst papers advertised it heavily as: "The only authorized and complete account of the most dramatic transformation of modern times—told by the courageous woman who was once a man."[18]

It had long been a Hearst policy to offer many supplemental feature sections in the Sunday papers. The flagship of these supplements was *American Weekly.* The content of the *Weekly* was intended to be entertaining, informative, instructive, and diverse. The snappy and pictorial articles provided practical help to the middle-class subscriber. For example, guidance was given in sewing, purchasing or repairing a car, planning travel, interior decoration, and do-it-yourself projects. There were always feature articles about personalities in the news, political leaders, pictures of important new buildings, and insider stories about movie celebrities.

Christine and Irmis Johnson seem to have worked together quickly and smoothly. Later, Jorgensen gave her credit for her work when the Jorgensen autobiography appeared. As we have noted, what Johnson wrote was highly influential in establishing the legitimacy of Christine as a person who had suffered a "mistake of nature" due to a "glandular imbalance," and who was said to be courageous in facing these difficulties and achieving a fulfilling solution through the help of her Danish doctors. These were the key explanations for her transsexual change that Jorgensen was to stand by throughout her life, and they helped to put transsexual issues firmly within the medical model. At the outset of her autobiography she offered this description of herself: "Although the term 'sex transformation' has been used by many people when referring to my case, even by me on occasion, mine was rather a process of revised sex determination, inspired by the preponderance of female characteristics."[19]

However, as clearly stated in Hamburger's 1953 medical report,[20] Chris never had the female characteristics that she alleged. Her notion that somehow the Danish doctors had carried out a "process of revised sex determination"[21] was far off base. Sex determination refers to the biological events fundamental to creation of a male or female fetus during gestation. Christine never abandoned her claim that she was an intersex person despite the medical record.

Throughout the spring of 1953, Christine was very socially involved and accepted invitations for luncheons with many celebrities, including Irving Berlin. With her winning smile and down-to-earth conversational manner, it seemed that one invitation always led to another. The once shy George Jorgensen, who apparently had never dined at the Waldorf-Astoria, was now, as Christine, breaking bread with Samuel Goldwyn, Dr. and Mrs. Ralph Bunche, Danny Kaye, and Milton Berle. Truman Capote invited her "to a delightful Sunday brunch." The Hollywood columnist, Elsa Maxwell, entertained her at a luncheon in her hotel-residence, along with Cole Porter. Ms. Maxwell later wrote: "Christine is definitely on the level. Her voice is soft and low. She is quite beautiful, very intelligent, has poise and very good manners."[22] Ms. Maxwell noted that upon leaving her luncheon, Christine had "thanked my maid who had cooked lunch, which no one else has ever done." Like Frank Sinatra, Christine showed exceptional respect for food and service personnel and was entirely without snobbery or pretentiousness. Soon thereafter, she was one of many major celebrities invited by Walter Winchell to headline a charity event at a Madison Garden on behalf of New York police and firemen. In March 1953, Chris was honored at a huge Scandinavian banquet to celebrate her selection as Woman of the Year. Despite the support shown by much of the press, the *New York Post* would soon publish a series of attack articles that questioned her entire account of herself.

Chapter 14

The *New York Post* Takes Aim

The *New York Post* ran six highly critical articles in an attempt to persuade readers that the Christine Jorgensen story was misleading, if not fraudulent.[1] Written in the style of an investigative reporter, the articles were largely based on remarks from her doctors in Copenhagen and comments from medical experts across the United States. According to the *Post,* Christine was no woman at all; it concluded Christine's claim of a sex change was without justification. Its main point was that Chris did not have a surgically created vagina nor was she a hermaphrodite. Furthermore, the *Post* argued, she most certainly could not become pregnant because she had no female reproductive organs. Hence, it concluded, Jorgensen could not possibly be a woman. The *Post* articles are worth review because they include the most extensive documentation of what the Copenhagen doctors had to say to the press immediately after Chris's case became public. They are also of interest as they provide a good example of the reasoning and logic employed by those who sought to defame Jorgensen. The *Post's* reports gave an accurate summary of Jorgensen's medical treatment, but they failed to show any understanding of gender-identity issues. *The Post's* definition of what constitutes a woman was entirely based on anatomy, and in its view, Christine failed the test.

The six *Post* articles began about two months following Christine's return to New York. The Jorgensen story had created an international thirst for more information about "changing sex," and anyone who had anything to say about the former George Jorgensen was interviewed by the *Post,* quoted, and sometimes photographed, regardless of what they actually knew about the case. Other papers, especially the New York pictorial tabloids, scrambled for follow-up articles ranging from some that were loaded with praise for Christine, to the

Becoming a Woman: A Biography of Christine Jorgensen
© 2008 by The Haworth Press, Taylor & Francis Group. All rights reserved.
doi:10.1300/5896_14

six hostile *Post* articles. Perhaps this frontal attack on Jorgensen was also a thinly veiled assault on the *New York Daily News,* which had scooped the *Post* by being the first to break the Christine Jorgensen story in this country. For the *Post,* it didn't seem to matter that Christine had never claimed transformation of her sex organs and she certainly never suggested the possibility of pregnancy. The *Post* hammered her without mercy using specious reasoning about her legitimacy as a woman, all founded on what it regarded as disqualifying anatomical deficiencies. Most of the facts of the *Post* articles are not in dispute; however, the generalizations and conclusions drawn from these facts would be an embarrassment to most high school debate teams. Trimmed down to their essential arguments, the *Post* series might have provided interesting content for discourse on an editorial page, but the articles could only appear as news reports or social analysis in a newspaper with remarkably modest journalistic standards.

In addition to finding fault with Jorgensen, the *Post* also made a target of endocrinologist Christian Hamburger, her principal physician in Copenhagen. His professional judgment was criticized by supposed medical experts who knew of Christine only through news reports. Further, while the *Post* stated that Christian Hamburger's explanation for undertaking to help Christine was supported by a psychiatrist and two surgeons, the articles largely discounted the medical decisions they had reached. For example, psychiatrist Georg Stürup had noted that he believed the doctors might have saved Jorgensen from killing herself, yet the mental health aspects of Christine's treatment were largely ignored in these articles. Alvin Davis, the writer of the articles, was accurate in saying that doctors in America knew little about the Jorgensen case when they made statements about intersex persons and linked them to Christine. This is hardly surprising since most members of the medical profession knew little about either intersex cases or transsexuality in 1953.

In examining Chris's motivation for selling her biographical story to the Hearst papers, the *Post* noted that her Denmark experience had produced a great deal of money, and by implication, that this was improper. We have noted that she was paid $25,000 by the Hearst publications for her exclusive story, but to imply that this was an important motive for her transsexuality or that it was improper was nothing more than a newspaperman's opinion. One of Alvin Davis' articles began with a sharp attack on Dr. Hamburger's endorsement of castration in Christine's case. Davis made several telephone calls to American physicians concerning the wisdom of this procedure; based on these telephone consultations he concluded that castration might have created unnecessary problems. Today, for male-to-female transsexuals, castration is a standard part of the surgical protocol, and this is now usually carried out during a one-step procedure. Davis remained concerned about the claims of some doctors who said they had been harassed by self-diagnosed prospective sex changers due to the Jorgensen publicity. He seemed more worried about the alleged demands put upon physicians than the persons who were asking for help.

The *Post* persistently emphasized that Christine was not a hermaphrodite and that she could never have been surgically transformed into a female. Taken alone, that statement is true, yet it does not justify the conclusion that Jorgensen was a fraud. The intersex question was never considered as a surgical justification by Christian Hamburger or any of his colleagues. According to Davis, Christian Hamburger wrote a New York psychologist explaining the three things that were done in an effort to assist Jorgensen. These included hormonal treatment, surgical procedures, and legal steps to allow Christine to appear in public as a woman. Hamburger's calmness, humility, and modesty contrasted sharply with Davis' attack on both the Copenhagen medical team and Miss Jorgensen.

The point missed by both the American doctors and the author of these *Post* articles was that Jorgensen had become an entirely different person from the ex-GI she had been. Her history was one of gender-identity discordance, and she had endured years of gender conflict, little of which was mentioned by the *New York Post*. One psychiatrist, who had not examined Christine, told Davis that he preferred to manage his male sex change applicants in the opposite fashion as was done in Denmark. He said that instead of castration, he prescribed male hormones to his male patients to emphasize their masculinity; he did not use female hormones. This approach seems to echo the rejection of Jorgensen's earlier pleas for both understanding and medical assistance in the United States. Some of Davis' psychiatric experts told him both homosexuality and transvestism could, in some cases at least, be helped through long-term psychoanalysis. Although this was a common view a half-century ago, at present, few psychiatrists would be so optimistic.

Davis gave much emphasis to the difference between an intersex person (in those days, a pseudohermaphrodite or a hermaphrodite) actually having ambiguous genitalia, in contrast with a person like Jorgensen who had no anatomic abnormality. In her June 8, 1952, letter to her parents, Christine alluded to herself as a person who might have both male and female organs. In this hand-written, four-page letter she surely had no way to predict this speculation might be used against her by a newspaper. She simply gave her parents her personal rationale for the emotions she felt and for the gender change she believed was essential. Alvin Davis, however, couldn't say enough about what he considered her misleading characterization of herself. He failed to explain to his readers that none of her doctors ever suggested anything pertaining to an intersex condition, nor did they want to participate in a trans-Atlantic shouting match with either a newspaper reporter or American medical experts, most of whom had never met Christine Jorgensen. Instead, Hamburger promised to publish a full account of the case; he did so in a highly informative and extensive report published later in 1953.

Davis asked Dr. Hamburger about his rationale for agreeing to take on Christine's case, and his explanation was more psychological than medical. He told Davis that he and the other doctors sought to help Jorgensen become a happier person. Most transvestites, he said, are very unhappy people and some may suffer even more than cancer patients.

Fifty years ago, both psychiatry and psychology regarded what was then called transvestism as a variation of homosexuality. For some of the doctors, their view of "sex changes" was based on lurid newspaper reports of distressed men in dresses who had committed crimes, or on the flamboyant drag queens and female impersonators in drag shows in the larger cities. The one thing that rang clear was the distinction between medical issues based on organ or tissue pathology, as contrasted with psychological issues based on claims of identity conflicts or homosexual attractions. For the American doctors, Christine's case had nothing to do with physical illness or disease. Many psychiatrists viewed her case as entirely psychological. Therefore, they argued, radical procedures such as castration were inappropriate and harmful. For decades, some prominent psychiatrists would argue against assisting transsexuals to make a gender change.

The *Post* offered its readers an opportunity to speculate about Christine's future. Would she try to live a more public life as a man masquerading as a woman, or would she choose a private life characterized by isolation or obscurity? Obviously, neither Alvin Davis nor his *Post* editors could envision Christine's future career. One thing is clear: they greatly underestimated her. Instead of remaining out of the public eye, Christine would soon start a thirty-year career in show business. As we have noted previously, perhaps she was rewarded by these gigs and by her speaking assignments at colleges and universities by a greater sense of self-worth, and, a necessary stream of income.

Alvin Davis didn't want to end the series without taking a slam at U.S. Ambassador to Denmark, Eugenie Andersen, concerning Jorgensen's passport. The *Post* erroneously told its readers that the ambassador had taken a personal interest in changing the passport of George Jorgensen Jr. to that of a woman. Apparently, no reporter asked to inspect Christine's passport, and as previously explained, Jorgensen's passport was applied for and issued to Chris Jorgensen, not Christine, and it did not bear any designation as male or female. The reporter went on to develop a supposed controversy concerning Mrs. Andersen's alleged role in giving permission for George's castration. Andersen had nothing to do with this. The *American Weekly's* description of George's meeting with the ambassador is described:

> I was still dressed as George, with my long hair tucked under a beret, when I kept the appointment Mrs. Eugenie Andersen, the American Ambassador at that time, so graciously accorded me . . . I was so distinctly feminized . . . that my apparel often confused people. When I told Mrs. Andersen my story, and presented her with letters from my doctors stating that my chemical and emotional body was that of a woman, she was most understanding. She told me to leave everything in her hands and not to worry. I made my trip home from the Embassy with a light heart . . . Two weeks later the approval was granted and I was free to dress as a woman, and take my place in society as a woman.[3]

When Dr. Hamburger was questioned by Alvin Davis about these letters, he explained that there was only a single letter, not to Mrs. Andersen, but to Vice Consul Lois Unger. He added that none of the other doctors had written anyone concerning the passport application despite what Christine had said. Finally, Hamburger explained that he had not declared Jorgensen to be either a male or a female. Furthermore, the question of who approved the passport application turned out to be a nonissue, and in any case, even if a new passport had not been issued, Chris could have returned to the United States using his/her existing passport. But in view of the thoroughness and persistence of Davis with his interviews, both in America and in Denmark, it is surprising that he did not discover that the passport did not carry any specification of sex. He could have learned this by simply inspecting his own passport. The disposition of the original passport is unknown, but there is a photocopy of each page among the photographs in the Jorgensen Collection in the Danish Royal Library. The Department of State was not able locate the 1952 application papers in response to our inquiry. Finally, it is highly surprising that the *New York Post* reporters researching the story failed to discover Christine's Copenhagen court appearance in 1952, (which was previously described). They also missed a great opportunity to tell about the background of the December 1, 1952, *Daily News* story by not interviewing Paul Ifversen, whose byline was on an informative December 2, 1952, article in the *New York Daily News*.

Davis also reported on his participation in an extensive interview with Christine held soon after her return to New York. This took place with a small corps of reporters in the living room of her sister, Dolly. This interview seemed to go from bad to worse. Christine was poorly prepared and inexperienced in dealing with assertive reporters. She was quoted as refusing to comment on all inquiries about the thousands of dollars she had received from the Hearst organization for her *American Weekly* series, while attempting to claim that this was not really cash. Of course, it was cash; she had been fully paid prior to leaving Copenhagen. She also emphasized that she had not received a cent for any of her public appearances on behalf of charities; this was a topic that had not been raised. Then, beyond financial matters, when the reporters asked for facts concerning her hormone treatments and surgery in Denmark, she refused to comment. Trying to smooth over the unpleasantness, her sister served Scotch to Chris and the reporters, but this did not soften the exchange which grew increasingly nasty, especially on Chris's part. She was chain smoking, and when she felt under attack, she switched into an assertive mode, becoming snappy, accusatory, and dismissive of her guests. Chris became somewhat carried away when she was told the American Medical Association was going to publish a full account of her case; she said she intended to put a halt to that. Soon thereafter she essentially dismissed the reporters. Chris was dealing with these newspeople without representation or coaching by anyone experienced in press relations. Clearly, she needed considerable assistance. Shortly after this interview she was introduced to the press-wise Charles Yates who taught her much about dealing with newspaper people, and also a great deal about making the most of her celebrity in show business.

The *Post* articles accurately documented the medical procedures that had been carried out, and they correctly explained that no one can actually change sex. By so doing, they provided sound information. However, the *Post* failed to go a step further and ask: What motivates the quest for gender transformation, and what makes a woman a woman? Fifty years later these question are as intriguing and controversial as they were in 1953. But the *New York Post* is not in the business of psychological or medical inquiry, and in 1953, neither were many psychologists, sociologists, psychiatrists, or attorneys. In large part, it was the Christine Jorgensen story that caused these questions to become part of the agenda for professionals, and to go beyond the issues raised by the press.

A little later in 1953, jumping on the anti-Christine bandwagon, *Modern Romance* magazine drew upon the *Post* material for a hostile review of her transformation. Its headline asked: "Christine Jorgensen: Is she still a man?" It informed its readers that very few photographs of Christine showed her hands without gloves, and that her voice was "husky." Seeing little hope for her, they predicted an unhappy future life.[3]

More hopefully, the Jorgensen publicity had awakened prospective transsexuals throughout the world to the fact that medical help might be available. Christine turned the letters she received over to endocrinologist Harry Benjamin, asking him to provide responses and referrals. It is not known how many letters she received. In Copenhagen, however, Christian Hamburger received mail from 465 individuals who presented themselves as prospective transsexuals. We know from his report[4] that the ratio of males to females ran three to one, and most of the letters came from the United States, England, and European countries where the Jorgensen publicity had been most widely circulated. Hamburger seems to have used a form letter for many of these responses, judging from the one received by a man in San Francisco.

The Hormone Department,   January 12, 1953
Statens Seruminstitut,
Amager Boulevard 80
Copenhagen (Denmark)

Many thanks for your letter. I must apologize for my delay in answering you, but I have, in the course of the last month, received several hundreds of letters, long reports of the life-tragedy of men, suffering from the same disease as you. I have been deeply impressed by these reports, and I feel that it is our duty to try and bring help.

At first it may be necessary to emphasize that it is not possible to transform a man to a woman. It is possible by surgical operations, including castration, to change the outer appearance of the sex organs to a completely woman-like state. By treatment with female sex hormones the feminine features are enhanced, and a swelling of the breasts frequently occurs. The hormonal treatment is not expensive, and the whole treatment can be carried out in any country.

The treatment is, however, not only medical, but to a large extent [is] also social. The authorities must allow the patients to wear women [sic] clothes publicly and to change their names. In Denmark the Ministry of Justice must give the permission (also to the surgical castration). Unfortunately the Ministry has decided, in the future, to give this permission to persons of Danish nationality only. Consequently, it is not possible for you to have the operations done in this country, for the present time at least.

It seems to me that it must be possible for you to get the help you need and deserve, in your own country. May I suggest that you write to Dr. J. W Jailer, The Endocrine Clinic, Presbyterian Hospital, 620 West, 168th Street, New York 32, giving him the same information as you gave me. You may tell Dr. J. that you wrote me, and what I replied.

With the best wishes for your future, I am

Christian Hamburger, M.D.[5]

His letter wastes no words in explaining what could and could not be done to change a man to a woman. He explained that hormones and surgery could alter the appearance of one's body, but that an actual sex change was not possible. In addition, Hamburger showed his awareness of the social and identity implications of a so-called sex change by emphasizing the social aspects of such a transformation. His humanity and concern for others comes across very strongly in this letter.

Chapter 15

Denmark, the Travel Film

One of the most important new friends Chris made, probably in March 1953, was a tall, gaunt, rather odd looking, fifty-something theatrical agent and horse-race enthusiast named Charles Yates. He knew a lot about show business, and within 100 days he would restructure Chris' career and help her to earn far more than the Jorgensen family ever dreamed possible. A mutual acquaintance had introduced him to Christine, and she recognized at once that he might be of considerable help to her, especially concerning the booking of her travel film. Yates was a well-established theatrical agent whose most famous former client was Bob Hope. He had also represented Beatrice Lillie and many other entertainers.

An inveterate gambler, Yates became one of the key players in helping to redirect and construct Chris's entertainment career, and he also became a close personal advisor and friend. He was quick to recognize two things: first, Christine had enormous name recognition and a facility for making news. The public was clamoring to see her and to hear her story. Second, while she was beautiful and newsworthy, she had virtually no performing experience, and her plan to launch her career with the showing of a travel film appeared to be a poor idea.

Yates and Jorgensen seemed to "click," and Christine immediately sought his help in arranging bookings of her Denmark film. She was convinced her movie would be of great interest in America, and that she could enjoy a career as a documentary filmmaker. Yates explained the show business disadvantages of initiating her career with this film, pointing out that Christine's major asset was her celebrity, and that the American moviegoing public had little interest in Scandinavian travel pictures.

Becoming a Woman: A Biography of Christine Jorgensen
© 2008 by The Haworth Press, Taylor & Francis Group. All rights reserved.
doi:10.1300/5896_15

Christine did not want to give up her dream of narrating her film and insisted that Yates arrange a test screening. In standing up to Yates, despite her lack of experience in the business of entertainment, Chris demonstrated her considerable self-confidence, while also showing a lack of business experience. She reasoned that while Charles Yates surely understood the economics of show business, he didn't know her well enough to decide what her career priorities ought to be. In the back of her mind was the conviction that her future would not be in show business, but in the making of educational and travel films aimed at school-aged audiences. Although she listened to Yates, she did not rush to sign an agency contract with him. She dreamed of becoming a minor independent movie producer, a career for which she had little talent, no training, and no track record.

Yates did two things: he emphasized to Christine that she had the potential "to earn a lot of money in show business."[1] He also arranged to preview her travel film in Connecticut, followed by a one-week run in Los Angeles. These screenings were exactly what Christine wanted. In Los Angeles, he booked her into one of the city's largest and most elegant downtown motion picture palaces, the RKO Orpheum. Yates also tried to assist her as she prepared for these presentations, while cautioning her that a career as a filmmaker might not be as easily developed as she hoped. While this was going on, Yates was working without any contractual arrangement. They did not sign a six-month representation agreement until late in April, 1953, possibly due to Chris's uncertainty about her future. Perhaps there was also a streak of cautiousness in Christine when it came to signing contracts like this. She had only met Charlie Yates eight weeks before she signed on with him. Although she was a risk taker, she was also a person, much like her parents, who thought twice about financial commitments. She was aware that agents received ten percent of a performer's gross.

As she began to work with Charles Yates, *Time* magazine[2] ran an uncomplimentary article based on the *New York Post's* series. *Time* reported: "Last week came the revelation that Christine Jorgensen was no girl at all, only an altered male." Chris turned to Yates for support and guidance, and he probably urged her to make no response to negative publicity. She remained silent. These articles were very hurtful to Christine, whose primary goal was to establish her legitimacy and respectability. Yates was immune to bad revues and shrugged off the *Time* article as yesterday's news. Concerned with her long-term success, he was trying to find a way to appease Christine's insistence upon trying out the Denmark film without damaging her importance as a celebrity.

Yates knew that a few motion picture theaters in the larger cities were among the last stages available for vaudeville acts or celebrity appearances. One of these was the huge, elegant, Los Angeles Orpheum Theater. The Orpheum presented four daily vaudeville shows along with a feature film and a live orchestra. Yates believed Christine could supplement the vaudeville acts by narrating her film. He negotiated a deal for thirty performances over seven days. As he saw it, if her film turned out to be well received, so much the better. On the other hand, if her movie and commentary flopped, little would be lost as Los Angeles was a long distance from the big theatrical centers of Chicago and New York City. Besides, she was simply appearing as a celebrity act supplementing a feature film and four vaudeville performances. What was there to lose?

Yates did the necessary contract work, arranged an opening date of May 8, 1953, and reserved an expensive suite for Christine and her mother at the newly constructed Los Angeles Statler Hotel, just minutes away from the Orpheum Theater. But prior to heading for the West Coast, a preview try out and rehearsal would be presented in Waterbury, Connecticut, with no advance publicity. On the day of that performance, while Christine was rushing to pick up a print of the film at Pathé Film Laboratories on 106th Street in Manhattan, her car was broken into and all of her costumes and jewelry were stolen. This was expensive jewelry, but not quite as expensive as Chris encouraged people to believe. The police report fixed the loss at $555. She obtained the necessary replacements in time for her evening show, although this time the jewelry was less expensive. The film proved to be much too long, and she was asked to cut it from nearly two hours to twenty minutes. At two showings in Denmark it had also been described as too long, despite some generous reviews.

In New York, the final editing was completed within two weeks and Christine began to pack for a flight west. Yates had planned to fly to Los Angeles with Chris and her mother to offer some press management assistance and moral support, but he became ill just before the trip. Yates had serious cardiovascular problems. Taking his place would be his brother, Irving Yates, who lived in Van Nuys, California, a part of the San Fernando Valley. But Irving was not a public relations man; he lacked the press experience his brother had acquired through years of working with the media. Nor would there be any Hearst public relations people on hand to assist Chris when she met the press in Los Angeles. Soon, it became apparent that in press conferences she had more confidence and less experience that was desirable.

Christine and her mother arrived at Los Angeles International Airport on the evening of May 6, 1953, and "were met by a crowd of more than 2,000 curious spectators."[3] We are not told what this estimate is based upon, or what publicity brought out the welcoming throng. A different report suggested a far smaller number of welcoming Angelenos. A *Los Angeles Times* story explained:

> The ex-GI, who claims surgery in Denmark changed her from a man to a woman, had all the aplomb of a movie queen as she prepared to capitalize on her change-of-sex experience with a personal appearance tour beginning tomorrow at the Orpheum Theater. Her surprisingly slim, straight legs were encased in sheer hosiery and she wore high-heeled brown and white sport pumps. Her hands were concealed by elbow length gray gloves. She limited her jewelry to modest ear clips.[4]

She told the *Times* her plan was to perform for a week at the Orpheum, make "an appearance or two in Las Vegas," and then leave for Denmark on May 17. A new wardrobe was promised for her Orpheum show. After receiving a large bouquet and chatting briefly with those who had come to welcome them, Mrs. Florence Jorgensen and her daughter walked slowly to a chauffeured limousine for the thirty-minute ride to the Statler Hotel. Could Chris have failed to recall her previous arrival in Los Angeles in 1947? Then, as George Jorgensen, the underweight, aspiring photographer who didn't have a job had stepped from a bus in a seedy part of downtown Los Angeles and into a crowded, somewhat smelly Greyhound bus terminal.

The Statler Hotel was upscale, impressive, and with a welcoming staff. The management treated them like royalty. Chris and her mother were surprised at the size and elegance of the top-floor suite Charlie Yates had reserved, but they each wondered what it would cost. Florence had always been a frugal mother and housewife, and to her this looked like unnecessary expense. Soon thereafter, they checked out and moved to a far less expensive Statler room.

They unpacked, smoked, had a snack, and then rested briefly. Later in the evening Chris changed into a shapely, lighter dress more suitable for nightclubbing. Mrs. Jorgensen went to bed. We learn from the *Herald and Express* that "Later, she startled the nightclub set . . . taking in the late spots on the Sunset Strip."[5] As described, a considerable crowd moved from club to club to catch a glimpse of the glamorous Christine. Since she was still operating on East Coast time we may assume that she was back at the hotel at a reasonable hour, but Christine had always been more of a night person than her mother. Even at this very early stage of her career, she enjoyed being a celebrity, and she seemed to gain energy and vigor from the excitement of being the center of attention. Perhaps the roar of the crowd signaled something to her about being appreciated and respected. She loved staying up until two or three in the morning. For her, being asked for autographs offered proof that the guilt and shame she had endured as a child was a thing of the past. She must have felt both excited and a little apprehensive knowing a large press conference had been arranged for the following day. Charles Yates had arranged for every newspaper in town to send both a reporter and a photographer. He was a pro.

In their suite at the Statler Hotel, the day before Chris was to open at the Orpheum, Florence Jorgensen welcomed eight reporters and photographers, explaining that her daughter would join them shortly. Nearly all were smoking when Christine emerged from one of the bedrooms wearing an ivory linen dress with a decorated bolero jacket, stockings, and high-heels, and a large hat. She had given extra attention to her eye makeup including the meticulously shaped curvature of her eyebrows, and as always, she was wearing some oversized jewelry. Greeting her guests with a sunny smile, she was surprised to see so many members of the press crowded into the suite. Irving Yates was on the side, looking a little lost. One reporter wrote that this had been the biggest press conference in Los Angeles "for months." The following morning's *Los Angeles Times* carried a three-column picture of Christine on the first page of Part II (local news) and described her very generously: "the first thing [the other reporters] asked her was what she was wearing, although it was obvious that she was wearing a specked linen summer dress with a bolero jacket."[6]

Chris had given some thought to what she wanted to say. Very likely, she led off with a routine that worked well for her, starting with a bit of self-effacing humor. Smiling warmly, perhaps she commented about the difficulties of transporting a large wardrobe, and how much easier this would be for a man than a woman. This banter usually helped to break the ice with reporters who she had come to both love and hate. She knew it was their job to get a statement that would enliven an article, challenge her account of her gender transition, or inquire if she would marry. Invariably, news articles alluded to her self-described status as a woman, but some still questioned her legitimacy. A few reporters still insisted on referring to her as "he."

Christine had heard several hostile questions in New York three months earlier, and she considered them "silly." Here in Los Angeles, her low-key humor seemed to help bring forth some smiles, and some of the female reporters began by asking details concerning her wardrobe. This was so-called girl talk about hats, hosiery, shoes, and gloves. This part was easy, but some unpleasantness soon followed. When the questions began to deal with the legitimacy of her claim to have become a woman, Chris quickly lost her composure. The press conference became something of a shouting match. The next day, one reporter described the session as "a head-on collision." The *Los Angeles Mirror* reported the following under the headline, "Christine Clashes with Inquiring L.A. Reporters."[7]

> The mass interview at the Statler Hotel began in an atmosphere of reserved cordiality but soon developed into a heated exchange between the reporters and the former GI who claimed to be a woman, after submitting to drastic surgery in Denmark. Speaking in what was said to be a husky contralto, Christine time after time returned to her stock phrase: 'After all, I'm a human being. I have certain rights. If you don't like me—say so. But don't dig. I hate digging.' At a glance, Christine looked like a well-groomed, slightly mannish young woman. She wore a white hat, beige linen dress with a bolero [jacket], tan and white sport pumps and elbow-length gloves. Seated in an arm chair, she was at first poised, pleasant and a trifle nonchalant. But as the reporters closed in and began to fire personal questions at her, she showed signs of extreme nervous tension. As she parried some of the barbed queries, she was in turn bitter, resentful, tolerant, and condescending.

Christine objected to all of the questions about her physical anatomy. This was the old issue of whether she was actually a woman or just a man in a dress. Although Christine did not usually reveal a low boiling point, these rather aggressive inquiries triggered her anger and she must have felt like she was fending off a gang of Main Street toughs. She especially objected to questions concerning whether she should be considered a male or a female, and what her justification was for defining herself as a woman. We can only imagine the concerns of both her mother and Mr. Yates as they listened to what was escalating into an unpleasant exchange. It was Christine versus a band of hard-charging reporters. By now, the room was filled with smoke.

What made this session unique was Christine's loss of composure in dismissing many of the reporters' moderately personal questions, few of which were new to her. After losing patience with them she began to beg for their understanding and sympathy, describing herself as a profoundly unhappy person who had to overcome " . . . a twenty year struggle . . ." and then taking a good deal of the credit for having accomplished a near medical miracle in Denmark.[8] Then, she shouted: "Now it seems to have become a great big joke." With her anger growing she pointed to a male reporter: "And don't look so skeptical, you there . . . You might have a child some day who would have the same problem." The reporter was taken aback, but quickly went on the offensive: "I'm sure, Miss Jorgensen, that if I did, my child wouldn't make it a public presentation at $12,500 a week." The interview then proceeded from bad to worse when another reporter quoted from a publication, probably the *New York Post,* describing Christine as "no more than a castrate male." For her, this was far out of bounds and she snapped: "I don't believe any of these people know enough about my case to make any statements. They don't quote authorities. What do they know about it?"[9]

The low point of the session was reached when the matter of her physical status was pressed, and particularly, when asked if she would submit to a physical examination by a physician. She responded, emphatically, "I'm not offering myself to anybody for examination!"[10] One of the female reporters tried to smooth things over by asking Christine to pose beside the new floor-length, much decorated gowns she would wear on stage the following day, while the photographers snapped their pictures. It didn't help much.

Irving Yates was distraught and wondered how his brother would have handled the unpleasantness. Would he have stepped in to cool off the press corps? Would he have passed some cigarettes or cigars around to encourage a break? Would he have asked that some drinks be served? Would he have joked and kidded with some of his old press cronies? Unsure of what to do, Irving did nothing.

Chris ended the interview soon thereafter, but it was a session she'd never forget. While she was eager for publicity and she had received much press attention, especially in New York, she was emotionally unprepared for the assertiveness of the Los Angeles press. The following day, the *Herald and Express,* a Hearst paper, reported that she had "clammed up . . . when reporters insisted on knowing whether [her] sex was really changed or whether 'he-or-she' is simply a male with the male organs removed."[11] In future unpleasant interviews her style would be to conceal her anger, bite her lip, take some deep breaths, and handle hostility with a smile and a few flippant, disarming remarks. This worked. She also developed a knack for vagueness to help deflect offensive questions about her anatomy, which she considered her own business. As far as she was concerned, those who wished to challenge her authenticity as a woman were free to do so: "It's their problem," she'd conclude.

Although the reporters in her Statler suite may have believed that a physical examination would put an end to all the speculation concerning her anatomy, her refusal was no different than would be expected of any public figure, or for that matter, of any person. But in early 1953 she was especially sensitive about her anatomy not only because of the attacks that had focused on her history as a man, but because she did not have a surgically created vagina. Basically, it was fair to ask if a male could be changed into a female. Even more difficult was the fact that Christine's body not only lacked a vagina, she had gained virtually no breast or hip development after years of taking female hormones.[12] She certainly was not about to reveal any of this to her critics no matter how insistent the reporters might be.

As soon as the last of her guests had left the Statler suite, Christine began chain smoking and feeling self-critical about her loss of composure. Yates may well have called room service for lunch, and after all three calmed down, they realized the press was just doing what reporters are expected to do. Lunch finished, Christine and her mother began to prepare the silvery-blue, spangled gown Chris would wear on stage the next day. Soon, all three went to the Orpheum to prepare her dressing room.

In Christine's view, her Orpheum act was to be the launch of a new career as a documentary filmmaker/narrator. It meant a great deal to her, and she expected to feel somewhat anxious about putting on a great show. Over and over, she rehearsed the lines from her script, but after smoking heavily she didn't get her best night's sleep. The next morning, all three left early for the Orpheum, only five minutes away by cab. The Orpheum was a complicated, busy place; it took 100 people to keep it running. Her first performance was to be at 10:30 in the morning, followed by a two o'clock matinee, and then two shows in the evening. There were to be five shows on Saturday and Sunday. It was a seven-day, thirty-performance contract.

Arriving by taxi in front of the Orpheum on Broadway, the Jorgensens entered the building through a doorway a few steps south of the ticket booth, and then proceeded through the unmarked stage-door entrance.

Feeling quite alone and a bit apprehensive, Chris and her mother walked to the rear of the motion picture screen and around to the east side of the stage. The audio of the feature film, *Count the Hours,* seemed very loud. Sliding aside the door of the 1926 hand-operated elevator, Chris rotated the control handle and they rode to the second floor. The dressing rooms in this enormous theater were far smaller than they had expected, and they all needed a coat of paint.

At the rear of the Orpheum, on each of five floors, there was one dressing room for headliners that measured about twelve by twelve feet and provided a small bath and shower. In addition, on each floor were two smaller dressing rooms, each with a tiny bathroom. The rooms were clean and adequately lighted, but plain and undecorated. These were working spaces built for the vaudevillians of the Western Orpheum Circuit, totally unlike the elegant Jorgensen suite on the top floor of the Statler with its fresh flowers and expensive draperies.

There was something both frightening and inspiring about occupying a dressing room that might have served the biggest of the former Orpheum vaudeville performers: Jack Benny, Eddie Cantor, Duke Ellington, Ella Fitzgerald, Lena Horne and even a youthful Judy Garland (who was first billed at this theater as one of the "Gumm Sisters").

Christine's sparsely furnished dressing room was highlighted by a vase of flowers and a good-luck telegram from Charlie Yates; he had thought ahead about anxiety-filled pre-show jitters. Yates was all too aware that Christine had no experience at this level of performance. On the morning of her first show, the sun was streaming in from the east-facing dressing room window overlooking the alley. In terms of space and comfort, Christine's dressing area was about the same size as George Jorgensen's fourth-floor bedroom at Naestvedgrade 21 IV in Copenhagen, but here at the Orpheum, happily, she had a private bathroom.

Neither Florence nor Chris had ever previously worked back stage in a theater; neither had even performed in a theatrical show staged by a church or a high school. Occasionally, at Askov Hall, there would be some homegrown entertainment, but none of this involved any of the Jorgensens in the roles of performers. Chris's entire theatrical preparation was limited to minor roles in elementary school plays, which she had enjoyed very much. Now, her stage debut was at hand. As she began to dress, the film ended and the first vaudeville acts began. The orchestra and the applause could easily be heard, and now, she could also sense the racing of her heart.

Christine dressed and did her makeup quickly and skillfully, but on May 8, 1953, she took special care with everything, thinking of what she'd been taught about the difference between stage makeup and day makeup for street wear. She knew that unless a performer used far more "color" and more eye makeup for the stage than for street wear, she would look washed out and older in the glare of stage lighting. Using the theatrical makeup they had purchased and practiced with in New York, she prepared for her first performance in this huge theater, before an audience of hundreds, and with theater reviewers from all the newspapers in attendance.

The makeup was finished, her earrings were in place, her hair was smoothed and pinned, and now her mother helped her step into a long taffeta petticoat to give the skirt of her gown a huge, sweeping, bell-shaped line from the waist to the floor. She was still in her stocking feet. She then slipped her arms into the dress and her mother fastened the waist; it was nearly off-the shoulder, and fitted snugly about her "falsies." Her waist was very trim. The telephone rang: "Ten minutes, Miss Jorgensen." Her silver, strappy two-inch heels elevated her to a full five feet eight inches, and she turned to see a full-body view in the wall mirror. Both Christine and her mother smiled. Her appearance was stunning as she reflected the sunlight. It was time for a cigarette.

Then, using the old elevator, they quickly reached the stage level, taking their assigned position in the wing, while watching the conclusion of Burke and Billie Marx' juggling act. The applause was bountiful. She felt a rush of blood to her face as the two jugglers stole an extra bow, then trotted off stage in her direction, smiling and nodding to her. The Orpheum's long-time orchestra leader for the seventeen-piece union group was Al Lyons, who had quickly left the pit and was at the microphone, center stage, about to introduce the star attraction. Christine swallowed several times, crushed her cigarette, and drank a sip of water from the cup her mother held. She heard Lyons' amplified introduction resonate throughout the cavernous, colorful, extremely ornate red and ivory vaudeville theater. He may have introduced her like this: "Ladies and gentlemen, the Orpheum Theater is proud to present, for the first time on any American stage, a woman you've all read about, and a lady we've all wanted to meet. And now, you are going to meet her in person in this exclusive presentation, the fabulous and beautiful, Miss Christine Jorgensen!" (applause).[13]

Imagine Christine, just three weeks before her twenty-seventh birthday, her shoulders back, her head high, blonde curls framing her face, trembling just a little, as she made her way to the microphone at center stage. With her pale shoulders reflecting a flood of yellow-white spotlights, and with her red lipstick accentuating her femininity, she was beautiful.

Al Lyons gave the downbeat and conducted a musical background as the title of her film, *Denmark,* flashed onto the screen. Stepping to the side, Chris began to speak into a handheld microphone, often struggling with her lines. In twenty-five minutes it was over.

Al Lyons conducted as the orchestra played Christine off the stage. We have no record of what the music may have been, but it surely was brisk, uptempo, and not more than sixteen bars. According to the reports of reviewers, many in the audience wondered why she didn't say more about her transformation in Copenhagen or take a few questions from the audience. After all, wasn't this the main reason they had come? That was one point Christine never fully understood. For her, it was all about her movie, not her transsexual journey. She wanted more than a feeling of being approved and respected as a woman; she wanted to be seen as a filmmaker and a narrator. Others, such as Admiral Richard E. Byrd and Lowell Thomas, had drawn large audiences for their lectures throughout the nation. They attracted people who had come to watch and listen as these national celebrities described their adventures in fascinating distant lands. But Christine's film and her personal experiences did not measure up to theirs. As judged by most of the audience, by failing to discuss her transsexual transformation, she completely missed the boat. This audience was not interested in the flower shops, the parks, or the statues of Copenhagen.

The feature film, *Count the Hours,* was about to begin again. Most of the audience from the first show streamed out onto Broadway, heading for lunch. Few noticed Christine and her mother leave the stage door and step quickly into a cab. They wanted to be on time for an exclusive press luncheon at the Statler that Charlie Yates had set up, and they both wanted something to eat. Christine lit a cigarette. She was not happy with her performance, especially her difficulties with the delivery of the narration, but she probably did not anticipate how negative most of the reviews would be. Without asking for sympathy she turned her attention to the forthcoming interview. This was a one-on-one exclusive "girl talk" interview with Fay Hammond of the *Los Angeles Times.* For decades, the *Times* had been the dominant, higher quality source of news for Southern California. Owned and edited by the Chandler family, the *Times* took pride in setting a higher standard of journalism than any of the other Los Angeles papers. Charlie Yates had phoned one of his Los Angeles friends to pave the way for this exclusive. There would be no nasty questions about anatomy. Accompanied by a photographer, the stylishly dressed feature writer, Fay Hammond, spent more than an hour with Christine, and then wrote a much more positive personal profile and a far more favorable review of her Orpheum act than any of the other news reports.

The next day, the front page of Part II of the *Times* featured a pair of side-by-side, two-column, full-length photographs of Christine in two new outfits.[14] One is described as "a favorite cocktail costume," and her theater dress was said to be a "ball gown of navy nylon tulle" with silver embroidery. The headline for the review reads: "Christine Gets Applause at Theater Debut." Above the report of the exclusive interview the headline read: "Christine's Femininity Charms Interviewer—She appears glamorous and beautiful at 'Woman and Clothes Chat in Hotel.'" The review in the *Los Angeles Times* read like the reviewer had watched an entirely different show than the other reporters. In the lead we learn that she "seemed to come off rather well" and that there was a "good house." In her opening comments, we're told "She alludes only briefly to her personal experiences in Denmark where sex-changing surgery reportedly transformed George Jorgensen, ex-GI, into a woman." It was the shortest of the reviews, but entirely upbeat. In a separate article, the exclusive "Woman and Clothes Chat" was even more enthusiastic, colorful, and complimentary. The lead read: "Christine Jorgensen is pretty, personable and pleasant—by any standard. She's courteous and intelligent too." This, Christine may have thought, is the way I expected to be treated. And for the most part, throughout her life, newspeople responded favorably to her, although the questions about her authenticity as a woman persisted for years. Aside from Hammond's generous article, virtually every review of her film and narrative was far worse than hoped for.

The *Los Angeles Mirror's* entertainment editor, Dick Williams, noted in his column the following day that "Not more than 500 persons . . ." were in attendance. The audience was described as less than enthusiastic, but courteous. Christine was said to have been "talking about everything in Denmark—except her operation. There was polite applause at the finish." Perhaps mocking her somewhat, Williams noted in his review, headlined "Christine's Act No Wow," that she was on the bill with four vaudeville acts that had a "musty whiff of the ancient 30s." Williams reported that the film had been shortened to eighteen minutes from an original eighty. He said she had filmed the travel scenes with an amateur movie camera, and that it consisted mainly of "a jerky panorama of castles, market places and fish vendors." Christine was shown briefly in three scenes. In all, it was a devastating review, and concluded that her twenty-five minute act "was not likely to set the show world on fire."[15]

The International News Service article also turned thumbs down on her Orpheum act and said the film was "amateurish."[16] The *Los Angeles Herald and Express* published a very poor review. Its *Entertainment Editor,* Harrison Carroll's evaluation was headlined: "Christine's Appearance Proves Disappointing." After telling about her silver-blue dress, and her live narration he wrote: "The appearance can hardly be called professional in any aspect. [She was] . . . extremely nervous, fluffing many times during the commentary. Her voice was husky, but not unfeminine."[17] The Associated Press wire service article that ran in scores of papers throughout America was even more scornful. After describing the partially filled Orpheum and noting that she made almost no reference to her Denmark "treatment," the report said:

> The film itself was amateurish, jumpy, and many times out of focus. Through it all, Christine gave a halting description— obviously nervous over her first stage appearance. Christine was accorded a fine hand, and expressed her thanks for the "wonderful California reception."[18]

Most of the newspaper accounts of her initial performance contained at least two or three items of misinformation. For example, it seems that her film was about eighteen to twenty minutes in length, while some described it as far longer or shorter. Also, there was disagreement on the number of patrons in the Orpheum for the 10:30 a.m. show. Was it 400, 500, or even more? Finally, several articles, both before and after the performance referred to a $12,500 "guarantee" for the week's work. Review of the contract shows that she was guaranteed a $12,500 fee, or instead, she could be paid fifty percent of the gross ticket receipts. As shown by her own income records, Christine did not receive the $12,500 guarantee.[19] We don't know the exact sum she was paid, but it was probably less than half of the guarantee. It was Charlie Yates' press release that stipulated the so-called guarantee, although in fairness to him, at least one newspaper added that her compensation could be fifty percent of the ticket gross. On one list of income prepared by Chris, wherein she showed every salary she received during 1953, her Orpheum income was simply shown as "50 percent."[20] We assume the Orpheum managers paid her as little as possible.

There was one unpleasant consequence of Chris's Orpheum performance. With the help of Charles Yates, she had signed a contract with the Sahara Hotel on the strip in Las Vegas for a two-week run. She was to receive a fixed fee of $10,000 for the first week and $8,500 for the second week. But after watching her lackluster act, the person responsible for booking her at the Sahara demanded cancellation of the contract.[21] As grounds for cancellation, the Sahara representative tried to rely on the theory that the hotel had been "misled" in its attempt to sign a woman performer, and that Christine was, in fact, a man and therefore "he" had misrepresented "his" status upon signing the booking contract. Its curt, rude letter of cancellation avoided any reference to "her" and was addressed: "Dear Sir." Christine was initially crushed and assumed she would not be going to Las Vegas, but Charles Yates, an old pro in such matters, immediately notified the Sahara that Christine expected to present "an appropriate act" to fulfill the contract and that the cancellation would not be considered. He made it stick.

Miss Christine Jorgensen (Credit: Photographer unknown.)

The Jorgensen residence, Bronx, NY. (Credit: Photo by author.)

George Jr. was athletic and well coordinated. c. 1942. (Credit: Jorgensen family archive.)

George Jr. was the best man at the wedding of his uncle and aunt, Robert and Amelia Andersen. (Credit: Courtesy of Robert and Amelia Andersen.)

George Jorgensen Jr., 1943. (Credit: Jorgensen family archive.)

George Jr. served as an Army clerk-typist for about ten months during 1946. (Credit: Jorgensen family archive.)

George Jr. as a photography student, 1943. (Credit: Jorgensen family archive.)

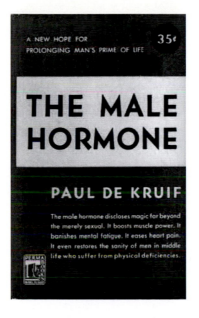

Paul De Kruif's book, 1949.

On board the Stockholm, 1950. (Credit: Jorgensen family archive.)

Christine's first press event, Denmark, Dec. 11, 1952. (Credit: Photographer unknown.)

The first studio photograph of Christine, summer 1952. (Credit: Jorgensen family archive.)

Dr. Christian Hamburger led Jorgensen's medical team. (Credit: Courtesy of Jesper Hamburger.)

Christine returning to New York on February 12, 1953. (Credit: Photographer unknown.)

Press session, Idlewild Airport, February 12, 1953. (Credit: Photographer unknown.)

Idlewild Airport, February 12, 1953. (Credit: Photographer unknown.)

Christine at the Las Vegas Sahara Hotel, 1954. (Credit: Photographer unknown.)

The Scandinavian Society of New York named Christine Jorgensen Woman of the Year, 1953. (Credit: Photographer unknown.)

On stage at the Los Angeles Orpheum Theater, 1953. (Credit: Photographer unknown.)

Christine at Los Angeles International Airport, May 6, 1953. (Credit: Photographer unknown.)

Credit: William Dellenback. By permission of The Kinsey Institute for Research in Sex, Gender, and Reproduction.

Howard J. Knox and Christine unsuccessfully applied for a marriage license in 1959. (Credit: Photographer unknown.)

Patrick Flanigan pursued Christine, c. 1960. (Credit: Photographer unknown.)

While visiting Dr. Alfred Kinsey, 1953. (Credit: Photographer unknown.)

From the play, *Oh Dad, Poor Dad,* 1964. (Credit: Photographer unknown.)

John Hansen and Christine while filming *The Christine Jorgensen Story,* 1969. (Credit: Photographer unknown.)

John Hansen and Christine, 1969. (Credit: Photographer unknown.)

With film crew from *Paradise Is Not For Sale,* Denmark, 1984. (Credit: Photographer unknown.)

Portraits
Through the Years

Various Promotional shots

(l to r) Sister Mary Elizabeth (formerly Joanna Clark), Christine, Lee Grant (film director), Jude Patton. (Credit: Mariette Pathy Allen.)

While filming *What Sex Am I,* 1984. (Credit: Mariette Pathy Allen.)

San Francisco, August 17, 1960. (Credit: Photographer unknown.)

Chapter 16

Developing an Act

For Yates, the real question was not how to rescue their booking at the Sahara Hotel, but rather, what to do to assist Christine Jorgensen to develop her considerable theatrical potential. He convinced her to put her dreams of making movies aside and to develop a nightclub act. With Yates' insistence, the two-week Sahara gig was set for the following November at the same fee as originally agreed. Yates knew how to enforce a contract. He was also invariably kind and patient with Christine, and she put her trust in him. Even better, he focused on the business side of Christine's celebrity. In late April, she signed a six-month, exclusive representation agreement with Yates, but he realized that Christine had a long way to go to become a successful performer, and he counseled her in a supportive letter:

> We need to work on improving the presentation of your act . . . you should give a lot of thought to how you present yourself, both in theaters and cafes. I have a great deal of confidence that you can make an awful lot of money in a high class manner in the entertainment field.[1]

Immediately upon completion of her week at the Orpheum, Christine was on a whirlwind international schedule, beginning with a flight back to New York City on May 15. She then participated in a brief meeting with Yates to discuss her future and to meet one of his clients, Myles Bell. Yates had proposed that Chris and Bell work together in the development of a nightclub act. Chris listened and promised to work with Bell immediately following her return from Europe. However, she made no specific commitment about the proposed nightclub

Becoming a Woman: A Biography of Christine Jorgensen
© 2008 by The Haworth Press, Taylor & Francis Group. All rights reserved.
doi:10.1300/5896_16

act. Her mind was on filming the coronation of Queen Elizabeth, which was to be her second travel film.

On the following day, she flew to London with her longtime RKO friend, to whom she had repaid the money he'd loaned George during his years in Copenhagen. The trip was a way to thank him for his kindness, and, additionally, she valued his practical know-how with a camera. Chris was still hoping that she had a future as a documentary filmmaker, but after shooting several hundred feet of sixteen millimeter footage in London, the project was dropped.

After less than a week in London, Christine flew to Copenhagen for a reunion with Drs. Hamburger and Stürup, both of whom gave her a cordial welcome. She spent a little time with each of her Danish friends, including Elsa Sabroe, and loved walking the narrow, twisting streets of the old city. Enjoying the beautiful spring sunshine in the land that had given her a rebirth of personal identity, she managed to meet and thank all of her Copenhagen relatives and friends. It seemed hard to believe that only 100 days earlier she had been selecting a fur coat, a hat, and a new suit for her return to the United States.

In early June, she flew back to New York and began serious work in the development of a twenty-five minute nightclub act. It was hard work, but she came to enjoy it, and to love the show business people she met along the way. In terms of talent, Christine was far more capable of becoming a success in show business than as a cinematographer or film editor, although she was not much of a singer or dancer.[2] She never again narrated her films to theater audiences, and most of the family pictures she took were thirty-five millimeter slides that few people have ever seen. They are now fading away in dozens of manila envelopes at the Danish Royal Library.[3] While all of this was happening, hundreds of letters from men and woman seeking information about their own transsexual feelings were being received, and Chris was happy to find one letter from a New York physician who offered his help. He was an endocrinologist; his name was Harry Benjamin.

Born in Berlin in 1885, Harry Benjamin is considered by many to be the "father of transsexualism." His first work with transgendered patients began when Alfred Kinsey referred a distressed young man to him in 1948. Benjamin and Kinsey were both staying at the St. Francis Hotel in San Francisco, and when Kinsey learned from one of his interviewees that he "wanted to change his sex," Kinsey asked Benjamin to see him. Some years later, Benjamin assisted this patient to arrange for partial transsexual surgery.[4] Benjamin subsequently became the principal physician and researcher who helped to lead the development of transgender studies. He also wrote the first modern text on transsexualism.[5] After completion of medical school in Germany, Benjamin came to the United States to participate in a research program on tuberculosis, but he was unhappy with the program's procedures and resigned. The ship he boarded to return to Germany was turned back to America following the outbreak of World War I in 1914, and he subsequently made America his home. In the early part of his career, Benjamin specialized in gerontology and the uses of hormones to assist the elderly. He was considered by all who knew him to be an excellent clinician and a highly compassionate advocate. Although he had seen only a handful of transsexual patients at the time Christine Jorgensen returned to New York in 1953, he offered his assistance. They met and discussed ways to help other transsexuals obtain information and medical referrals. Benjamin was aware of the international confusion associated with the term "transvestism," and therefore he proposed distinguishing between periodic cross-dressers (formerly termed transvestites) and individuals such as Christine Jorgensen who made a complete reversal of gender role (termed transsexuals). This language was widely accepted and remains in use today. Concerning transsexuality, he came to believe that biological determinants were the most likely causes, while noting that social and cultural factors also played a role. Benjamin described a continuum of transgender identity beginning with fetishistic cross-dressers and "transvestites," and at the opposite end of the spectrum, what he called "true" transsexuals, such as Christine Jorgensen. Later, he helped to establish the Society for the Scientific Study of Sex and the international association that has provided standards of care for transsexuals: The Harry Benjamin International Gender Dysphoria Association. Contributing by telephone to a memorial gathering for Benjamin in 1986, Chris explained that "he was a Godsend . . ." in helping with the "mountain of mail" she had received from self-identified transsexuals.[6] Harry Benjamin lived to be 101.

Charles Yates, then in his late fifties, didn't need to say much to Christine after they had read the disastrous reviews of her week at the Orpheum. Even her mother, the eternal optimist and unfailing source of encouragement, realized that the Los Angeles week had not been a success despite the lighthearted words of Fay Hammond of the *Times*.

A new plan was needed. Chris not only trusted Yates, she knew she needed his expertise, his fatherly guidance, and his steady hand as a leader. Chris also needed a future that included earning money, as the generous payment for the *American Weekly* articles had largely been invested in her new home. Yates explained his ideas in a thoughtful, low-key letter: "You have the potential to earn a great deal of money in show business, but you must earn it with an act that people want to see, and that means starting from where you are now, and building an act."[7]

He saw the intimacy of the smaller nightclub-cabaret-supper clubs as an ideal venue for Chris, and tried to show her the economics and the practical side of exploiting this entertainment market. In the days before television, there were hundreds of these clubs throughout the country, all competing for live entertainment and for acts that were fresh, musical, and unique. His judgment about a cabaret act was sound, but at first Christine saw many reasons to reject his recommendation. He emphasized the considerable income she could generate, but down deep, the prudish and moralistic Chris believed nightclub work was the sleazy side of show business, often featuring performers with modest abilities. Always the dreamer, she had hoped to appear in a Hollywood feature film, or in a Broadway play, but neither of these star-struck dreams was ever realized. On several occasions, she told news reporters that she was close to signing a contract to star in a major Hollywood production, but this never happened. In her view of herself, Christine exaggerated her importance, convincing herself that she had the potential for a highly paid career as a legitimate actress. In the future, she would cancel all but the most lucrative cabaret bookings in exchange for a few weeks on stage in a summer play that paid only a fraction of her regular fee. To complicate the planning of her new career, her family didn't think much of the proposed nightclub work. Her sister, Dolly, never attended nightclubs, and Christine knew nothing of working in the cabaret scene. Yates helped her to distinguish between the high profile theatrical career she dreamed of having, and the actual opportunities to earn money, pay her bills, and sustain her celebrity. Chris agreed to take a few singing lessons and to practice some elementary dance steps.[8] Yates paid a song writer to sketch out some brief original songs and lyrics to help introduce and conclude a proposed act. More important, he asked her to start collaborating with Myles Bell, an experienced song and dance man who had appeared in vaudeville and nightclubs in every major city in the country.

Good looking, in his late forties, and always optimistic, the gregarious Myles Bell was born in Uniontown, Pennsylvania, one of four boys in a family of nine children.[9] His father worked his entire life as a coal miner and each of the four sons had followed him into the dusty, dangerous mines. But Myles did not plan to spend his life underground. He was a happy-go-lucky, song-filled, story-telling comedian, and even as a teenager he was asked to entertain at fairs, dances, and church socials. By the time Christine was introduced to Myles and his wife, Nan, he was looking for a new challenge. He still had a very charming smile and a lots of good humor, patience, and eagerness to help in the development of an act featuring Miss Jorgensen as the headliner. Myles Bell was happy to be her straight man because he was a real trooper, and he knew the importance of working regularly regardless of who came first in the billing. He also agreed with Yates that Christine's name could be a powerful draw on the nightclub circuit. They could earn good money, week after week.

In 1953, before television arrived in a big way, every major city in America had an entertainment district that included nightclubs where couples would go out for dinner, drinks, dancing, and to enjoy a live performance. Today, perhaps the smaller show bars of Las Vegas are glitzy reminders of the nightclub life of a half-century ago, but there is little of what existed prior to television.

Charles Yates had helped Bob Hope organize a troupe of show girls, dancers, and musicians for appearances at United Service Organizations (USO) shows during the Korean war, and one of the people he tapped was the versatile, reliable, and easy-to-work-with, Myles Bell.[10] He phoned Bell who was "between engagements" at the time, and proposed the two-person Jorgensen act. Bell accepted at once, and within a few days Yates, Christine, and the Bells met to outline an act and draft a script. The basic components and style of the act were quickly agreed upon. It was to be musical, lighthearted, and humorous. Christine would describe enough about her Danish transformation to satisfy the curiosity of the audience. Like it or not, many who came to see her wanted to judge if she was, in fact, the woman she claimed to be. Yates, a strong father figure, suggested that some short musical compositions be written to make the act unique. They soon had a few original songs, such as "Welcome to My World"[11] that Chris would sing, inviting people to recognize that she lived in something of a different world and that she was eager to make new friends and welcome them to join her. It would be an act suitable for family entertainment. It would be flashy and full of fun, but not one in which Chris would ever show much skin, despite the later urging of many club owners.

Initially, Christine felt very inadequate, even clumsy, both in handling the simple script with Bell setting up her punch lines, and with her singing and dancing. Dancing as part of the new act was totally different from the ballroom steps she had mastered at Askov Hall as a teenager. But she learned quickly, and she showed aptitude not only for delivering her scripted lines with verve and appeal, but for improvising humorous asides. Her sense of timing was excellent. The vocal assignments were another matter, for she had never done any singing, not even in a church choir or school glee club. Like many actors, she learned how to sing a song by talking her way through it. Bell had been dancing on stage since he was a teenager, and his movements were fluid and professional, and his baritone voice was steady and resonant. He found many ways to help support the headliner of the act without upstaging her.

Nan, Bell's wife, demonstrated some steps for Christine, very simple at first, and she worked on her moves individually before attempting to pair up with Myles. It wasn't easy, but improvement could be seen as they worked both mornings and afternoons, usually with a piano accompanist, smoothing out their presentation. Yates paid little attention, except to offer consistent encouragement. He also reminded Christine of the wisdom of keeping the act brief, and the fact that in the golden days of vaudeville, an act was strictly limited to eleven minutes. The vaudeville motto could have been "Get out there, be funny and make 'em laugh," "do a few very fast costume changes and then get off the stage."[12] No one argued with his direction.

Yates was busy sending out flyers promoting the act, and he spent a lot of time on the telephone explaining to his friends how they could make a great deal of money by hiring Christine Jorgensen. Some contracts were being signed, but most club managers wanted to see the act or read a review before booking an unproven newcomer. Happily, good reviews would come very soon, and by then, Yates' price would be higher.

Bell and Chris perfected a short music and dance act with humorous dialogue built around Christine's presentation of herself as a courageous person who had struggled with life's challenges and won. It was the story of converting sadness into triumphant joy, and of struggling to find one's real identity. Now, she was asking for others to appreciate her as a successful survivor. Here, she said, was a woman who asked nothing more than to be treated fairly and to be shown the same respect all women want. The act was a musical, lighthearted, highly American treatment of the familiar tale of transforming one's difficulties into personal success through hard work. Bell would begin with some light humor and a bit of song and dance, and then introduce Christine. After a few welcoming remarks, she'd slide into the Rogers and Hammerstein song: "When You Walk Through a Storm."[13] This was followed with some light banter and some self-deprecatory humor, signaling the audience to relax and enjoy a special evening. As Bell took over for another song and a little dancing, Christine would do an "instant" costume change behind a screen, then float back to center stage to help Bell wind up his song. A little more patter would follow, then another costume change, a snappy solo by Christine, and finally a windup finale with a plead for mutual respect, compassion for all, and love for our fellow man. Somewhere along the line she would usually sing, "I Enjoy Being a Girl." It was over in forty minutes.

Christine designed and sewed most of her costumes, none of which revealed more than bare shoulders and arms; she never wore revealing outfits and none of her dance moves approximated a bump or a grind. Her costumes were spectacular in fabric, color, design, and decoration, emphasizing her trim waist and flaring out to the floor. They resembled the satin formals that the women in the audience had sewn or purchased for their high school proms. Christine loved big, flashy jewelry to accent her costumes.

But by the end of June, Chris wanted to take a few days rest, so she traveled to Indiana University in Bloomington to spend nearly a week with sex researcher, Alfred Kinsey. He was about to issue his second report, a study of the sex lives of human females. Kinsey obtained her complete sexual history, but it's not clear whether he placed her coded white data sheets along with the records for his 12,000 American men, which he probably did, or his 6,000 females. As a thank you gift, Kinsey sent Christine a copy of his 1948 report inscribed by himself and his two co-authors, Clyde Martin and Wardell Pomeroy.

While visiting a motion picture theater in Bloomington one evening, Chris attracted a large crowd and the following day, news reporters swarmed the Institute for Sex Research's campus offices seeking interviews and pictures.[14] Although she loved the publicity, most of the staff would have preferred less press attention, especially since Dr. Kinsey had become seriously ill and required hospitalization. Like Charles Yates, Kinsey suffered from major cardiovascular problems. Photographs taken of Chris at the Institute show her wearing the same trim linen dress and bolero jacket she wore at her troublesome press conference a month earlier in Los Angeles. Her public presentation in places where she was likely to be photographed invariably showed her as very buttoned up, typically covered by a jacket or a full length coat. She tossed aside her prudishness, however, when Kinsey convinced her to allow a professional photographer to document her body shape from every possible angle. This is the only series of revealing Jorgensen pictures known to have been acquired.[15] At about the same time, she had posed for some skimpy cheesecake pictures for a proposed spread in a girlie magazine, but they were never published.

Alfred C. Kinsey, the greatest collector of human sexual histories and the first scientist to document the prevalence of homosexuality in both males and females, was born in Hoboken, New Jersey, on June 23, 1894, the eldest son of an abusive, highly religious, and authoritarian father. He died in Bloomington, Indiana, in 1956, having spent his entire career as a professor of biology at Indiana University specializing in taxonomy. All who knew him agreed he was a workaholic, a compulsive collector, a harsh critic of the work of others, and a demanding taskmaster with a bossy, formal, know-it-all style. But as a researcher, he held himself to the same high standards he demanded of others.

As a teenager, Kinsey developed an intense interest in biology, especially the study of birds. He excelled as a student and became one of the nation's first Eagle Scouts. His father demanded that he become an engineer, and forced him to enroll in the well-known Stevens Institute where the senior Kinsey was a faculty member. He hated this, and after two unhappy years, he left to major in biology at Bowdoin College, in Maine. Here, he was an exceptional student scholar. He then earned a PhD from Harvard University and was appointed to a biology professorship at Indiana University in 1920. As a young faculty member, he carried out a definitive study of the gall wasp, ultimately collecting, measuring, and describing 37,000 of these non-flying insects. He found vast variation within this species, a view he would carry over into his sex research. Kinsey and his associates wrote: "It is a fundamental of taxonomy that nature rarely deals with discrete categories. Only the human mind invents categories and tries to force facts into separate pigeonholes."[16] In his two major sexual reports, he focused on the irrationality of dividing humans into two supposed groups: homosexuals and heterosexuals. Kinsey insisted on thinking in terms of a spectrum of sexual orientation, not in discrete categories. This view is widely accepted today.

At the time his sex research was published, Kinsey was a well-established research biologist and tireless collector of sexual histories. One of his goals was to acquire 100,000 histories from male volunteers, an objective most scientists considered unjustified. His sexual studies began in the late 1930s and were sponsored by a committee of the National Academy of Sciences and by the Rockefeller Foundation. At that time, the sponsorship of human sexual research was highly controversial. It was not until four decades later that his well-hidden gay weekends in Chicago and the wife-swapping escapades of his research team were documented in a massive biography by James Jones[17] and in a largely confirmatory account by Gathorne-Hardy.[18] The extent to which his own sexual interests may have influenced his work remains poorly understood, although there is no evidence that he slanted his data. Another question is whether his results should be generalized beyond the samples of subjects from whom his sexual histories were obtained. Even with many thousands of subjects, his male and female samples were far from being representative of the nation at large. But it is generally agreed that his two reports are not only the most voluminous, but also among the best sexual research ever reported.

The first two biographies of Kinsey tell a good deal about the institute he founded but very little about his personal or sexual life. One of his former students and co-workers, Cornelia Christenson,[19] wrote the first, and psychologist and colleague Wardell Pomeroy[20] authored the second. They described Kinsey as an extraordinarily dedicated researcher with the highest personal and professional standards. In the third biography, by far the most complete of the four, historian James H. Jones presented an extraordinarily detailed life story. He concluded that Kinsey's sexual interests and his bisexual motivation clouded the objectivity of his studies and improperly influenced his conclusions. Jones' work also gives a thorough history of Kinsey's difficulties with various sources of funding. The fourth biography, by Gathorne-Hardy, considered Kinsey's homosexual adventures and unconventional sexual practices to be a complement to his sex research.

In 1948, Kinsey published a best-selling book that summarized his findings based on 12,000 interviews with American males.[21] A central point was that human males, like other mammals, manifest a great range of sexual behavior, and that two dichotomous categories such as heterosexual versus homosexual are not warranted. He also interpreted much of what had historically been termed "sexual perversions" as common, nonpathological behavior that should be de-criminalized. Cloaked in the language of an objective scientific report, this book was a thinly disguised plea for the liberalization of social attitudes about sex. Five years later, his report on human females was published based on about 6,000 interviews.[22] This sample reported roughly half the rates of orgasms found in males, and about the same was true for homosexual experiences.

Critics who spoke from a religious perspective condemned Kinsey as an advocate of free love and accused him of presenting misleading data that tended to weaken the moral foundations of the family. His professional critics were also outspoken, focusing on the troublesome problems of sampling and the format of his interview procedures. By today's standards, some of Kinsey's procedures and sampling would surely be done differently, but when judged by the standards of the 1940s, most of his conclusions are considered accurate.

Back in Manhattan, Charles Yates had wondered if the Bloomington trip should have been postponed while the act was being polished and fine-tuned, but he said nothing. He had become aware that Chris not only had a mind of her own, but that she was not likely to be persuaded to alter her plans once her mind was made up. She was very much like all of the Jorgensens, whose neighbors later described as "take charge people."[23] On her way back to New York, she spent a few days with family members in Chicago where an aunt had died earlier in the year. Always faithful to her family, Chris believed that if virtually all of July was dedicated to working on the act it would fall into place very nicely, and it did. Together with Myles Bell, the act was tested in a Detroit nightclub with little fanfare. They made a few changes and then concluded they were ready for the season.

Yates knew Lenny Litman, the owner-manager of the Copa Club in Pittsburgh and sold him on booking the act; they quickly agreed on a fee of $3,500 a week for the first presentation of the Christine Jorgensen Show.[24] The standard American Guild of Variety Artists (AGVA) contracts were always written for her entire show, not simply Chris's fee, and they did not provide for travel or hotel costs unless this was stipulated. Chris often tried to get club owners to "comp" (complimentary free services) her bar tab.[25] She may have paid Myles Bell either a fixed performance fee or a percentage of her fee, and she also probably picked up the cost for travel and for some of the meals. At some gigs, she paid the piano accompanist. In clubs that had a small musical ensemble, Chris usually gave each musician a five dollar tip at the end of the evening. The debut was to be August 5 (or perhaps August 9, 1953; the record is contradictory).[26] After weeks of rehearsal with Bell, she had become far more comfortable with her singing and dancing, and she had little difficulty handling the patter. With experience, Christine proved to be a very entertaining performer; she relied more on her sense of humor and her glamorous appearance than on her singing and dancing.

Gathering her new costumes, a few pages of sheet music for the house piano player at the Copa, and summoning all of the courage she could after the disastrous week at the Orpheum, Chris was off to Pittsburgh and the beginning of a new phase of her life. It was a way of life that she quickly came to enjoy, because she found the take-life-as-it-comes outlook of many show business people fitted her own preferred lifestyle. In this way, she differed entirely from the nine-to-five style of her parents and her sister, all of whom sincerely believed in the Protestant work ethic.

At this time of her life, Chris kept looking forward to a happier tomorrow, but she didn't worry much about how to make this happen. She loved to travel, to enjoy the novelty of new people and new places, and most of all, she loved the applause. For her, applause was proof of the respect and admiration she was always striving to capture. Never before had she realized what this applause could mean to her. The entire experience of working in an intimate cabaret or nightclub was just the opposite of the intimidating and impersonal Orpheum, where she hardly saw the faces beyond the footlights. The Copa week swept past in a haze of cigarette smoke, cocktails, and conversation. Her Denmark film and the coronation footage along with the dreams of becoming a documentary filmmaker had all been put away.

Before the Copa week ended, Yates had signed contracts for at least five other club dates, most of them in the $5,000-a-week range. This was an enormous fee in 1953 for nightclub work; adjusted for today's dollar value it would come to about $30,000 a week. Off the top, however, Chris had to pay Yates his ten percent, and although she never reveals what her deal was with Myles Bell, she was doing very well. But income taxes would always be a headache for Chris. The gross always looked fantastic, but after her travel expenses and sending money to her parents for household bills, she wondered where so much of the big money had gone. Sometimes she failed to give Uncle Sam all he expected.

For the rest of August the act was booked for five nights in Detroit ($3,500), Westhaven, Connecticut, for a night ($1,000), and then three days in Belle Vernon, New York ($2,500). The act was rolling along, peppy, full of laughs and quick moving song and dance combinations; the audiences loved it. The reviews in the nightclub newsletters were very good, and Christine was changing her view of cabarets. Instead of seeing them as dingy and not very respectable places where churchgoers were not expected to spend enchanted evenings, she was now seeing them as one of the after-dark playgrounds of the middle-class. The patrons, she concluded, were nice folks who were similar to the Askov Hall crowd. They went to nightclubs to enjoy a few beers, an evening of entertainment, and a little dancing. She liked being with people who were having fun, and she loved to feel that she was one of the reasons they were smiling, clapping, and always asking for autographs. After the show, she enjoyed hanging out and having a few drinks with other performers and some of the patrons.

Even the travel seemed exciting. She was making many new friends, being treated as a celebrity, and given a special suite in most hotels. By the end of August Chris was in Philadelphia ($4,000), then on to Atlantic City ($4,000) and Buffalo ($5,000). During September, she entertained in Washington, D.C. ($4,500) and Springfield, Illinois, ($5,000). It was time for a breather, so she took a quick detour for a $6,500 week at the upscale Tropicana in Havana, Cuba. Before the end of October she and Myles had added gigs in Toronto ($5,000) and three days in Canton, Ohio ($1,500).

Chris then took her mother and one of her nieces for two weeks in the sun at the Sahara Hotel in Las Vegas. This former Mormon railroad town was just beginning to be an important destination resort. Yates had negotiated the highest fee Christine ever received for her act: $10,000 for the first week, and $8,500 for the second. Financially, for nightclub gigs, this was her high-water mark. Perhaps as she danced, sang, and joked with Myles in the showroom of the Sahara she took a moment to remember that it was exactly one year earlier that she was preparing for her penectomy at Copenhagen's Royal Hospital. Performing with Myles Bell was a lot more fun than being an in-patient on Pavillion IIc East, and her mother was enjoying it too. Never one to turn down a visit to a new city, Chris closed out the year with December gigs in Montreal (fifty percent of theater ticket sales) and Quebec City ($1,500). The show did not do well in Quebec City which she attributed to one thing: "They spoke French."[27] No need to worry, Charlie Yates had booked dozens of clubs for 1954, and besides, she'd be home for Christmas for the first time since 1949. She had already invited dozens of relatives to come for a huge Christmas party at their new, spacious Massapequa home.

For most of her relatives, the new house was a showplace. A few of the relatives who looked upon their gender-transformed cousin as having defied God's will announced they would not be sharing the holidays with her. But nonetheless, life was good. For the record, Christine grossed about $70,000 during a five month string of performances toward the end of 1953. The Orpheum disaster had been washed away by a flood of green cash. Christine was seldom certain of what income taxes she owed, and she tended to put off paying the Internal Revenue Service. Taxes aside, for 1953 she probably netted at least $45,000. As judged by all of the Jorgensens and most Americans, this was a very substantial income.

These were happy days for Christine for she was meeting people who placed a great value on live entertainment. Imagine young couples in a cabaret, seated at tiny round tables each with a candle and a rose, all surrounding the small spotlighted stage. They were curious about how the former GI would look in person. Then, when the music began, most audiences were stunned to see the dazzling, radiant, and elegant Christine looking more like a movie star than they had ever imagined possible. As she danced and sang, nobody asked if she was "really a man." In fact, throughout her adult life, that was a question that simply did not come up, at least, not when she was performing.

Like all celebrities, especially the youthful and attractive ones, Christine received telegrams and letters from male admirers urging marriage, business propositions, or simply asking for a date. One of the most persistent admirers was Patrick Flanigan, an aspiring portrait painter she had met in Washington, D.C.[28] Born in Indianapolis, Flanigan was a slender, handsome, married man expressing his passion for Christine. Flanigan persistently showed up at her performances and managed to chat with her in her dressing room at the conclusion of many of her shows. He said he had fallen madly in love with her and that he was considering divorcing his wife to marry Christine. He then presented her with a diamond engagement ring, but judging from news reports she seems not to have accepted this. She did maintain a correspondence with him for many years, and referred to "Flannery" as one of the relationships she had had that nearly led to marriage.[29] They never sought a marriage license. Flanigan remained in contact with Christine for many years through correspondence, and she responded to him with warm and friendly letters. There is nothing sexually explicit in their written communications although their relationship appears to have meant a lot to each of them. Mr. Flanigan occasionally showed up at Jorgensen family events.

Most of the nation seemed little interested in whether Christine Jorgensen was a good and respectable person, but she had to deal with some unpleasant rejections during her early years in the national limelight. As seen by some people, there was always the vague accusation that she was not a fully legitimate person. These individuals and groups seemed to believe that transsexuality was somehow unclean. For example, in California the previous May, Yates had signed a contract for her to appear as a featured performer on the main stage of the California State Fair in Sacramento. But the contract was cancelled by the senior fair managers, none of whom had seen her act, citing her gig as something inappropriate for a family audience.[30] Later, she was banned in Boston when theater censors feared her presence might fail to meet their standards although, again, they had not seen her act. Throughout her life, the former GI with an Honorable Discharge was also barred from appearing at shows on various military bases, apparently to protect the young servicemen from her supposed uncertain moral influence.[31] One lesson of these rejections may be that while Chris and her admirers saw her act as simply enjoyable entertainment performed by an interesting transsexual woman, others ignored her actual performance while rejecting her as an immoral influence. Perhaps those who put a moral spin on her suitability as a singer and dancer believed that having her appear on their stage was like bringing the money changers into the temple.

But most of America really didn't care to sit in judgment of this "sex change" lady who was fascinating, a little titillating, and a little confusing. Her audiences showed a high interest in seeing Christine, and this contributed to high-fee bookings throughout 1954. But in the back of her mind, Christine was planning for additional surgery. Strongly motivated to have a surgically created vagina, she had previously consulted one of America's first surgeons to perform transsexual operations, the late Dr. Elmer Belt, a prominent Los Angeles urologist. To her dismay, he had told her he could not be of assistance.[32] The surgery she sought was obviously not intended to improve her appearance as the creation of a vagina would be unknown to the public for many years. Chris wanted to be a woman in every way possible, including having the genital anatomy of a female. Therefore, she urgently sought the surgical construction of a vagina. Most of all, this was another step in the solidification of her gender identity, and perhaps it also had something to do with her sex life, or at least, with some anticipation of what her sex life might become. Her actual sex life was a topic she never discussed, not even with her family, or perhaps especially not with her family. After all, these were middle-class Presbyterians.

Chapter 17

On the Road

There were three segments to Christine's year in 1954. First, she was earning her peak income. Second, she obtained additional surgery. Third, she experienced a theatrical flop with a new act she had tried out in England. The year began with Chris and Myles continuing to perform across America, from New Year's Day until the end of June, playing a dozen cities and grossing at least 70,000 dollars. These were six wonderful months, accompanied by great income, many laughs, and never-ending requests for autographs. But this was an unsettled time for Christine. She was in the process of ending her relationship with Myles and Nan Bell. At least in part, this may have involved the one priority that took precedence over her career: Chris felt anatomically incomplete without a vagina.[1] Not only was this a matter of her self-image, it may also have affected her sex life. She turned to a New Jersey plastic surgeon and booked an operation for late May 1954. Later, Christine described it as follows: "The extremely complicated operation took seven hours to perform. With skin grafts taken from the upper thighs, plastic surgery constructed a vaginal canal and external female genitalia. It was a completely successful procedure."[2]

There is no record of exactly what surgery was attempted during her New Jersey visit, nor was the name of her physician revealed. It is clear, however, that over time the results were not satisfactory, and she sought additional vaginal surgery twice: reportedly, at Johns Hopkins Medical Center in about 1970,[3] and in 1980 in Oklahoma City. We may assume that Christine's self-evaluation of the 1954 surgery as "completely successful" complemented both her desire to be seen as a complete woman, and also her idealized description of her-

Becoming a Woman: A Biography of Christine Jorgensen
© 2008 by The Haworth Press, Taylor & Francis Group. All rights reserved.
doi:10.1300/5896_17   *179*

self as a woman fully capable of responding sexually. However, in reality it was unsuccessful plastic surgery.

Just as the facts of the surgery are unclear, the details of her deteriorating relationship with Bell are also incomplete. Possibly, he objected to her refusal to accept bookings during the three months set aside for her surgery and recovery. This was during a period of peak earnings and a three-month layoff that Bell would not have welcomed. To make matters more complicated, following the three-month convalescence, Bell went to England with Chris and the two tried out a new act at a Manchester theater. This was unsuccessful. There had been amicable discussions during 1954 about his leaving the act, but because some contracts called for both of them to participate he appeared with Christine now and then through the early part of 1955. Looking ahead, Christine had hired a replacement in January of that year.

In mid-August, after three months of recovery at her Long Island ranch house, Chris booked a first-class passage (costing $445) on the pride of America's Atlantic passenger ships, the exceptionally fast *United States,* and sailed to Southampton. Myles Bell may have also been aboard, but that's not clear. Upon her arrival in England, several of the low-brow English scandal sheets published outrageous tales about her supposed personal life that were all fictitious. These articles described her in insulting terms, insisting that she was not only a "freak," but a threat to public morals. Chris was hurt by these attacks, but she had other business on her mind. Together with Bell, Christine had contracted for a six-day run at the Manchester Hippodrome, a large theater somewhat reminiscent of the Los Angeles Orpheum, but far smaller. She had a variety of flashy new costumes and a revised, fast-moving, two-person song and dance routine. Her goal was to jump-start a hot new act designed for theaters. She wanted to earn smash reviews in Manchester and then take the act to a London theater. Ideally, in the future she would be spending far less time in nightclubs.

But her new act not only didn't go over well, it was a money-losing flop and this triggered a serious episode of depression. Plans for the London opening were cancelled, and instead, she proceeded to Stockholm where she met some old friends. Soon thereafter, her act, apparently without Bell, played to enthusiastic audiences in Sweden for over a week. Meanwhile, feeling depressed, she had been pouring her heart out in letters to both Christian Hamburger and Charles Yates.

She had told them both that her mood was only at "the 80 percent level" following the Manchester failure. From Copenhagen, Hamburger wrote a warm and supportive letter, assuring her that an "eighty-percent" mood level was all she should expect at times, and noting that had she not made her earlier visit to Denmark, even that level might not have been achieved. Yates knew of the ups and downs of show business, and he was more direct:

> You say you feel you are somewhat on the skids. You are bound to feel that way anytime you have had a flop . . . Don't worry about your own disappointment with the way things went in Manchester.[4]

Chris bounced back within a few weeks and then took her friend, Helen Johnson, to Venice, Rome, and Capri before returning home. While Chris dated men, her travel companions and housemates were usually women. Following her excursion in Italy, she enjoyed a luxurious return to the United States aboard Italy's proudest, biggest, and most expensive Atlantic liner, the impressive *Andrea Doria*. Meanwhile, Myles Bell moved to Chicago to start a new career as a stock broker.

In the fall of 1954, Roy Ald, an associate editor of *True Confessions* magazine, visited Chris three times in her dressing room at a New Jersey nightclub to gather material for a feature article. Her father was present for at least some of these interviews. Ald described her as a person who was very much "in command" as a performer. He added that she showed much self-confidence, while respecting others. As she often did, her conversation with Ald included extensive name dropping, a favorite lifelong tactic to establish how respectable and well-connected she had supposedly become. And when it came to dollars and cents, she was especially well-informed. According to Ald. "She showed much interest in knowing the number of patrons who had paid to come to each performance, and she was very aware of money matters."[5] The two seemed to become very friendly, and Ald developed a sympathetic and supportive view of Christine. He was surprised, therefore, to hear her father consistently refer to her as "he" or use the pronoun, "him." On his final visit with her, Ald took away a less cheerful impression than he had held earlier: "All at once, she seemed to me like a lonely, lanky boy in make-up . . . she seemed so utterly lonely." Why he arrived at this conclusion is unclear. Perhaps

Ald had managed to tap into Christine's emotional life at a level seldom revealed to others, especially newspaper people.

There were plenty of bookings for the final three months of 1954, as Christine tried out a new partner, Lee Wyler. They performed in eight venues, taking in a gross of about $27,000. In her autobiography she praised Wyler, but he was no substitute for Myles Bell. Her total gross for 1954 appears to have been about $100,000, and she may have netted at least $60,000 to $70,000 after expenses. By any measure, this was an enormous income.

With the coming of winter, it was time for another Jorgensen family Christmas reunion in Massapequa. Unfortunately, some of the relatives who were angry with Christine continued to boycott parties at her residence.

Christine was dependent upon Charles Yates for much more than his know-how as a booking agent: he had become her second father, her occasional social escort, a close friend, financial advisor, and the person who took care of whatever business problems arose. When she would call from some distant city, complaining about something he would remind her: "Chris, stop worrying! Remember that I'm always back here doing your worrying for you."[6] No matter what the difficulty, just having Charlie reassure her by telephone was enough to cheer her up. While golfing with Bob Hope in Palm Springs, Charles Yates suffered a fatal heart attack in January, 1955. Christine learned of this while preparing to open a play in St. Louis.[7] That night, proceeding with her performance was one of the toughest assignments of her life, but she carried on as best she could. During the following months, Yates' son, Steve, was of some help but he was not a substitute for the many roles his father had played.

At the Empress Theater in St. Louis, the play *To Dorothy, With Love,* had a moderately successful run for a few weeks, but after the cast party on the closing night, Chris felt less certain of her future than she had since 1952. She returned to her Long Island residence, spent long hours in her upstairs room, smoked a great deal, and tried to conceptualize what she should do with her life. Christine was again depressed. She had ample cash for living expenses, so money was not an immediate problem, although having an income would surely be a long-term requirement. Florence and George were worried, but they said little.

In February, she and Lee Wyler played a one-week engagement at a theater restaurant, but it all seemed like a broken record. The bookings were not coming in as hoped, and Christine seemed unsure of how to proceed. A $5,000 fee for a one-week gig helped to brighten her mood. She knew the financial health of the nightclub circuit was taking a beating from the competition of television. Fewer of the couples who had been the backbone of the cabaret business were going out on the weekends; they were staying home, watching *Your Hit Parade* or *Your Show of Shows* on Saturdays, not to mention *The Ed Sullivan Show* on Sunday nights. Even the Jorgensens were glued to their new black and white television set on Saturday and Sunday evenings, and they never missed Wednesday nights with Milton Berle and *Your Texaco Star Theatre*. Perhaps some of them might have wondered what Chris thought when Uncle Miltie did his over-the-top drag acts.

Concerning her future, Christine was trying to be as realistic as possible, and she was asking herself some tough questions: Was the market for her act contracting? Was the fascination with seeing a transsexual person of less interest than it had been a year or two earlier? What was the significance of having Myles Bell out of the act? Many times, she must have longed for the opportunity to have a conversation with Charlie Yates. There was no one with whom she could consult that offered the combination of experience, wisdom, and friendship that he had provided, all for ten percent of the gross.

Without rushing into any final decisions, Chris formulated a plan: She would develop a single act, turn the affable Lee Wyler loose to find his own way, try out the new act during May at a club in Indianapolis, and put a lot of other questions on the back burner.

On May 5, 1955, she opened her single-act show featuring song, dance, and transsexual patter, together with rapid-fire costume changes behind a spangled on-stage screen, unzipping "industrial quality"[8] fasteners in what seemed like "instant" costume changes. The audience loved it, and so did the management. But unfortunately, the Indianapolis club where she had performed became bankrupt even before Chris's salary check had cleared the bank, so her efforts had to be charged up to rehearsal and experience.

At least, she felt a lot better about singing and dancing, hearing the laughter and applause up close to the tiny stage, being in the spotlight again, and having a few drinks after the show. Chris had a lot of insight into her own feelings, for she had been struggling with inner conflicts during much of her life. Perhaps she reasoned that she had been working through an identity crisis, and that the worst of this process was behind her. Part of this identity struggle involved the challenges of being a woman, of having men find her attractive, yet harboring concerns that her body was not entirely the body of a female. Beyond the curiosity of newspaper reporters, she wondered if she could ever meet a heterosexual man who wanted to marry her.

During this period, very little income was booked, but at least she had a new act. She then decided to try her hand at the booking business by sending out brochures, writing letters, and badgering club owners for work. Since she was no longer paying an agent or a partner, she reduced her fee. Some of the club managers she was doing business with became good friends and booked her annually.

Steve Yates, lacking international experience in show business, sent her on an unrewarding trip to Venezuela, hoping to open up engagements in South American nightclubs and theaters. It was an expensive disaster and provided no income. Returning home, she and a friend stopped in Trinidad for a few days of vacation. No club dates were on the books until November 1955, when Chris was contracted for a $10,000 four-week stretch at the Las Vegas Silver Slipper. Very likely, she was aware that during that month, she earned more than twice the annual income of most Americans. Money had been a problem, so the Las Vegas income came at a good time. Her Las Vegas dates spanned the Thanksgiving holiday, so she took her father along, both for companionship and so he could enjoy a vacation in the sun. Later, on the East Coast, he would often drive her to gigs and operate spotlights for her act. Both parents were always close, supportive, and sensitive to helping Chris work her way out of a troubling passage, but neither felt comfortable when she wanted to share her feelings about being a transsexual. They simply didn't know what to say. During December, she took in another $5,000 for two weeks at the Koko Club in Phoenix, Arizona. This totaled $20,000 for 1955, a small fraction of her financial successes in the two previous years. Was her earning power at risk? Ever realistic, Christine later wrote "the fact of the matter was that the offers simply weren't there."[9] Except for the Silver Slipper, the contracts she was receiving were from the smaller, less successful clubs, and her fee was averaging about half of what she had been getting.

In September, Christine responded to a letter from Dr. Alfred Kinsey explaining that "my book is in the process of being written ... I'm doing it myself with editorial assistance."[10] However, judging from the comments of actress and writer Lois Kibbee, this biographical effort was never successfully completed. During the next decade there would be other comments at press conferences alluding to an autobiography that was soon to appear. According to Kibbee, Jorgensen had paid Irmis Johnson, the author of the 1953 *American Weekly* series, $5,000 for a "worthless" biography that was never published.[11]

Jorgensen missed her friend and manager, Charles Yates, a great deal. In her letter to Kinsey, she explained how the death of Yates had been a major emotional blow to her, and that she had not worked in nightclubs for several months. She wrote that Yates' death had "left me barren of feelings for show business."[12] Although she had only met Kinsey once, she sent him Christmas cards and brief letters until his death in 1956. One of the things Chris did very well was to keep in touch with famous people, relatives, friends, and business acquaintances; she valued these relationships and nurtured her network of supporters. True, it probably was important to her career, but she also stayed in touch with many friends who had nothing to do with show business. A lot of the Jorgensen family loyalty was shown in her social skills and her kindness to others.

In Las Vegas, Betty Walton,[13] a hard-driving personal manager for entertainers had swept into Christine's life like one of Nevada's gusty, superheated, desert breezes; these winds were refreshing after dark, but overwhelming in the middle of the day. A bright, fast-talking self-promoter and entrepreneur with considerable newspaper and publicity experience, Walton set out to make herself indispensable. Walton was looking for work, and Christine needed help. It was a partnership that had to happen. She began by organizing a list of prospective nightclubs where Chris might appear, and by speeding up the mailing of promotional brochures. Christine not only recognized that Walton could help produce bookings, but she also valued the companionship and initiative of her new friend. The energetic and controlling Walton also offered suggestions about costumes and makeup and kept a list of telephone calls and mail to be answered. Walton could not replace Charles Yates, but soon her efforts were producing bookings and income. She had big plans for a new act. She wanted Christine to add a male singer and hire three Las Vegas show-girls as singers-dancers to create a bigger, flashier, more expansive musical show. She wanted to construct an act that could be booked to run for several weeks at the big showrooms of Las Vegas, Honolulu, New York, or Miami. Of course, she also expected Christine to finance all of this. Neither Walton nor Jorgensen had ever put together such a show.

They hired the necessary performers, then previewed and fine-tuned the expanded act in Portland, Oregon (three days at $1,000), then played in Vancouver, BC (two weeks at $1,000 per week), and then in Eugene, Oregon (six days at about $2,000), before returning to San Francisco. One thing Christine understood was that this act was much larger, flashier, and more musical, but it was also a lot more expensive than a one-woman show. She also knew it felt wonderful to be back on the road, meeting new people, enjoying the support of this new group of friends, learning new routines, and feeling there was a promising future ahead. Perhaps she hoped this new act and the new cast could do the same thing for her that linking up with Myles Bell had accomplished. Although expensive, the act seemed to be an improvement. There was a lot more dancing and it was a much more ambitious and glamorous show.

But within weeks the male singer had dropped out, which Christine considered an improvement. Then, with high hopes, in March 1956, the four performers, along with Walton, boarded a plane for an engagement in Honolulu (three weeks at $2,000 per week). Chris's autobiography cites an eight-week gig. But whatever the length of the run, it went very nicely, despite the high overhead. The club owner in Hawaii had carried on a long negotiation with Chris concerning the fee for the act and when that was settled, Chris requested airline tickets for all five of her troupe. "Fine," said the club owner, "but I am only providing coach seating." Chris accepted the deal. With the help of this person, Christine was later booked for a one-night, one-person show at the Honolulu Civic Auditorium, ($1,000); this was also well attended. Without the overhead of three cast members, it was also more profitable.

It was time to move on. The Las Vegas showgirls decided to remain in Honolulu, a decision that spared Christine the unpleasant duty of firing them. In April, Chris and Walton flew back to Massapequa. New cabaret bookings, all arranged by Walton, were coming in. The new work would be in Florida, New York, and Atlanta; things were continuing to look up. There was a week in Tampa ($2,000), eighteen days in New York City ($2,500), six days at the Steak Ranch in Atlanta ($1,500), a one-nighter in Charlotte for $350 which was a new low fee, eleven days in Baltimore ($2,500), three weeks at Chicago's upscale Black Orchid ($1,750 per week), six days in Toledo ($1,250), and finally, at the club where she had first broken in her show with Myles Bell, the Copa, in Pittsburgh (six days, $2,000). The money was not insignificant, but it was less than half the revenue she felt she should be earning. Both of her parents pitched in to help address envelopes and to mail brochures to large and small nightclubs and vacation restaurants in out-of-way places; they produced some attractive bookings for 1957. The trouble was that hundreds of nightclubs were closing their doors. Television was killing them. Although Christine received many very favorable reviews and generally helped to pack customers into these clubs, her mid-July appearance at Chicago's Black Orchid, a highly publicized jazz club, was panned. The *Chicago Sun Times* entertainment writer, Bentley Stegner, was not much impressed:

> The former George W. Jorgensen Jr. is a tall one with a low contralto [voice] and big feet carefully covered by an oft-changed wardrobe of red, white and gold gowns. She does singing and dancing takeoffs of Johnnie [Cry] Ray, Martha [Mr. Paganini] Raye, Legs Dietrich and Danny [Wonderful Copenhagen] Kaye. Christine runs a poor third to two other acts in the revue . . .[14]

Surely, by this time, Christine had come to know that people paid to see her perform because she was a beautiful transsexual, not because she was one of the nation's outstanding singers or dancers. But no matter what the motivation of the customers, she was helping to pack them in. Chris's records for 1957 show her playing nineteen engagements ranging in length from a single night to four weeks in a large New York club. According to her records, she appeared in Denver, Montreal, Louisville, New York City, Rochester, Williamsport, Providence, Binghamton, Norfolk, Brooklyn, Lawrence, and on Long Island. She also performed one-night stands in several small cities. The total revenue listed on Christine's worksheets show a gross of about $17,000 which is almost certainly on the low side. We cannot be certain that these financial accounts are complete, although she typed them herself. Occasionally, she did not show the total fee for her work, especially for dates overseas. Among her papers and records in the Danish Royal Library there are no day-to-day records of her expenses. Christine had continued to have problems with her "favorite government agency," the one she called "The *Infernal* Revenue Service," and this may explain the absence of some financial records.

Christine showed no recorded income beyond the first two months for 1958, although she probably had a week booked here or there. Referring to 1958 in her autobiography, she explained: "For the past year, I'd noticed that my nightclub dates were becoming shorter in duration, and my salary had diminished somewhat during that period, too. I often wondered if I was really progressing or simply treading in one spot."[15]

Without fully realizing it, Chris's income from performances had passed its peak; most of her earnings from show business during the years ahead would slide downward. To add to her headaches during 1957, the IRS had continued to challenge her about whether she had ever actually "intended" to become a resident of Denmark, seven years earlier. That's a hard thing to prove, especially since there is little to show that she ever had this intention. Although the topic of her American citizenship and her 1952 U.S. passport is extensively described in her autobiography, there is no mention of actions taken to establish her intent to become a permanent resident of Denmark. Brenda Lana Smith[16] explained that Christine had "told me" that as George Jorgengen, Jr., he had "passed muster" concerning proof of his intention to become a permanent resident of Denmark by taking three actions: becoming employed, paying Danish income taxes, and acquiring a burial plot. If any of these three steps actually occurred, there is no record of them among the Jorgensen papers in the Danish Royal Library. Some of her United States tax difficulties began with the receipt of $25,000 provided by the Hearst organization during the months of December, 1952 and the following January. She claimed this income had been earned in Denmark and was not taxable in the United States, but the IRS saw it differently. Christine was losing her tax battles despite costly legal and financial advice. Her letters to her tax representatives in Washington, D.C., were filled with self-pity, unrealistic demands that were rather childlike, and poorly reasoned counterarguments.[17] After failing to pay an IRS assessment of about $30,000 that included tax claims for several years, a tax lien was placed against her residence, her wages were garnished, and her bank account was seized. Now, just meeting her bills was a problem.

Late in 1957 she agreed to do a recorded interview to be titled: "Christine Says, with Nipsey Russell," advertised as the first and only recording ever made by Christine Jorgensen.[18] According to her autobiography, this long-playing record generated few sales and she reported she had never received a penny from the project. This was described as "a candid and truthful" account of her transformation, although it fell far short of being either complete or fully accurate. Russell, who later earned recognition as an actor and comedian, led off with two important questions, and Chris's responses illustrated her skill in leaving the impression that one way or another, she was an intersex person:

RUSSELL: Are you a woman?

CHRISTINE: That's a good question. We seem to assume that every person is either a man or a woman, but we don't take into account that from a scientific standpoint, each person is both, in varying degrees. Now, this sounds a little evasive, but I don't mean to be. My only answer is that I am more of a woman than I am a man.

RUSSELL: I see. Speaking from a medical and physiological standpoint, do you have female organs?

CHRISTINE: In my particular case, let me explain it this way. Under the various tests and examinations I have encountered, it is believed by my doctors that somewhere within my body these organs exist, or parts of them exist.

RUSSELL: The ovarian tissue?

CHRISTINE: Yes. Due to chemical results they have gotten, there is nothing definite in there. And of course, several people, even medical people have said, why not undergo an exploratory operation? But as one of my doctors said, it is utterly preposterous that a person should undergo such an operation simply to satisfy a newspaper.

This convoluted and contradictory double-talk was Christine's way of defining herself as an intersex person, implying that "doctors" had identified female organs, or parts of organs using "chemical" measures, while adding: "there is nothing definite in there." This explanation to Russell was a replay of the same ideas she used in describing her transsexual passage to her parents in July 1952, when she emphasized that a glandular imbalance was somehow a reason for her sex change. While never fully claiming to actually have female organs, Chris came as close as she could to saying this while relying on "chemical" findings to support her claim. In response to Russell's questions, Chris gave her standard story of receiving hormones and surgery. Attitudes toward homosexuals, she stated, called for a change in social beliefs. Russell's questions were very personal and often sexual but they evoked little information about Chris that had not been previously reported. He rushed through a series of softball inquiries with virtually no follow-up questions. Christine showed no intention of telling much about her personal life and easily outsmarted Russell with vague responses that often failed to deal with the question. However, throughout the interview she presented herself as sincere, intelligent, and willing to "tell all" without actually saying much. Sometimes she became tongue-twisted. For example, in attempting to clarify the difference between a so-called true hermaphrodite and a pseudo-hermaphrodite, she reversed the correct definition. On the recording, her voice, selection of words, vocal range, and speech pattern sounded like an entirely convincing woman and not the "husky" contralto so often described by reporters. It was sometimes said that she spoke with something of a European "lilt," but to my ear her speech seemed to include more of the speech of Bostonians. For example, she dropped or softened her final "r" sounds, saying "be-foah." Perhaps dropping the "r" would be especially easy for someone who grew up in the Bronx where the word "interesting" might be pronounced: "inner-estin," or the word, weird, would sound like "wie-yud."

Responding to Russell who remained highly courteous and deferential, she said she used "breast padding" especially when on stage due to the weight of her costumes, and that while many women seek plastic surgery for breast enhancement, she did not plan to do so. Russell asked about the motivations of those who came to see her perform, and she explained that her typical audience was made up of "middle-aged couples." In nightclubs, she added, she was treated with respect and that rude remarks were virtually nonexistent. In fact, however, in some of the blue-collar cabarets she did encounter abusive personal remarks. She cautioned that while she had earned "a great deal of money in show business," her expenses were also high and no entertainers worked continuously. Chris claimed many Hollywood people had contacted her concerning her possible work in films, but no contract had been forthcoming. When asked about her parents, Chris said they were very supportive, but within the family, she explained, there was no discussion of her transsexuality. More than anything else, this recording reveals Chris's skill in calmly handing troublesome questions and her knack for changing the subject.

During this time, the policies of America's medical associations concerning the treatment of transsexuals were not supportive. The American Medical Association, for example, retained its policy statement cautioning against physicians undertaking "experimental surgery" on behalf of transsexuals. The University of California, Los Angeles School of Medicine adopted a policy blocking transsexual surgery, and it would not be until 1966 that this country's first surgical Gender Identity Program would open at Johns Hopkins School of Medicine.[19] Harry Benjamin kept Christine informed of these developments, but she never became involved as an advocate for policy changes.

During the first months of 1959, nightclub bookings were few and far between. At first, Chris enjoyed this more open schedule and the opportunity to spend more time in her solarium and to work in her garden. As always, she was getting up late, reading, and making a few phone calls to friends. But soon she realized that a busy schedule was something she really missed. She also missed the applause and the late-night drinks with the audience. Chris was very much a people person, radically different from the supposedly shy and socially isolated child on Dudley Avenue that had been portrayed in her autobiography.

Several church and community groups had asked her to speak and she accepted some of these invitations. She spoke of the problems of children who are born with special needs and of her own struggle to overcome personal problems. She learned that while these speaking engagements did not contribute to her income, they provided a feeling of shared intimacy that was not fully matched by nightclub audiences. A decade later she would diversify her career by becoming a well-paid celebrity lecturer on the college and university speakers circuit. She thrived on the applause of every audience.

Chapter 18

The Marriage License

In early 1959, several friends came to stay with the Jorgensens for a long weekend. One of these individuals was a tall, good-looking, well-dressed, statistician and former merchant mariner from Waukegan named Howard J. "Jim" Knox.[1] Chris had dated him several times when she was performing in Washington, D.C., where he worked for a railroad employees union. Knox had the soft-spoken style of the Jorgensen men, easy-going, quiet, and friendly, and he seemed to hit it off nicely with her parents. Christine had come to feel unsure of both her professional and personal future; the nightclub bookings had slowed markedly. Somewhat impulsively, the two began to talk of marriage. She wrote of Knox: "we had enjoyed a friendly relationship for some time . . . I was at the point when I thought life was passing me by." Further, "I'd reached the point where I thought every woman should be married . . . [perhaps] it was the excitement of a new and fulfilling adventure."[2]

Knox proposed marriage, and soon the two were off to the New York City Hall to apply for a marriage license. However, "We were informed that as the gender designation on my birth certificate had not been changed to read 'female,' they couldn't issue us a license to marry."[3] After protests and the threat of legal action by Chris, a city attorney provided a written opinion that the license application should be rejected until Miss Jorgensen submitted "legally competent evidence . . . [that she] may qualify for a marriage license . . ."[4] in accordance with applicable statutes of the state.

This came down to requiring that the sex designation, male, be changed to female on her birth certificate, but this was something that was not permitted in New York State at that time. Christine obtained a statement from Harry Benjamin that seemed to be powerful support, but the city officials were not impressed and no license was issued. Benjamin wrote:

> This is to certify that I have known Miss Christine Jorgensen for over six years. It is my opinion that she must be considered female. I have examined Miss Jorgensen and have found her in a condition that would fully enable her to have normal marital relations.[5]

They were out of luck. The *New York Daily Mirror* ran pictures of Chris and her boyfriend, with the headline: "Bar Wedding for Christine . . . All Because of Her Boyish Past."[6] The city attorney who met with the press relied upon a second issue to back up his recommendation: Howard Knox had been married previously, but he had not brought his divorce papers when they applied for their license. But this paperwork was not the real problem. Chris's legal status as a male proved to be an insurmountable barrier. In explaining the marriage license difficulty in her autobiography, Christine glosses over the central reason for the denial. The city clerk quite properly relied upon her birth certificate as the primary evidence of her sex. Chris passed off her male birth designation as "a happening" some thirty-three years earlier, and, according to her, of no consequence as far as the license was concerned. She claimed the birth certificate "was in no way a legal sex determining document," which was simply her own opinion.[7]

As she saw it, the really important evidence of her sex was the passport issued by the State Department in July, 1952, which she repeatedly and erroneously implied had classified her as a female.[8] As we've explained, it said no such thing. She had misstated this so often that she may have believed the sex reclassification had actually occurred. We have previously noted that in 1952, the United States passports did not bear any sex designation; sex could be inferred from the attached and signed photograph, or by a clearly feminine first name, but not otherwise. Her 1952 passport photo left no question about her self-presentation as an attractive woman, but a passport is not a birth certificate even if it had shown her sex. That's something she would not acknowledge. Her New York driver's license said she was a female, but this is far from a certificate of birth. How ironic that this same-sex marriage license controversy continues to be a divisive public policy issue forty-five years later. At both the federal and state levels, there has been great inconsistency concerning how sex should be defined. Some judges have relied on supposedly objective biological differences to differentiate males from females, while others have emphasized gender identity and gender role. Sex designation continues to be an unresolved issue in America.

Changing the sex on a birth certificate is also highly controversial. For example, some states, such as California, will amend or modify a birth certificate on behalf of a transsexual or an intersex person, at least, under certain conditions. Other states, such as Ohio, will not do so. Even today, the question of what constitutes a male or a female, or a man versus a woman, for purposes of a state-recognized marriage and for other legal reasons remains in a judicial never-never land.

Within weeks of applying for a marriage license, Howard and Chris had mutually agreed that marriage was not to be a part of their destiny, leaving us to wonder how deeply they had been in love. In her autobiography, Chris stated they shook hands, kissed, and "parted as warm friends."[9] But news reports and statements from Mr. Knox tell a different story. Apparently, something happened between the two of them that caused Christine to cut off communications entirely. She was on the road and she saw to it that Knox had no way to reach her. It's not clear what was behind the break-up of their relationship, or why it fell apart when it did. Apparently, the flames of romance only burned brightly for about six months. Knox told a reporter on September 8, 1959, that his many telephone calls and telegrams to Chris had gone unanswered and that he was therefore asking for her to return the "22 karat" engagement ring he'd given her.[10] By this time, Knox had begun dating a Chicago model, and Chris was driving her Cadillac to some undesignated nightclub booking. Judging from her autobiography, they never met again.

Throughout her life, Chris had many dates with men including a few well-known actors, but she never appears to have had a love affair that lasted more than a few months except for a highly romantic and sexually expressive year with an attorney, Moton Holt. She described herself as prudish. A good question is whether some childhood conceptions of morality along with her Presbyterian sense of propriety played a part in limiting her adult sexuality, or were there other factors at work? Another explanation would be that she was sexually inhibited, in part, because of discomfort with her somewhat unsatisfactory neo-vagina. When asked about her romantic life her standard and well rehearsed response was this: "I have been engaged twice and I have been deeply in love twice. I was never engaged to the men I was in love with, and I was never in love with the men I was engaged to."[11]

Chapter 19

Exit Betty Walton

In early April, 1959, Chris gave an interview and a house tour to *Massapequa Post* reporter Arnold Weiner in response to her announced plans to marry Howard "Jim" Knox, and Weiner's story gives us a picture of her home and of what she then called "Real country living."[1] The house was decorated with many paintings and photographs of Christine and her family along with landscapes by various artists. She showed the reporter some samples of her needlework, including one representing Abraham Lincoln. "If more people would follow the example of Lincoln," she lectured, "we would all be better off today." This was about as political as Christine ever became. While she always followed world news closely, she never revealed much about her social or political views. Although 1959 was a slow year for her, she told Mr. Weiner that "I don't want to give up my career entirely, but I would like to give up five or six dates a year so that I can devote more time to my family." She was referring to week-long nightclub bookings, not social dates. While commenting upon her transsexuality, she told the reporter that "people have both sexes, some a little more predominant than others. It's a matter of degree." Never did she depart from her insistence that we all are partially female and partially male, and that the balance between the two had produced her own transsexual status. For her, transsexualism was entirely a matter of biology. Concerning her childhood, she again stuck to the themes first clearly emphasized in the *American Weekly* articles, and later in her 1967 book, commenting that as a high school youngster "I never dated or went out, I guess I was just shy and inhibited. I still am to a degree but not as much as I used to be." The thousands of patrons in the nightclubs where she entertained didn't see anything shy or inhibited about Christine the performer; they saw a

Becoming a Woman: A Biography of Christine Jorgensen
© 2008 by The Haworth Press, Taylor & Francis Group. All rights reserved.
doi:10.1300/5896_19

foot-tapping, upbeat, smiling, and altogether confident entertainer, loved her work, and made people smile, laugh, and applaud.

As they walked through her spacious living room, Chris pointed out Loraine Merritt's large oil painting of Christine in a strapless evening dress with a mink stole, one of her favorite portraits. This painting was later displayed in the foyer of Chris's Laguna Niguel home, and it expresses her vibrant energy, the movie-star-like glamour of her youth, and a sense of near-regal importance. It now resides in the archives of the Danish Royal Library. Less than a decade before, George had his picture taken beside a life preserver on the *Stockholm* wearing a baggy overcoat, his hair blowing in the wind; it was a typical shipboard Kodak moment, probably taken before they had cleared the harbor, and it was not glamorous.

When the reporter asked about her feelings when she had to face criticism and rejection, she philosophically explained: "In [some places like] Boston, for example, they make a lot of noise you know, they ban books and other things but they are very hypocritical [sic]." Years earlier, the Boston religious leaders had come down hard on Christine, accusing her of being a poster girl for a less than virtuous life style. She ultimately experienced the cancellation of some important bookings because someone feared she was not a proper example. In fact, her act was invariably as clean as a whistle. She didn't even smoke on stage, and that required much self-discipline.

Toward the end of the interview, Chris again went beyond truth by saying she had completed "two movies [that] haven't been released to the public yet." Christine never appeared in a Hollywood feature film. She told the reporter that her manager, Betty Walton, "at one time handled the publicity for Rosemary Clooney, had a column in the *Los Angeles Herald-Tribune* [sic], and also had a personality show on KFOX in Long Beach." The interview ended with this summation: "Show biz has been good to me in more ways than one. It also afforded me the chance to live in Massapequa. Real country living. I love it."

The slow bookings continued during the summer of 1959, although Betty Walton[2] had lined up a gig for a week or two at Hollywood's Interlude Club. The two flew to the West Coast, rented an expensive cottage at the fashionable Chateau Marmont just north of Sunset Boulevard and a well-known address for show business people. The act at the Interlude was very successful and she agreed to a twelve-week run. It was one of the best money makers of the year.

Most of her bookings during 1959 were for weekends only, substantially reducing her income. There was Hollywood chatter of her being offered a part in a major film, but nothing came of it. Talk of such "offers" had been described in the press beginning with the first major publicity she received in 1952. A film contract or a part in a Broadway play were assignments she always sought but never realized. The same disappointment followed her summer theatrical experiences where she earned good reviews, but none of these led to the major offers she longed to receive. In Hollywood, Christine believed her film opportunity had been damaged by unfavorable remarks in the columns of Hedda Hopper and Louella Parsons, but other factors were probably more important, especially the fact that the projects she wanted to participate in were never produced.

Betty Walton, her agent and personal assistant who sometimes lived in Chris's upstairs guest bedroom, had spent a good part of her own career in Southern California and she convinced Christine to establish a second base of operations in Hollywood. Miss Walton, of course, was not paying the bills; it was expensive to maintain residences both on Long Island and in California. There was some success in booking Jorgensen into nightclubs where she had come to feel both welcome and professionally comfortable with her one-person act, but the fees were now negotiated for about two-thirds of what they had been five years earlier. Happily, during 1959 there was sufficient income to fully pay off the substantial assessments of the Internal Revenue Service. Christine hated this unpleasantness and was glad to bring the tax dispute to a close, although it hurt her in the pocketbook. Throughout this period, in far-away Casablanca, surgeon Georges Burou had developed a radically different way to create a vagina for male to female transsexuals. It was surgery she surely would have preferred had the option been available in 1952.

Born in France in 1910, Georges Burou's parents were both teachers who encouraged him to become a physician. After serving as a military doctor in France during World War II, Burou opened a surgical practice in Casablanca in 1950 specializing in obstetrics and gynecology; he named his center Clinique du Parc.

In 1956, he introduced what was later called the penile inversion procedure of sexual reassignment for males. This was based on the use of the skin of the penis and scrotum to create a neo-vagina and labia. In brief, the skin encasing the penis was separated from the interior cartilage, while maintaining its tube like shape and retaining its blood and nerve supply. This tube was then packed to provide the shape of a vagina and then inserted into the abdominal cavity as far as the prostate gland. The skin of the scrotum was used to shape the labia. First described at the biannual meeting of the Harry Benjamin International Gender Dysphoria conference at Stanford University in 1975, Burou's method was quickly emulated by surgeons worldwide.

Surgeon and historian, Joris Hage, reported at the 2003 meeting of the Harry Benjamin Association in Gent, Belgium, that an English medical team had performed a similar procedure in "1952 or 1953" but this work was not published until 1957 in a book on plastic surgery.[3] Therein, the authors of the book described surgical procedures for both female-to-male, and male-to-female transsexuals. Hage noted that Burou was not aware of the earlier work. Burou's penile inversion operation was widely adopted as the surgical preference for male-to-female transsexuals.

Christine fulfilled contracts with clubs all over the nation during 1960, usually leaving Betty Walton at home to continue beating the drums for additional bookings. Walton hated flying. While Chris never wanted a seven-day work schedule, she very much wanted to be busier than she was. Even more troubling, her fee schedule was far lower than she was used to receiving, and with the expenses of two residences, two cars, and the salary she was paying Walton, there was often tension about cash flow and meeting the current bills. Christine was not one to waste money, although she was not as frugal as she liked to claim she was. As viewed by their relatives and neighbors, her parents had been very watchful in the management of income, and they rarely dipped into their savings. In contrast, Chris found it necessary to borrow small sums of money from her parents now and then, and larger amounts from her life insurance policies, including her 1945 GI life insurance.[4] This policy had been a headache for her because the Veteran's Administration refused to change the policy holder's name from George to Christine Jorgensen. Decades later, one relative commented that when Chris found something she really liked in a department store, such as sweater set, she'd order one set in each color, running up a substantial bill.[5] Invariably, she was generous with her youthful relatives on shopping trips, always urging them to pick out a new dress. She retained receipts for gasoline purchases, car washes, dry cleaning, and many other daily expenses and these reflect far more modest expenditures than most celebrities would choose. For example, in 1955 her records show she bought a purse for $4.90, and a new pair of shoes for $12.[6]

In April 1960, one peculiar incident occurred in Long Beach, California, where a city ordinance prohibited male employees of nightclubs to perform cross dressed. Christine fulfilled a contract to do her usual act in one of the city's cabarets, unaware that two detectives had been dispatched to determine if she should be arrested for violation of the cross-dressing ordinance. After taking in the show, no arrest was made, and the undercover officers avoided a showdown by reporting to the City Council that Christine was an independent contractor, not an employee of an "entertainment cafe," and further that Jorgensen had "papers from a New York doctor that showed she was a female."[7] Asked for her comment after being told she would not be charged, Chris laughed and told the *Long Beach Independent* reporter: "Boys will be boys."[8] A decade later, local ordinances of this kind were a thing of the past. With the many national struggles of the 1960s, courts of appeal nationwide concluded that standards of attire did not require governmental supervision.

The gaps in the nightclub schedule for early 1961 bothered her, but the good news was that Betty Walton had lined up another trip to Honolulu, followed by excursions to Australia and the Orient. She loved Hawaii, and travel had a way of bringing Christine out of a gloomy mood. She was a person who loved the idea of escaping to a tropical paradise, free of all worries, but she never established a residence anywhere other than New York and California.

Christine and Betty Walton flew to Honolulu in June of 1961, did a gig or two there, and then six weeks later they flew to Australia. They remained there for six months, seeing much of the country and fulfilling many publicity-making opportunities. Generally, she enjoyed having Walton along, although the tightly organized and managerial business woman often got on her nerves. Walton was more of an early riser than Christine, who lived everyday as if she were still doing nightclub performances on a regular basis. Chris liked to get up very late, shop or visit for an hour or two, then have a few drinks before dinner.[9] Socializing with friends, she would smoke and chat until all hours of the night, long after Walton had retired. Arising at about noon or later, she'd put on a house coat, have coffee, toast, and glance through a newspaper, looking unlike the sparkling, carefully made up celebrity of the night before. But she could dress and do her makeup in record time when there was some place to go or someone to meet. These late starts annoyed Walton and more unpleasantness developed. Money had also become a problem. Chris felt Walton tended to be "extravagant" with her daily living expenses, seldom seeking the less expensive restaurants and lounges, but Jorgensen failed to note that she also enjoyed the more upscale spots. Neither of them ever stayed in budget hotels. Betty, on the other hand, believed that Christine was a celebrity, and that part of the "image" she needed to project required being at the better hotels and eating places and leaving large tips. Remember, Walton's background was in publicity. From time to time, there were unpleasant words between the two ladies.

One gig in Australia was at a Sydney night spot that Christine enjoyed doing very much, except that they gave her a bad check that was never made good. She asked Walton, who had booked the job, some pointed questions about this difficulty and there was a hostile exchange leaving Chris feeling more irritated than ever. The relationship was deteriorating. Putting these problems aside, it was time to pack and leave the land "down under," and so, on "a rainy January day in 1962, we boarded an Australian freighter for the trip northward to Hong Kong."[10] For the moment, she appreciated the planning Betty Walton had done to arrange this interesting mode of transportation. She had traveled across the Atlantic several times aboard major liners, and now, this was a chance to find out what it was like to ship out aboard a freighter. She enjoyed getting to know the other passengers and several members of the crew. The friendliness and informality of the trip helped to compensate for some overcast weather and rough seas. On the other hand, her relationship with Walton was getting worse. Chris had a tendency to allow minor irritations to be passed over without resolution, something she had learned to do as a teenager at Christopher Columbus High School. In the style of her mother, Chris was the peacemaker. She was inclined to use a smile and silence to diffuse an unpleasant situation. On the other hand, when pushed too far, her anger could come to a nasty climax and she would sound off loudly, especially after a few glasses of wine. Christine felt that Walton had become more and more demanding, controlling, and less respectful of the preferences and priorities of her boss. Christine was now asking herself, why am I traveling with Betty Walton? However, she said as little as possible when the tension was high. After all, they were on vacation.

There were several nightclub jobs in Hong Kong that turned her attention away from the problems with her manager, and it was wonderful to have money flowing in. As you'd predict, Betty had arranged for rooms in one of the most expensive hotels. Since the exchange rate was highly favorable, she reasoned that their living expenses were a great bargain, and they were. The two went sight-seeing during the afternoons, and did show business until the early morning hours. The next stop was Manila, where the Filipino people and the newspapers gave Chris a warm welcome. The mayor rolled out the red carpet, and the governor invited her to a luncheon and praised her as "the best Ambassador" they had received in years.[11] Soaking up the sunshine and the praise, Christine felt proud, strong, and very independent during the four months they stayed in Manila. While there, she had sufficient free time to help make a motion picture. But she had come to believe Betty Walton was more of a headache than she wanted to bear. Close to the end of their vacation, she fired her.

During her four-week run at Manila's Safari Club, she was much too busy to dwell on the Walton matter. She offered her a plane ticket home but Walton said "no thanks," and they went their separate ways. Alone again, Christine soon felt the loss of her former friend. She plunged into one of her weeks-long depressive episodes, returning to Los Angles "with five dollars in my handbag."[12] Without an agent, there was no one responsible for drumming up business, and there was little prospect for a good year ahead. She found it difficult to shake the dark feelings of discouragement, even at times, a sense of hopelessness. As always, she was smoking heavily, and finding it hard to keep her vow to drink only after the cocktail hour. Calling some of her Southern California contacts, she managed to find a few nightclub gigs during the summer and she promised herself to make drastic cuts in her expenses.

Upon returning to Massapequa in September, she asked her dutiful mother to take on management responsibilities for Christine Jorgensen Enterprises, something Florence did very well. There was a week of work in a Midwest club. Then, on her return trip home, she stopped for a visit with Aunt Augusta in Minneapolis who was seriously ill. This was to be their final visit. Chris had never forgotten the understanding, warmth, and the kindness Augusta had shown in 1947 when George Jorgensen had stopped to visit her. Now a celebrity, Chris was in a far happier passage of her life, and she did all she could to assist her Aunt. There were several more weeks of show business appearances during the fall, and after the income and expenses were compared, she found that by eliminating the costly Hollywood residence and office and reducing her fixed expenses, her net income compared favorably to previous earnings. It wasn't a great year, financially or personally, but she was home with her parents and there was ample money to meet the bills. It felt good not to have Betty Walton running her business or sharing their Massapequa home.

Chris was aware that her show business career had hit a high point almost ten years earlier, and she realized that this could not be revived. She was longing to branch out and to move on to a different kind of stage. Throughout this year of self-examination, of depression and declining bookings, how many times must she have longed for the guidance and steady hand of Charles Yates? Both her mother and father were eager to help her in any way they could, but neither had any insight when it came to show business. They simply had no idea of how their daughter might restructure her career. Just as the teenage George Jorgensen Jr. struggled to shape a sense of identity, now, at the age of thirty-seven, Christine felt she must face a similar redefinition of her professional identity. But this was an assignment she didn't know how to handle.

Chapter 20

Summer Stock

The brightest highlight of the summer of 1963 was meeting Bill Hunt, and it happened entirely by accident. Hunt was the producer-director for summer shows at two small theaters on Long Island: The Red Barn in Northport, and a second one known as Tinker's Pond. Hunt recognized Christine when she arrived to see one of the plays he had produced. He was very welcoming and invited her to meet soon thereafter for coffee. This led to an offer calling for Christine to play the leading role in an Arthur Kopit comedy, *Oh Dad, Poor Dad.* Not everyone connected with this production was enthusiastic about Chris taking the part, for while she had appeared in some stage productions, she certainly had not established herself as an actress, except, perhaps in her own thinking. Hunt's offer provided a big professional shot in the arm at a time when she was discouraged and uncertain of her future. In their rehearsals it was rewarding to hear Hunt give her praise, encouragement, and to offer guidance; he reminded her of Charles Yates. Her role required some real acting ability, excellent comedic timing, and a sense of command as a performer; she felt certain she could do a fine job and so did Hunt. The production was planned for early in the summer of the following year. Meanwhile, Chris would go back on the road.

With her smile and confidence on the rebound, Christine made a quick trip to Anchorage, Alaska, to fulfill several weeks of nightclub work. The gigs were working well, with appreciative audiences, good pay, and a reasonable amount of time for sight-seeing and playing the part of the celebrity-tourist. This was the kind of therapy she needed most, and when she flew back to New York in October, her parents could see that the energy she needed to keep her career moving had been restored. There were a few bookings during the rest of the fall

Becoming a Woman: A Biography of Christine Jorgensen
© 2008 by The Haworth Press, Taylor & Francis Group. All rights reserved.
doi:10.1300/5896_20

and she performed these with the verve and fun that helped to make her nightly work enjoyable. In return, the audience gave her the applause, and more important, the admiration she so urgently sought. With the laughter and approval of audiences, along with a few drinks with friends after the show, Chris was again the happy-go-lucky party seeker her parents expected to see. In the cabarets she knew so well, the applause was bountiful, sincere, and most gratefully received. As 1963 came to a close, she looked forward to having Christmas at home with so many of the relatives sharing these good times.

The good news was that her mood was joyful, and the family circle was complete. But the bad news was that just before the end of the year, the Internal Revenue Service managed to seize Chris's entire bank account; she had incorrectly believed her tax problems had ended. By April of 1964, she had again "settled the whole affair" with the IRS."[1] The tax struggles had been going on for more than a decade.

Hopes and dreams for a different career dominated Christine's daily life during the first half of 1964. There were a few offers for nightclub work, but she turned down most of these. Her goal was to become the best actress she could possibly become, and to put on her finest performance when *Oh, Dad, Poor Dad* opened at Tinker's Pond. She loved participating in the rehearsals, making new friends, and following a different schedule. She found the cast delightful, but most of all, she found the direction of plain-spoken, stage-wise Bill Hunt to be very educational. For Chris, it was important for this show to present her as a real actress, not a remake of the nightclub performer who had worked the cabaret circuit for a decade. To her, this new opportunity represented a complete departure from her role as a beautiful celebrity transsexual; instead, she had become, simply, a beautiful woman and a legitimate actress. This was the big difference between performing in nightclubs and working on the stage. But one unrewarding difference was in salary: as an actress she was earning $125 a week. It was barely enough to cover her living expenses.

Having a lead role in a play was Chris's big chance for a fresh start. Her upbeat style, her ready smile, her intelligence, and her respect for a highly experienced professional cast, all worked to cement the close relationships so important in the presentation of a play. She even bought several electric fans to refresh her fellow actors during rehearsals. The show opened at Tinker's Pond on June 30, 1964, and

Bill Hunt saw to it that her cigarettes were near at hand, and that she had her costume changes properly organized.

The reviews were excellent and so were the ticket sales, once the word got around that Miss Jorgensen was fully up to the part. The show did well in its scheduled run of four weeks. It didn't bother Christine that her total compensation for a month's work came to less than she had usually earned in a single evening on the nightclub circuit. Besides, her expenses were low; she was living at home and driving herself to the theater. After seeing Chris in action, a producer from Ohio invited her to perform the *Oh, Dad* role in a summer production the following year at a small theater near Columbus, Ohio. It was a considerable distance from the lights of 42nd Street, but being signed for this role confirmed her belief in herself as an actress. Bill Hunt was so happy with the buzz created by his *Oh, Dad* show that he added a two-week run at the end of the summer, with Christine in the leading role; they drew a full house every night. Chris gave Hunt much of the credit for her development as an actress. He had much of the same respect, patience and kindness she had found in Charlie Yates.

A year or so later, when Christine was performing at Northport's Red Barn Theater, her dresser was a high school student intern named Elizabeth Finken who spent a good deal of time with Jorgensen, both in connection with her performances and in a more relaxed setting at a favorite Northport watering hole, Gunther's Bar.

> She was a very delightful, funny lady, and a really good listener and she made friends easily. She was always very well-dressed, usually in a dress, Capri pants, or a suit and with a large hat. Sometimes, in a friendly way, one of the guys would grab her hat and toss it around like a Frisbee.[2]

Finken, who is now Mrs. Elizabeth Levitt, told me Bill Hunt was very protective of Christine and that Hunt and the cast regarded her as a very good actress. "In a play she could transform into an entirely different person," Mrs. Levitt noted, "and it meant a lot to her to be a fine acress."[3]

Performing in plays was Chris's passion; performing in nightclubs was her job and continuing employment was essential. Using the corporate name, Christine Jorgensen Enterprises, Inc., a slick pictorial brochure was printed with the goal of stimulating more work than had been booked the previous year. This publication offers a lesson in self-promotion which is one of the essential skills for anyone in show business. The several headlines were: *About Christine . . . The Critics Rave . . . What Does She Do?* Replies and inquiries were to be directed to her home address in Massapequa, and she reminded her nightclub prospects that "Christine is as close as your telephone (or call your nearest agent)."[4]

The colorful brochure begins with rave notices about a radio interview with New York columnist, Hy Gardner,[5] that was described in the most glowing language. The brochure quoted one reviewer: "I recommend for study Hy Gardner's gab session with Christine Jorgensen. It was an adult, intelligent exchange of opinions concerning delicate topics, unsullied with Burkers or the slightest touch of prurience."[6]

Furthermore, Gardner claimed Chris had received "many favorable remarks" about this radio interview. Citing her twelve years in show business, the brochure reported that nightclub audiences have been "well satisfied with Christine's act . . . which is still a hot attraction." Taken as a whole, the more experienced Christine was said to be an "act that stands on its own merits [and] is a strong entertainment package." The brochure also told about her successful performances around the world and of a film she made in Manila. This is followed by quotations of rave reviews of her work in *Oh, Dad, Poor, Dad* and of her progress in writing an autobiography. Seven reviews of her nightclub work proclaimed her excellence and versatility as a performer, and we are then told that her "30 to 40 minute performance . . . was especially written for her." Nightclub owners were assured that Christine's act was designed for the "family trade" and that she maintained strict standards of decency. "She sings and also has light comedy material [so] there is no way the act can be called offensive." Hy Gardner, a good friend, gave her the highest marks: "Christine Jorgensen has an act, polished and poised. The sophisticated audience loves her. That Chris can attain (sic) such warm response shows that she has been accepted into the realm of the true performers."[7]

The back page featured short quotations from reviews that appeared in newspapers from all over the world. These self-promotion efforts appear to have worked reasonably well, for they resulted in additional bookings. Over the years, Chris had sought the assistance of booking agencies in Los Angeles, Kansas City, Chicago, San Francisco, and other major cities, usually without giving an exclusive contract to any single agent. These efforts produced several bookings during the early months of 1965, but more than anything else, her mind was focused on the Columbus, Ohio, production of *Oh, Dad.*

Christine maintained a lively correspondence with relatives, friends, and virtually anyone she thought might give a boost to her career. However, an unusual rebuff occurred when she wrote an overly personal note to a Hollywood director with whom she had some kind of romantic relationship during the late 1940s, as George Jorgensen.[8] Upon learning that this man was about to direct a feature film, Chris wrote him a breezy letter reminding him of their earlier time together.[9] However, his secretary, correctly interpreting Chris's allusion to an earlier romantic episode, did not pass the letter along to her boss but returned it to Chris, asking her to send a less personal letter. As you might guess, Chris was asking to be cast in the film, but no assignment was offered. Hollywood was never very kind to her.

During the spring of 1965, summer stock producer Bill Hunt called and offered her a part in *Mary, Mary* which was scheduled for a June opening at the Red Barn in Northport. She jumped at the chance, letting Hunt know how much she appreciated his confidence and assuring him she would help to make this another success. The rehearsals went nicely, and again, Chris helped to weld the cast into a family-like unit with lots of laughs, doughnuts, and coffee. Everyone liked Chris. She was a joy to be around and she brought confidence to the entire group. The audience loved the play, and so did the reviewers. It was scheduled for an eleven-week run, but due to her contract to play in *Oh, Dad* in Ohio, she had to leave during the fifth week. They all hated to see her go. As we shall describe later, another member of the cast was the well-established Broadway actress, Lois Kibbee, who would soon begin to ghost write Chris's autobiography; this turned out to be an exceptionally lucrative step in Jorgensen's career.

Ted Tiller was her director for the Ohio version of *Oh, Dad,* and they immediately developed an easy rapport. He had some excellent suggestions for Chris about the part she would play, and his ideas were accepted and implemented with gratitude. As with her relationship with Charles Yates and Bill Hunt, Chris had no problem taking direction from people who knew what they were doing. Again, the audience and the critics raved about the play, and the praise for Christine was even more generous than expected. On the closing night, Tiller handed Chris a script he'd just completed. It was his adaptation

of the eighteenth-century novel, *Tom Jones.* She loved the script and
negotiated a major part. The play was to be staged in mid-August. At
last, she must have thought, I'm being noticed as an actress. Although
the income was not impressive, it was very important that her success
in these two plays in Ohio was a major boost to her identity as an actress. With a cast of thirty-five and Tiller's direction, they opened to a
full house. It was entirely successful and generated excellent reviews.
Christine wrote: "I felt much regret on the night we had to close after
a two-week run."[10]

Returning home, she learned that her father was suffering from a
blood disorder involving the regulation of red cells. Dealing with the
health of her parents was an entirely new role for her; Chris had always considered the family circle as permanent. Now, she had become the caregiver, driving both her mother and her father to doctor's
appointments, picking up medication, and arranging for brief periods
of hospitalization. At first, she tried to deny the reality of her parents'
deteriorating health, but the truth was soon apparent. In addition to
taking more responsibility for their care, Chris knew she had to remain professionally active. The summer plays were over now, and
once again she turned her attention to generating some nightclub
dates for the remainder of 1965 and throughout 1966. One of her
agents called to offer fourteen performances at military bases in Germany. The money was good and a contract was signed. But it was
cancelled six days prior to her scheduled departure. She learned that
the Army higher ups in the Third Armored Division had nixed the
deal, supposedly to protect the morals and health of the tank corps.
The former GI had been rejected previously as an entertainer of military personnel, and while this was nothing new, it hurt to realize that
the old issue of whether she put on a clean show still dogged her.
When performing, Chris did not smoke, drink, swear, or tell off-color
jokes. On stage, she presented little risk to an audience and surely not
to the youthful tankers of the United States Army.

After a decade of entertaining all over the nation and in many foreign countries, she wondered what could be done to change some of
these rejecting attitudes. She also wondered whether the cancellation
of her contract could be reviewed or appealed. There followed a succession of correspondence with various Congressmen and Senators,
but none of this made any difference. As much as she hated to be rejected, she also resented the loss of income; financially, this had not

been a good year. Even more difficult was her realization that her kind and gentle father was slipping away; he died on January 8, 1966. Christmas was not the same that year, despite the forced gaiety. At least, it was again a very cohesive family with Dolly and her husband, Mrs. Jorgensen, the nieces and more than a dozen other relatives helping to cheer up one another.

For Christine, there were a few club dates during the early months of 1966, and most of these were on the East Coast allowing her to work close to home. At last, some consistent money was again coming in, and there was ample applause from her cabaret pals. In April, she did two weeks at a club in Hawaii, and as always, she came home with a tan and stories of happy times with her many island friends. But for several years, it had become increasingly difficult for her to command the compensation she felt she deserved, although she was a tough negotiator and won her share of business dealings with club managers. In salary discussions she would emphasize that "my book is about to come out" which she assumed would increase her visibility as a celebrity. For more than a decade she had told reporters her autobiography was about to be published, but this time it was true. Actress and ghost writer Lois Kibbee was close to completing a first draft.

Nineteen sixty-six must have seemed like a busy year. Bill Hunt had called in the late spring to ask her to play a role in his summer production of *A Nice Place to Visit;* she eagerly accepted the assignment, and the four week run was very successful. Especially following the death of her father, Chris enjoyed living at home with her mother, one person whose loyalty and affection was never in doubt. Florence Jorgensen was still the main person to keep the household affairs in order, although her health was declining. For years, ever since the departure of Betty Walton, Florence Jorgensen had managed Christine's business affairs, and under her supervision Christine Jorgensen Enterprises was a very thrifty and efficient organization. In contrast, Chris never had much interest in the management of her financial assets. No one foresaw that within eighteen months of the death of her father, her mother would be gone as well.

At some point between January and March 1966, Richard Lamparski called on Christine at her home to record an interview that later was aired as part of his series on radio station WBAI. The name of his series was: "What Ever Became Of . . . " and that's how he began his discussion with Jorgensen.[11] She responded with a quick summary of her surgery in Copenhagen and then described her thirteen-year career in show business. In their thirty-one-minute conversation, Christine was articulate, informative, very humorous, well organized, and showed much self-confidence. Lamparski asked her a familiar question about why people want to change sex. As she had explained so many times before, Jorgensen simply stated "we are all both male and female." She then explained that she had never regretted giving up her life as a man, and that she had always believed she was a girl. As noted, she relied on De Kruif's book, *The Male Hormone,* to explain her first realization of the profound significance of the sex hormones. It was this book, she told Lamparski, that had the greatest influence on her decision to proceed with a transsexual change. The interviewer asked her a series of questions concerning homosexuality, and whether, as George Jorgensen, he had been a homosexual. Without giving a direct answer, she said she had experienced "strong emotional ties with men, [and that] some people might have labeled her as homosexual." Somewhat more revealing, she added: "I was afraid I might be a homosexual." A little later she concluded, saying: "Most of my emotions [as George Jorgensen] would have been considered homosexual." This was a topic she rarely discussed with such candor. Quite generously, Lamparski ended the interview by complimenting her for her frankness, and added: "You are more than just an interesting person: you are a perfect lady." Christine had the last word: "At least, I'm me."

Meanwhile, there were other important developments concerning transsexuality. On November 21, 1966, the *New York Times* carried a front page account of the opening of a gender identity clinic at Johns Hopkins Medical Center in Baltimore, offering surgical services for a small number of carefully selected transsexuals. This was the first program of its kind in the United States, and very likely, this would not have occurred without the pioneering example of Christine Jorgensen. The medical format developed by Christian Hamburger and his associates fifteen years earlier, in Copenhagen, and later improved by Georges Burou in Casablanca, had finally taken root in the United States. Starting with the initiative of this prestigious university hospital, other gender identity clinics and surgical programs would soon be announced. An important prime mover behind the Johns Hopkins team was psychologist John Money.

John Money went on to become one of the world's foremost sex and gender researchers, producing a highly regarded series of books and papers. He also managed to become one of the most controversial gender theorists. His difficulties began with an unusual Canadian case. Serving as a consultant, Money urged the parents of a male infant whose penis had been nearly burned off in a botched circumcision procedure to raise the child as a girl.[12] However, this didn't work out at all well, and by the age of fourteen, "Joan" announced "she" was abandoning the role of a girl in favor of living his life as a boy. For some, the outcome of this case throws light on the question of the relative importance of social learning versus biological influences that shape gender identity. Money was convinced that gender identity could be molded by the "sex of rearing" provided this was imposed in a consistent fashion prior to age two and a-half.[13] This had been done in the John/Joan case, but the extreme discomfort "Joan" felt while trying to live as a girl seems to be a strike against Money's "sex of rearing" theory. Most of his critics have argued that this case may be best interpreted as supporting a biological conception of gender identity.[14]

Chapter 21

Autobiography

During the 1950s, Chris attempted to have Irmis Johnson, the author of the *American Weekly* series, expand those articles into a complete autobiography. However, this was never accomplished.[1] Although Chris repeatedly told reporters that a biography was forthcoming, little beyond the *American Weekly* series had been written. The story of how her autobiography was produced is important, for not only did this book generate considerable cash, it also led to the sale of the motion picture rights. All of this happened at a time when her income had been sharply reduced, and her career future was uncertain. New York book editor/agent Warren Bayless, now retired, explained how this happened.[2] In 1965, Christine appeared in a summer production of *Mary, Mary* at the Red Barn Theater in Northport, Long Island, and there she met red-haired Lois Kibbee, a highly successful actress. Kibbee's mother and uncle, Guy Kibbee, were also well-known show business personalities. Miss Kibbee was better known as a stage, screen, and television performer than as a writer; she had appeared in more than 250 stage productions, including several Broadway plays. She had also been a long-standing regular on two television soap operas, *The Edge of Night* and *One Life to Live*. Her work in television earned her five Emmy nominations, four for acting, and one a shared credit for writing. She also appeared in motion pictures, including the 1980 movie, *Caddyshack*. The 1967 autobiography for Christine was her first book. In 1970, she wrote a biography of Joan Bennett but this attracted little attention. Kibbee died in 1993 at the age of seventy-one.[3]

While performing with Christine, Kibbee became more fully aware of the story of her transsexual transformation, and at a Thanksgiving dinner party hosted by June Bennett Larsen and her husband, she pro-

Becoming a Woman: A Biography of Christine Jorgensen
© 2008 by The Haworth Press, Taylor & Francis Group. All rights reserved.
doi:10.1300/5896_21

vided an animated description of Chris's life story. At the time, Kibbee was not aware that Mrs. Larsen was an assistant to Warren Bayless, head of the literary department of Creative Management Associates. A day or two later, June Larsen enthusiastically told Bayless about her dinner conversation with Kibbee, and proposed that a Jorgensen biography be developed with Kibbee assigned to do the writing.[4] Bayless responded favorably, and Kibbee was asked to write the biography. The next step was to meet with Christine and arrange a contract. June Larsen, who later earned a doctorate in theater history, now lives near Houston. She recalls the first time Christine came to their New York offices:

> I was nervous, waiting for her at the elevator at about 6:15 in the evening. We wanted her to have a private meeting and for her to feel at ease. She came alone, and when the elevator door opened, I was amazed to see a stunning woman, elegantly dressed to the nines, who was unusually beautiful and sophisticated.[5]

Beyond her "stunning appearance," both Bayless and Larsen emphasized that Christine was exceptionally capable in putting those around her at ease. Larsen explained:

> She had a way of dispelling my nervousness, and everyone who met her seemed to gain the same impression. She was very well spoken, intelligent, very well mannered, and she presented herself as a lady of refinement, a very feminine person but also a strong person. There was nothing whatever about her that suggested a man in drag. She was slender and she was dressed elegantly.[6]

Warren Bayless had much experience in the development of book publishing and screenplay proposals, and he worked with both Christine and Kibbee to push the project forward. Soon, Kibbee was at work on the manuscript. Jorgensen and Kibbee seemed to work together easily, although Kibbee complained that Christine virtually refused to provide personal information essential to telling her life story. From time to time, Bayless took Jorgensen aside and explained the importance of including more emotional and personal material in the biography, but "this never seemed to work," Bayless said. "She just didn't want to open up her personal life."[7] When the manuscript was nearly completed, Chris invited Lois to join her along with several family members for a cruise to the Bahamas. The trip was very sociable, but Christine revealed little of her personal life to Kibbee. She was most comfortable providing a history of events, especially comments about the people she had met, show business gigs, and major developments in her life. In addition, she had provided Kibbee with the letters she had written to Dr. and Mrs. Joseph Angelo that gave details of many of her Copenhagen experiences. However, when it came to discussing her innermost feelings, her conflicts, or anything dealing with her sexual life, both Bayless and Kibbee felt she was inhibited and unresponsive. Bayless put it this way: "Christine was very self-protective about her private life, and even after I talked with her about the importance of including some of this in the biography, she shared very little with Kibbee."[8] As work on the manuscript proceeded, Kibbee complained to Bayless and Larsen that she was " . . . not getting the full story . . . " and that "I can only deal with what she is willing to tell me." According to Bayless, Christine wanted to describe George's persistent attraction to men, but on the other hand, she wanted to do so without any implication of sexual behavior. Apparently, Jorgensen's view of these relationships was that the youthful George was experiencing intense love affairs just as a woman would, and therefore they had nothing to do with homosexuality. Rather, it was a matter of a "woman" being in love with a man. Try as she might, Kibbee did not find a key to unlock the inner feelings of her friend.

While Kibbee worked on the manuscript, Bayless contacted a friend at Bantam Books, one of the biggest paperback publishing houses, and proposed that Bantam be assigned the paperback publishing rights in exchange for helping to finance the publication of the hardcover edition. This proved to be an excellent idea, and it helped to put a great deal of money in Christine's bank account. It also led to considerable profit for both the hardback and paperback publishers. Lois Kibbee had promised to complete the manuscript by the end of November 1966 although it was only "sixty percent finished" ten weeks earlier.[9] This may explain why the final chapters of the autobiography seem rushed to a conclusion, and why there doesn't seem to be a real ending.

"We shopped the manuscript to eighteen New York publishing houses," Bayless told me over lunch at Billy Reed's in Palm Springs, "and June Larsen and I became very concerned with all of the negative responses."[10] It seemed that Bayless's innovative approach of having Bantam Books provide some of the hardcover financing did not sit well with some of the major publishers. Unexpectedly, one of Bayless' friends stepped forward to play a critical role. Howard Cady,[11] an editor at the publishing house of David McKay, phoned Bayless and explained that while his firm was not interested in publishing the Jorgensen book, he liked it and he recommended that Bayless contact publisher Paul S. Eriksson. After hearing Bayless's presentation of the project, Eriksson agreed to undertake the publication of the hardback edition. The autobiography first appeared in book stores in September, 1967; soon thereafter, Eriksson escorted Christine on a publicity tour to twenty of the largest cities in the nation.

Paul Eriksson knew he was unlikely to lose money by underwriting the hardcover version of the Jorgensen book. The deal called for him to receive $15,000 from Christine's initial Bantam guarantee of $75,000. He also reasoned that this was the unique story of a major American celebrity with strong name recognition. He saw no negatives in the deal. From Bantam, Christine was to receive additional royalty payments if the paperback edition sold more than 500,000 copies. Additionally, Bantam agreed to pay Christine $25,000 if a feature film was released within three years of the book's publication. Since this did happen, Chris was paid as agreed. Ultimately, she received $100,000 from Bantam[12] and about $30,000 from Eriksson,[13] making the book the most profitable undertaking of her entire career. According to Paul Eriksson, the hardcover edition sold 24,500 copies. The 1974 royalty report from Bantam Books shows the total paperback sales reached 427,000 copies. After expecting a "blockbuster best seller," some of the Bantam people were disappointed despite the financial success of the book. Ever eager to inflate her earning power and her importance as a public personality, Chris told a Hollywood newsman that the Bantam editions of her book had sold two million copies; this was subsequently reported in a Hollywood trade paper.[14] She also informed booking agents and nightclub owners that her performance fees had been increased based on the popularity of the book.[15] For a time, she made it stick, although within a few years her nightclub work would be almost entirely gone. As so many celebrities have discovered, it's hard to stay on top.

On her national publicity tour with Eriksson, Christine gave dozens of newspaper and radio interviews including one for the *San Francisco Chronicle*. She explained that following her surgery she achieved "full sexual satisfaction as a woman," leaving the details to the imagination of the reader. This was almost surely a misleading statement. The reporter added that "Her gestures and her mien were feminine but she did not overdo it."[16]

In early 1971, in accordance with their contract, Eriksson billed Christine for $4,500 representing his percentage of the $25,000 Bantam paid her as additional compensation upon release of the Christine Jorgensen motion picture. Her lawyers responded that nothing was owed Eriksson, although their contract clearly stated what he was due. He then gave serious consideration to suing her, but in the end the matter was dropped. Eriksson's attorneys were certain they could win in court, but the potential recovery was insufficient to justify the litigation.[17] Throughout her life, as seen by Chris, a dispute of this kind was not a contractual problem to be negotiated and resolved. Rather, in her view it often became a question of survival or defeat, right or wrong, decency versus ingratitude. These were the two sides of Christine Jorgensen. In most of her human relationships she was cooperative, helpful, and ready to compromise. She was skilled in working with people in much the same way she had learned to work an audience, relying on warmth, honesty, and self-effacing humor. If this was the Christine you knew, so much the better. But she also had a hostile streak, and she could turn and attack a friend when this was least expected. In this dispute with Eriksson she became dismissive and refused to recognize the considerable investment he had provided to help make her book a success. She even criticized his choice of hotels as "too costly," and found fault with the price of meals during their extensive publicity tour. There is no question that Christine failed to pay him what he was due.

Before long, the same pattern of turning against a close friend and co-worker was shown with Lois Kibbee. Experienced in business matters, Kibbee had an iron-clad contract spelling out exactly what percentage of the gross sales she was to receive from the hardcover copies, the paperback edition, overseas sales, and the possible sale of the film rights. At first, all went well. Kibbee and Christine were on the best of terms, exchanging Christmas cards and expressing concern about the health of various relatives. But when Kibbee's final check for the film rights was sent by Christine, she had withheld $500 from the amount Kibbee's contract required.[18] Kibbee was infuriated. As the level of mutual resentment escalated, and the unkind words began to fly, Christine claimed that Kibbee was supposed to repay her for gifts and for occasional cash she had given her friend. Kibbee replied that all of the gifts had been unsolicited, and that the withholding of money she had earned was unfair. It seems that Lois Kibbee lost both the money and the friendship they had once enjoyed. Jorgensen then telephoned Warren Bayless and demanded that he no longer have anything to do with Kibbee. When he explained that they were already working on another book project she told him their relationship had come to an end. However, by rejecting the help of Bayless in the negotiation of her film deal, Christine almost certainly cost herself many thousands of dollars. Bayless knew a lot more about the structuring of these deals than she did.

The autobiography was an unrevealing historical account of Chris's life through the age of forty, including lengthy descriptions of childhood experiences, some name dropping, extensive quotations of newspaper articles and letters, and thousands of words from the *American Weekly* stories. Little of this illuminated the private side of Jorgensen's life. The book provides a chronological account of what she was doing year by year, the ups and downs of her nightclub act, and various disappointments and high points. Her tax problems are mentioned, but little financial information was included. As previously described, she excluded important events in Denmark that contributed to newspaper publicity in 1952, while offering a coverup story about the origin of the "tip" to the *Daily News*.

Some of Kibbee's description of the youthful George Jorgensen was accurate, but some was not in harmony with the reports of relatives. For example, as noted previously, as a youth George was a "loner" in many social situations, while at other times he showed strong social skills.[19] The childhood story of effeminacy and physical weakness seems overstated by Kibbee. This profile reflected the childhood image of herself that Christine favored: a sad, underweight youth who later overcame every obstacle through fortitude, courage, and a reversal of sex. Her rags-to-riches story required a supposedly traumatic early childhood. In contrast, neighborhood friends and relatives who knew George well during these early years invariably report that he was typically confident, well-spoken, funny, and friendly. And while it's true that following his high school graduation, George jumped from job to job and place to place for about four years, all of this reflected his strenuous efforts to formulate his own identity. George was a work in progress, and once he identified transsexualism as a goal, he plowed ahead, assertively seeking both information and medical assistance. Later, Christine kept her name before the public with the publication of her autobiography and this helped to make her the first surgically reassigned transsexual to hold the attention of the public over several decades. She had become an accidental icon for transsexuality, and she achieved far greater celebrity than any other transsexual.

Following the publication of her book and the death of both her mother and father, Chris decided to make a major change. In 1968, she sold the Massapequa house and moved to Southern California. Gone were the memories of Christmas reunions with the Jorgensens, as she packed her costumes and moved temporarily to Riverside, California. Initially, she stayed with her close friend, Peggy Olsen.[20] The two had met years earlier when Olsen had become a Jorgensen fan. Soon thereafter, Jorgensen and Olsen rented an apartment in Hollywood. For Chris, the sale of her Long Island house meant leaving the trees she had planted in the front yard, which are still thriving, and giving up the handsome cabinetwork built by her father. She wanted to set her course toward a new horizon, to define some new goals, establish a different residence, and more than anything else, to prepare for the next phase of her life. Chris was bored; she wanted new challenges. For all of these reasons, there was great excitement when independent producer, Edward Small, proposed a motion picture based on her autobiography. The proposition arrived at just the right time. It all began with a telephone call from film director Irving Rapper, an associate of producer Small, from Hollywood's Brown Derby restaurant to Warren Bayless in New York City.[21] But since Christine had dropped Bayless as her literary agent, she unwisely negotiated directly with Small.

Chapter 22

The Christine Jorgensen Film

Edward Small was one of Hollywood's most prolific independent producers,[1] although few would recognize his name.[2] Born in 1891, Edward was highly industrious youngster and immediately set about earning what little money he could on the streets of the city. He was drawn to the theaters of Manhattan, hoping to become an actor. At the age of fifteen, Small landed a job in the theater district as a messenger boy, and before long he began to learn the business of representing actors who were seeking theatrical work.

As a young adult, he was offering advice to clients that went beyond simply finding another theatrical job. His view was that an agent should be involved in the selection of theatrical and musical properties, and in bringing together the talents of directors, designers, and actors. Essentially, Edward Small helped to invent the business of a full-service theatrical management company. There was plenty of agency business in New York City, by all measures the theatrical capital of America. But Small looked westward as the earliest film producers in Manhattan packed their gear and moved to Hollywood. He came to Los Angeles in 1923 and built a highly successful agency. He also began investing in Southern California real estate, a tactic that paid off in a string of lucrative investments. At the age of twenty-six Small produced his first silent film: *Who's Your Neighbor?* It earned a profit, and before he died in 1977, he had produced 116 other films. Only a few were memorable, such as *The Man in the Iron Mask,* but nearly all of them were money makers.

In his autobiography, Small wrote that he had seen a television interview with Christine during the mid-1960s and then read her autobiography. "I became intrigued with the battle this game woman had put up," he wrote, ". . . and after meeting her it was hard to imagine

Becoming a Woman: A Biography of Christine Jorgensen
© 2008 by The Haworth Press, Taylor & Francis Group. All rights reserved.
doi:10.1300/5896_22

she had ever inhabited a man's body."[3] Small paid Jorgensen $3,000 for a one-year option for the film rights to her story. He also worked out an extension for a second year by paying her an additional $2,500. As it turned out, he needed the full twenty-four months. The first treatment of a proposed screenplay was written by Malcom Marmorstein, an up-and-coming screenwriter who was a former Broadway stage manager.

As a young man, Marmorstein had helped to stage many highly successful Broadway musicals and plays, including *A Streetcar Named Desire.* Eager to become a screenwriter, he moved his wife and four children to Hollywood and set up an office at Samuel Goldwyn Studios. This was the same building where Edward Small had his offices. Unlike Goldwyn, Small favored a modest office furnished with antiques; he had very few employees. Marmorstein quickly wrote a proposed screenplay that used flashbacks, the creation of three-dimensional characters, and a plot that revealed the major complexities of Christine's story. He envisioned an ambitious and cinematically challenging motion picture. Unfortunately, Small considered his ideas and storyline too complex and too expensive. Marmorstein told me this:

> Eddie thought in terms of showing a doctor in a white coat, holding a pointer, and telling about how an operation was to be performed. . . . He never realized that Christine's story involved more than telling the day by day events of George and Christine in a rather pedestrian fashion. He was a guy who knew how to make money, but he had little interest in trying to make outstanding movies. The sets for the Christine movie looked cheap, but for the same money he could have told the story in a more complex and interesting way, but that just wasn't Eddie's style. He didn't understand that the more subtle psychological aspects of George Jorgensen's transformation into a woman were at the heart of the story.[4]

I also discussed with Marmorstein the love-hate theme that ran throughout Chris's life, especially when she felt mistreated, and he noted the tension between needing to be loved, and having difficulty trusting others.

> Christine was a person who more than anything else wanted people to love her, and to let her know that she was a respected

person. But perhaps her difficulties with trusting others interfered with receiving love. She was never quite sure what people actually thought of her, so sometimes she turned against those who actually cared about her very much.[5]

Marmorstein had quickly put his finger on one of the core personality difficulties that made Christine a far more complex individual than the smiling, glamorous woman she revealed to the public, or the vanilla-like, sexless profile offered by Lois Kibbee. Edward Small had no time for these psychological fine points. After rejecting Marmorstein's proposed scenario, a second script was written by Robert E. Kent and Ellis St. Joseph.[6]

Writing after the Jorgensen film had been released, Small noted that upon meeting Jorgensen he had been impressed by her femininity. He saw her as a totally convincing woman despite her "husky" voice. In planning the production, it was his view that the film would "work" better if Christine's part was played by a man, and so he held auditions for several male actors who aspired to play the leading role. However, he later observed that "Christine Jorgensen made all our male actors look bad."[7] That turned out to be a considerable understatement.

Meanwhile, before the casting had been completed, Chris was campaigning hard for Small to feature a female in the lead role; she urged him to cast Mia Farrow as Christine.[8] Working toward this goal, she urged Harry Benjamin to contact Small and the director, Irving Rapper, in an effort to convince them of the importance of this approach. Benjamin then sent Jorgensen the letter he proposed to send to Rapper and Small. It included this paragraph:

> If a male actor, even if young enough and not too masculine appearing would play your [Christine's] part, it would be most unfortunate . . . the essential message would be wrong; it would be that of a successful female impersonator. . . That is unthinkable [because] . . . a male transsexual is a [real] woman with the wrong anatomy.[9]

Benjamin may have given the matter more thought than Small, for he went on to suggest that the ideal choice of a star would not only be an attractive female, but one who was not known to the audience and who would leave them guessing "is so and so a boy or a girl." As this was going on, Warren Bayless also weighed in with his recommendation, urging that the lead role be played by a woman.[10] Small gave little attention to the advice of others.

After considering many male candidates for the starring role, Small selected John Hansen, a film novice. Small was convinced he was capable of portraying a transformation from an unremarkable male, George Jorgensen, into the feminine and beautiful Christine. Small was aware that Hansen was "huskier than Christine." Indeed, he was far huskier and lacked Christine's attractiveness. In the eyes of most reviewers, Hansen appeared to be a man in a dress. He had almost no theatrical background and had never appeared in a film. Small later wrote that "we had many problems with the Jorgensen picture [and] our truthful narrative sounded like an episode from a soap opera."[11] Actually, his telling of the Jorgensen story was far from the truth. For example, at the end of the movie he showed her marrying her agent which, of course, never happened. Christine assured relatives not to worry, describing several fictitious and misleading scenes as "poetic license."[12]

Small considered the film "only a moderate success."[13] However, as a record of the *Christine Jorgensen Story* or as quality cinema, it was a dismal flop. Edward Small died at eighty-five on January 25, 1977, after a half-century in the motion picture business. As might be predicted, he made money from the film which proved to be his last production.[14] His extensive personal papers and a three-volume biography were donated to the University of Southern California Cinema-Television Library.

At about the time the film was made, Christine rented a spacious two-bedroom Hollywood apartment: North Laurel Avenue, about six miles northwest of the house where she had lived during part of 1947. Close to the Paramount studios where her film was made, she enjoyed the sunny weather and made good use of the oversized swimming pool. Some of the money from the sale of her Long Island home was invested in rental properties in the Northridge area, but according to a close friend, "Christine was a good investor, but not a good landlord."[15] These properties were sold within a few years.

In making the film, most of the interior scenes were done on the historic Paramount lot on Melrose Street. According to the production records, the first location scenes were taken at what was then The Jamaica Inn, a motel overlooking the harbor at Marina del Rey, beginning on October 6, 1969. The final day of filming was eight weeks later, on December 2, 1969, a date slightly later than the one given by Christine.[16] Other location scenes included the Army footage which was shot in Franklin Canyon and the playground scenes filmed at Pointsettia Park, close to the Paramount studios. The many lakeside scenes of a rustic house were taken at Malibu Lake in Ventura County.

The first public showing was in Hollywood on July 18, 1970; the reviews were mostly discouraging. Later that year, when asked her view of the movie, Christine quipped to a reporter: "Well, it isn't *Gone with the Wind*."[17] During the months that followed, Christine traveled to many of the world's largest cities to help publicize the various openings. Her newspaper interviews at this time almost always included a short summary of her life along with answers to questions and a photograph or two. In addition to Small, the key participants in the making of the film were Irving Rapper, Robert Kent, and John Hansen. Ironically, for all except Rapper this movie was their final motion picture assignment. Among those who worked on the film, Rapper's reputation for quality motion pictures was by far the most impressive.

Principals in the Making of the Jorgensen Film

Irving Rapper, Director

Born in London in 1898,[18] Irving Rapper broke into Hollywood as a dialogue director working on twenty-seven films between 1936 and 1941. Just before World War II he was chosen to direct his first feature film, *Shining Victory* (1941). He went on to direct twenty-one other features including many that were highly regarded, including *The Corn is Green* (1945), *Rhapsody in Blue* (1945), *Anna Lucasta* (1949), *The Glass Menagerie* (1950), and *Marjorie Morningstar* (1958). After the *Morningstar* film, he directed five additional pictures including *The Christine Jorgensen Story;* he was seventy-one when Edward Small gave him this assignment. Given his direction of many films of high quality, it would seem likely that producer Small gave him the wrong script, the wrong cast, and the wrong budget for the Jorgensen project. Irving Rapper was capable of directing a far better movie than this one turned out to be. In 1978, at the age of eighty, he directed his final film, *Born Again.* Rapper lived to be 101.

Robert E. Kent (AKA James B. Gordon)

Screenwriter Robert E. Kent was born in the Panama Canal Zone and became a prolific contributor to the world of entertainment as a writer, a producer, and as the composer of the lyrics for two title songs for 1950s films. He was a journeyman, earning screen-writing credits for ninety motion pictures. In all, he participated in the production of forty-one films. All of his work was on so-called B pictures with titles such as *Hot Rods to Hell* (1967) and *Hootenanny Hoot* (1963). Following *The Christine Jorgensen Story* he never wrote another screenplay, but he assisted Edward Small in writing his personal history which remains unpublished at the University of Southern California Cinema-Television Library. Kent died in 1984. His screenwriting co-author, Ellis St. Joseph, died in 1993. One of Kent's literary beneficiaries was James B. Gordon who sustained a membership in the Screen Writers Guild. However, Gordon was not a person; he was Kent's invention.[19]

John Hansen, Actor

Edward Small was frustrated in his search for a male actor who could carry off a convincing presentation of Christine Jorgensen. After several false starts, he met a totally untested nineteen-year-old youth hoping for a big break. He hired John Hansen, described in some newspaper reports as a former member of the Disneyland musical group, Kids of the Kingdom.[20] Hansen lacked any background as a movie actor, but Small liked him and arranged for screen tests with full makeup and costume, both as George and Christine. The still pictures of those tests are part of the Edward Small papers at USC. They show Hansen as a moderately passable, oversized version of Christine.[21]

Given the criticism in reviews of Hansen's portrayal of Christine, along with the benefit of hindsight, it is difficult to understand what guided Small to choose this actor. Christine was a slender five-foot-six and one-half inches, a beautiful woman with the charisma and sophistication of a movie star. Hansen was far heavier and taller, and his efforts as Christine failed to capture her exceptional beauty. Her sparkling appearance undoubtedly contributed to her acceptance wherever she appeared. Publicity releases described Hansen as a former high school quarterback, but regardless of his athletic background, he seemed to have lacked the right body to play Miss Jorgensen. His selection for this role, together with an unimaginative script and modest production values, doomed the picture. Over the following twelve years, Hansen appeared in several television programs and then dropped from the Hollywood scene.[22] When Chris's close friend, Stanton Bahr, spoke with Hansen at Christine's memorial luncheon in 1989, he said he was working in Utah on educational and corporate films. However, a note in a newspaper article concerning Christine's memorial event said Hansen and his wife, Sue, were living in Fullerton, California, and that he was involved in real estate development.

With one or two important exceptions, *The Christine Jorgensen Story* received poor reviews. It was flawed in plot and character development and also in acting and set design. The *New York Daily News* published a searing evaluation:

> Unfortunately, the movie itself is technically a disaster. The dialogue is so bad it is hilarious. The acting is painfully amateurish. John Hansen is very feminine as George, but as Christine, with his football shoulders, he looks more like a man trapped in the body of a woman.[23]

Surprisingly, the *New York Times* liked the picture. The *Times'* film reviewer, Howard Thompson wrote:

> Here is a quiet, even dignified little picture handled tastefully . . . this is essentially a decent film that says a bit and implies much about human courage, sensitivity and plain pluck.[24]

While praising the movie, the *Times* did complain of "an economy of settings." Small, it seems, was used to doing low-budget westerns and using the wide-open spaces for his sets, along with inexpensive location shots on the streets of Los Angeles. *The San Francisco Chronicle* said this: "a fatuous, simplistic bore . . . not overly bright children might make up its preferred audience . . . [it was] hopelessly written [and] moved at a snail's pace."[25]

Daily Variety, didn't think much of the movie but gave it a thumbs up as a potential money maker. Their prerelease headline summary read: "Saga of the first sex change emerges as an unintentionally campy,

1930ish melodrama with enough commercially exploitable curious interest and documentation of the facts to be a profitable programmer."[26]

The Motion Picture Association of America rated the film Restricted (under age seventeen requires accompaniment by parent or adult guardian).

Harry Benjamin, who worked in San Francisco during the summer months, considered the *Chronicle* review so unfair that he drafted a strong rejoinder, but Christine, having learned from Charles Yates not to publicize bad news, urged him to ignore the review, and he did. Christine Jorgensen tried to take the high road when speaking with reporters about the purpose and significance of the movie. "Look at me as a person . . . We made the film to help people better understand transsexualism . . . I want to create a healthier view on [sic] the problems of people like me," she told the *Washington Post.*[27] The article added that Chris "Looks a lot like Lana Turner."

Some of Chris's relatives attended a preview of the movie in Hollywood and after the show the Jorgensen family members went out for dinner. According to one person who was present, Chris poked fun at the amateurish aspects of the film. Several members of the cast had become friendly with Christine during the filming, and as the final days of filming wound down, there was a cast party. The actors who had played members of Chris's family presented her with a large gold poodle pin with an attached gold heart. On one side the heart was inscribed:

> "Love and appreciation for the peace you kept. From the family. November 19, 1969." [On the reverse they had listed their names] Ellen Clark . . . John Hiams (sic) . . . John Hansen . . . Lynn Harper . . . Don Pierce.[28]

In 1971, Chris gave an interview to the *San Francisco Examiner and Chronicle* in which she was described as a "stately lady of middle years."[29] The interview touched on many aspects of her life, including prior engagements and romantic attachments. She made it clear that during her teenage years, before becoming Christine, "I never had homosexual relations with a man. I was always a loner." As we have noted, she gave a different story when Christian Hamburger took her medical and sexual history in 1950. He described the youthful George Jorgensen as having had a homosexual history although he later declined to describe her in those terms. Whenever she was interviewed by the press, she stuck to her story of total sexual restraint, no matter with females or males.

Although Edward Small's movie was relatively inexpensive to produce, it didn't earn a profit and Chris was paid far less than one might expect. Her deal was this: she agreed to be paid a pre-production fee of 3½ percent of the total production cost, plus 10 percent of whatever Edward Small derived from his share of the profit following its international distribution by United Artists. However, the total Chris was eligible to receive from Small's share was limited to $115,000. As previously noted, Warren Bayless assisted Christine in her earliest communications with Small, but he was not involved in her final agreement. He explained that when Jorgensen refused to pay Lois Kibbee the final $500 she was owed, he had sided with Kibbee and "Christine just dropped me . . . it was as simple and as sudden as that." It was Bayless' belief that her contract with Small should have been based on 5 percent of the total production cost, just as he had arranged in several previous book option deals. But since Chris stopped speaking with him and negotiated directly with Small, she wound up with less money than Bayless might have arranged. Finally, Small's share was to be 75 percent of the net profit with United Artists retaining the rest. Such profit would be based on income exceeding all production costs, loans, and distribution expenses.[30]

In 1970, based on the completed screenplay and the recommendation of United Artists, Small obtained a one million dollar loan from a New York bank to underwrite the filming. According to the Superior Court documents submitted by both Small and United Artists in 1977, the total cost of making the film was about $850,000 plus $150,000 Small paid himself as compensation due the producer. Christine was paid her 3½ percent which came to $35,000, and as agreed, the book option payments totaling $5,500 were treated as part of this sum. Chris believed Small had profited from the film and that he still owed her money, but during the early 1970s she was busy with college lecturing, and she took little or no action to clear up the problem. Adding to the misunderstanding, Small may have failed to keep her informed of the financial results from the picture. He later claimed that financial data had been sent to her agent in New York, but that issue was never resolved.[31]

In the early 1970s, Christine had occasionally telephoned Small to complain that she believed additional money was due her. But after he told her that the movie had lost money, and that he had received no income from United Artists, he stopped returning her calls. According to United Artists, the distributor, the gross receipts amounted to $1,544,756 yielding income of $449,823, all of which was said to be expended on distribution expenses. According to Warren Bayless, a distribution expense in this range would seem appropriate given the international distribution of the movie. The reported box office revenue was considerably less than Christine believed had been taken in, although she had no facts to back up her position. The *Daily Variety* reported that the movie finished fifty-seventh in income for 1970 feature films, taking in $1,500,000 which was undoubtedly based on the same financial records later submitted to the court in response to Christine's suit. As a sidelight, the top grossing film that year was *Airport.*[32]

Convinced that Small had not been honest with her, late in 1976, Christine retained an attorney to sue Small and United Artists. Through a friend, she was referred to Moton Holt, a charming, good-looking lawyer trained at Stanford School of Law. He was a friendly and extroverted young man, but he had no experience with suits against major motion picture studios. Earlier in his career, he had served for three years as a corporate attorney for the Union Oil Company; he then went into private practice. Upon meeting Chris to discuss her proposed law suit, Holt impressed her not only with his legal knowhow, but with his ease of conversation and his awareness of national and international affairs. She quickly recognized some of Holt's interesting qualities. For example, his hobby was collecting western history books, paintings, and sculpture. The two seemed to have a lot in common.

Interviewed at his home, Holt, now about seventy and still practicing law, spoke openly while describing both his professional relationship with Christine and the intense romantic relationship that ensued. "We seemed to hit it off right away," he said with enthusiasm, "and very soon our legal discussions included a lot of personal matters including the fact that I was divorced."[33] Christine signaled an interest in dating and soon they became very affectionate. "When I'd appear at her door with flowers or a bottle of wine, she would hold my head firmly with both of her hands and kiss me passionately . . ." Their dating moved from coffee shops and restaurants to dressy evenings at the Los Angeles Opera. Christine was so taken with Holt that she wrote a letter to then California Governor Edmund G. Brown, Jr., urging him to appoint Holt to one of the state commissions; she subsequently received a polite form letter of thanks. Holt was flattered to be dating a beautiful celebrity. "She was always tastefully dressed," he noted, "and for special dates she was very glamorous." He said she told him of her face lift obtained a year or two earlier, and that so far as her breasts were concerned "you should be aware that what you see is not all me." Holt told me Christine had a "great figure," although he thought "her shoulders were a little wide for a woman, and her voice was a bit on the husky side."

In January, 1977, Holt filed Jorgensen's suit in Los Angeles Superior Court seeking various financial reports and possible compensation from United Artists and from the estate of Edward Small. Ironically, Small had died the day the suit was filed. The thrust of the legal initiative was to learn whether Small had received any film profits that Chris was entitled to share. However, no evidence was developed to show this had happened.[34]

Beyond these legal steps, Christine and Holt fell in love with each other, and this became one of the most passionate love affairs of her life. "She was vamping me, and I was falling for her ... we had some very romantic times, and I'll never forget the excitement we both felt when we first kissed," Holt recalled. "But sexually, she was a fragile person, and I don't think she was confident about expressing her own sexuality," he added. "I respected that, and I tried to be a gentleman, but as our relationship heated up, we'd have times when it became very physical—almost leading to going all the way, but not quite. My hands would be all over her and she would be half-undressed. God, it was exciting and I don't know where it might have led ... even to getting married."

Holt explained that on one occasion Christine began to perform oral sex with him and he responded by attempting to have vaginal intercourse. "But she stopped that. It was something she wasn't comfortable doing." Chris explained to Holt that she was sensitive about "lacking a clitoris ... that's what she called the 'trigger or the button' of vaginal excitement ... a topic she constantly brought up. That's why I treated her so gently," he said. As judged by Holt, Christine's self-described lack of a clitoris was at the heart of her sexual inhibition so far as sexual intercourse was concerned. In her many private discussions with him, she remained silent concerning sexual practices with other persons. Holt never learned whether she had a functional vagina. It's entirely possible that she did not, for three years later Chris sought additional vaginal surgery.

Holt told me he saw "two sides of Christine: one was the high-intensity Pearl Mesta-type hostess for her own parties, in a flowing gown and looking a little like Rosalind Russell."[35] The other was a more reflective and quiet person, musing about her feelings, her future, and her impressions of the people she knew. In his view, she needed a good deal of excitement in her life, but on the other hand, she was "tired of the constant hustle of show business. . . . She tried to develop a two-person act with Dorothy Lamour, but nothing ever came of it," he explained, "except some suggestions about improving her costumes." During the year that he was close to her, Holt never observed her drinking heavily except at one of her Fourth of July parties. According to him, she was tight-fisted concerning the money she owed for legal services, yet "she was quite good as a business person in buying cars or real estate." It was his impression that her main source of income at that time was from a "brokerage account."

There had been both television and newspaper coverage of the initial filing of the lawsuit, and so far as Holt was concerned, this welcome publicity was the only benefit to him or Christine. In 1977, attorneys were not permitted to advertise in California, and the considerable newspaper and television coverage gave him substantial public notice. Throughout the final months of 1977 and during 1978, Holt had invested much professional time in the lawsuit, and upon review of the responses from United Artists and Small's estate, he concluded that there was very little likelihood of success and he then urged Jorgensen to drop the case. He advised Christine that if she elected to move ahead in a court battle, it would be essential for her to invest several thousand dollars for expert witnesses to testify about both the financial accounting and the distribution expenses claimed by United Artists, and there was no certainty that such experts would demonstrate United Artists had done anything wrong. However, she was not willing to drop the case. Guarding her cash, Christine failed to pay Holt the retainer they had originally agreed upon, and she also managed to have him absorb the expenses of preparing the case, and also paying the court filing fees and other expenses. "She managed to get me to use my money to cover all the legal costs," sighed Holt. In 1978, she agreed to drop the suit. The case was subsequently dismissed.

Concerning their personal relationship, a complication was that Holt had not terminated another romantic partnership that was deeply meaningful to him, and when he revealed this to Christine, she became furious. Following their breakup, she contacted the State Bar and filed charges against him, claiming that he had failed to complete the legal work for which he was responsible. The Bar investigated her claims but took no action against Holt.[36] He said, "I think her fury was to be expected under the circumstances. It was all about a woman scorned." Their relationship was clearly one of the high points of his life: "I blame myself for the way it ended . . . and despite the unpleasantness, it was a wonderful summer. Perhaps I was a fool, and had we stayed together I really don't know where our love affair might have led." It was Holt's impression that Christine particularly favored a romantic relationship with a "heterosexual man . . . I think it meant something special to her to have a man like me fall in love with her." She told him that several prior love affairs with heterosexual men were just "youthful flings."

If Christine maintained any records of her employment in the 1970s, such documentation has not been found. Perhaps she discarded those files when she moved to Laguna Niguel in the mid-1970s. At this time the nightclub work was much less available, but she was still sending out brochures, writing to agents throughout the country, and calling on some of her old accounts to solicit work.[37] With much less time on the road, Christine hit upon the idea of obtaining representation from one of the agencies that arranged for college speakers. After exploring some options, she signed an exclusive contract with one of the largest agencies; they prepared an excellent sales brochure showing a very youthful and glamorous Christine Jorgensen on the cover.[38] The bookings came in by the dozens, paying roughly $1,000 per campus visit.[39] At that time, a few of the most prominent speakers were getting twice this fee or even a bit more, but Christine was happy to be branching out, meeting large crowds of young people, doing interviews with college newspapers, traveling, and having some fun. As always, the applause was plentiful and it meant a lot to her. These lecture assignments went on for about ten years. In all, she appeared on about thirty college and university campuses.

Christine was an excellent public speaker, grasping the mood of the audience, playing off the events of the day, and making her remarks meaningful to different kinds of audiences. In her talks, Chris made extensive use of humor, a skill that had paid off well throughout her show business career. She was also articulate, well-informed of world events, especially the intense and conflicting attitudes toward the Vietnam War. Marilyn Courtney, a second cousin of Christine's commented: "She had a huge presence. You knew she was there, and that she was the star of the show."[40] Marilyn continued: "At a party, Chris would join in and have a ball, talking all evening to anyone and everyone. After they went home, she'd analyze each one, and then she'd comment on what made each person stand out."[41]

A business activity that brought diversity to her life throughout the 1970s and 1980s involved the purchase and resale of houses. Chris bought several houses near university campuses and rented them to students. The real estate market kept rising during the decade of the 70s, and she made a profit buying and selling properties, often in the San Fernando Valley. But seeing little reason to live in Hollywood, in 1975 Chris and Peggy Olsen decided to buy a home about an hour's drive down the coast from Los Angeles. Her parents had always explained that owning a home was far wiser than paying rent.[42]

Chris missed living in the spacious house her father had built in Massapequa, and she was delighted to find an impressive, large, home in Laguna Niguel. A deal was struck and the escrow papers and financing were completed. But within a month she received an offer from an eager buyer to purchase the home at a substantial profit. "Sold," said Christine, switching into her real estate sales persona, and she set about to buy a different residence having duplicate two bedroom wings separated by an atrium entry. Peggy looked after her side of the house and Chris took care of hers; they divided the cost of the mortgage and the upkeep. The relationship between Jorgensen and many members of the Olsen clan was as close, or perhaps even a bit closer, than the ties between Christine and her own family. Brenda Lana Smith, who lived with Christine during the final six months of her life, explained it as follows:

> Peggy's daughter, her grandchildren . . . and their friends in Riverside became CJ's often visited surrogate family . . . unlike the relationship I observed between CJ and her sister and nieces . . . it was a familial environment where, poorly or not, CJ harmoni-

ously felt she was not obligated to live up to the 'Christine Jorgensen Myth' . . . Peggy's home was a home away from home to CJ. . . .[43]

Smith may have been unrealistic about how much time the East Coast Jorgensen family members could spend with Chris on the West Coast. A few years later, facing some health problems, Peggy moved back to the Riverside area where her family lived, and Chris bought her share of the residence. Initially, there was some misunderstanding about the compensation that Peggy deserved, but unlike some of her other financial disputes, this was quickly ironed out between the two longtime friends.

During the 1980s, Christine looked for ways to reduce her monthly expenses, which had never been lavish. She consistently sought tenants to occupy the side of her home Peggy Olsen had lived in, but few remained longer than a year. During the 1984 Olympics she advertised rooms at "Casa Christine" which she described as a homelike alternative to the far more costly hotels of Los Angeles. Money was a concern; she was living on the interest from funds that had been set aside for her retirement.

Chapter 23

Retirement and Illness

Marilyn Courtney, an attractive Brooklyn real estate agent and interior design color consultant dined with me at the Beatrice Inn on 12th Street in Greenwich Village where Christine had dined often, and where Marilyn is treated like a member of the family.

Marilyn traveled on vacations to Hawaii with Chris, and in 1984 she accompanied her on the trip to Copenhagen for the making of the documentary film, *Paradise Is Not For Sale*. In Denmark, she had several opportunities to visit with Christian Hamburger and to meet Georg Stürup, who was not in good health. She described Hamburger as "a jolly gentleman . . . very dignified and devoted to his golden retriever . . . he loved to take his dog everywhere with him . . . he was a dedicated medical researcher and also a sculptor."[1] She showed me a photograph of one of his sculptures of a human form that was almost as tall as Marilyn.

As a small child, Marilyn, a relative of Christine's, and her sisters often spent vacation days at Chris's Massapequa home, playing dress-up with Christine's costumes and pretending to be royalty while wearing her oversized jewelry. She hosted birthday parties for her nieces and cousins in her backyard and invited many of the Jorgensen relatives. Marilyn especially remembered her aunt as a "generous, warm and out-going person . . . a real lady, who cared deeply about all the members of her family." Having attended several of Christine's nightclub performances, she noted that when men occasionally poked fun at her, "she knew how to put them in their place, and that was the end of the rude remarks." She told me none of the family ever thought of Chris as having been a homosexual youth, and that "when I traveled to Hawaii with her as a young adult, I still didn't even know what a gay person was." Years earlier, her father had told her of the scene when Chris returned to New York in 1953:

> She went to Denmark as a young man, and when she came back she was a whole new person, with not only a different appearance, but with a new personality. Chris quickly put the family at ease.[2]

But learning that George Jr. was now his daughter was difficult for the senior Jorgensen, according to what her mother had told her. Marilyn put it this way:

> Her father was devastated and it was all a big adjustment for him, but they loved their child and they were very supportive of Christine. She made a wonderful home for them on Long Island and later, her mother became her secretary and business manager.[3]

Commenting on family relationships, she told me that Chris's sister, Dolly "was a far more socially reserved person than Christine . . . she never went to nightclubs . . . her relationship with Chris was sometimes a little tense, but they really loved each other." All of the living relatives emphasize Christine's love for her family and her eagerness to have family members accompany her on trips, both within this country and overseas. "Christine was very old fashioned in the way she cooked, kept house, did needlepoint, and she really loved to read American history, especially the theories of the Kennedy assassination," Marilyn said. "We became her children."[4] Marilyn learned of Christine's Denmark experience from finding old movie magazines in her basement telling the whole story and providing before and after pictures. "It didn't change a thing because everyone who knew Chris just treated her entirely as they would any other female member of the family,"[5] added Marilyn.

One of Christine's goals from the time she first returned to New York in 1953 was to hold out the promise of a better life for other transgendered people. This was one of the main reasons she met often with endocrinologist Harry Benjamin and enlisted his assistance in responding to correspondence from persons seeking guidance or medical referrals. In later years, Marilyn became aware of her aunt's concerns for others: "She came to see how some transsexuals wanted to be on a fast track and cut corners in preparation for making a change, and that worried her a lot."[6] Moving to a different topic, Marilyn explained: "It was hard for me to watch Chris grow older. I felt she was smoking way too much."[7]

She strongly emphasized that "Chris always wanted to be taken seriously as a person and never to be seen as some kind of a freak." Although she met many celebrities throughout her show-business life, Marilyn said her aunt valued the times with family members the most. In some important way, according to Marilyn, Chris was quite different from her sister. She put it this way:

> Dolly was very religious and she had a very normal home life. Dolly always avoided conversations about the show business side of Christine's life, preferring to stick to family matters.[8]

In correspondence, Dolly always addressed her sibling as "Chris," and never questioned the legitimacy of her transsexualism. A dedicated genealogist, Dolly wrote an award-winning history of the Jorgensen family that included names, birth dates, children, and other facts about all of the family members, and in this book she invariably refers to Chris as Christine Jorgensen. Whatever their ups and downs, Dolly was a peacemaker and one who stood up for what she believed in, while always striving to pour oil on troubled waters. Just weeks before Chris's death, she flew to Southern California from her home in the East to assist her to put her affairs in order. One of the things Dolly did was to convince Chris that her niece would have difficulty serving as executor of her estate since she had small children and was living on the East Coast. Christine agreed, and a close relative of Peggy Olsen accepted this responsibility. As our conversation wound down, Marilyn had one final thought: "Oh, I do remember that my father told me that when he knew Chris as a teenager, he was more introverted, but when she returned from Denmark she was a whole, new, more outgoing personality."[9]

Peggy Olsen's health problems may have motivated Chris to think about her own mortality, and to seek out the Neptune Society in 1979. This is an organization providing low-cost cremation services. At this time, Chris was in good health. I discussed Chris's "pre-necessity planning" and her contract with the Neptune Society with the executor of her estate, asking why she would have been likely to make arrangements for her own cremation ten years before her death. His answer was direct and humorous: "Well, if you really knew Christine Jorgensen you wouldn't even have to ask. Of course she'd do that, even without any need to do so."[10]

Christine received an exciting offer in 1981 inviting her to do a two-week gig at Freddy's, an intimate night spot in Manhattan. The New York newspaper publicity for her Freddy's performance referred to this as a "comeback," but whether she had actually sought a show business "comeback" is very questionable. She was not actively seeking additional bookings and she wasn't represented by an agent. Her two week run at Freddy's was successful, but mainly as a Manhattan nostalgia event.

She arranged for a videotaping of her Freddy's performance, providing a full-color record of her finest self-designed costumes, sparkling as always, her oversized necklaces, bracelets, and rings, and her shining golden hair with carefully interwoven extensions and falls. These were all performance devices she had long relied upon. The videotape of this performance is among her photographs and other films including a copy of her documentary, *Denmark,* at the Danish Royal Library.[11] The opportunity to perform again in Manhattan must have been exhilarating, even triumphant. As always, she loved receiving the applause of the audience when her accompanist played "Welcome to My World," a song he had composed for Christine thirty-one years earlier. She was back as a headliner in the core of the Big Apple. It was her world and it was where she was most comfortable. Could she have possibly foreseen her show business career spanning almost three decades when she met that noisy press gathering at Idlewild airport on a cold, breezy morning in February 1953?

On her opening night at Freddy's, a table close to the small stage bubbled with the joyous chatter of twelve of her many cousins, some of whom had never seen her perform.[12] Others, however, had enjoyed playing dress-up with her costumes during summer visits to the Massapequa house, or joined her for cruises or trips to Hawaii. Her relatives loved the show, but one of the most important reviews was respectful, but cool. This unsigned review is from a March 1981 newsletter written for nightclub booking agents.

> Her act comprises song and story. The singing is not far removed from a conversational patter. Her pipes do not always do the bidding of the music, but in this room, it seems acceptable. She has brought on the stage a screen, behind which she makes about five

changes of costume, displays comedy props and does impressions. Her garb switches are of the onion type: each layer is peeled off and draped around her shoulders. It works out effectively with feathers and boas around the head and shoulders. She also tells show biz stories between tunes. However, it's at the end of the act when she asks for questions that her performance begins to take on greater interest. She answers questions frankly and entertainingly. The article notes that Christine has not been on the nightclub circuit for "many years," that she has been speaking on the college circuit, and that now, at 55, she is "again trying her hand at variety." Summing up: "She is not a singer, but she speaks entertainingly and toward the end, deeply and frankly. It is better material for the college than the cafe circuit. Bill Lockwood is her accompaner [sic] at the piano."[13]

After a performance at Freddy's, Chris relaxed by having a cigarette and a few drinks with her fans, many of whom had followed her career for years.[14] For Christine, the respect and kindness shown to her at Freddy's was like a capstone for a career that had played such an important part in helping her prove to herself that she had earned the respect of others. In fact, she had come to not only feel respected by people everywhere, but to have developed a strong feeling of pride and self-esteem from her many years of successful performance on the public stage. The personal uncertainties, the self-doubts, the shame and guilt of her teen years, all had been washed aside along the show business trail. She loved the applause, the friendships, and the financial rewards, all entwined with some late-hour drinking and clouds of cigarette smoke. During the early 1980s, she appeared for a week or two in several small nightclubs throughout Southern California, but her career as a performer had essentially ended.

Although the billing of Christine Jorgensen could draw an audience in nearly any part of America and in many other parts of the world, both her importance as a celebrity and her novelty as a transsexual faded during the 1980s. As the footlights dimmed, her personal life also became less rewarding. Worse, some of the pleasures she had long enjoyed, smoking and drinking, started to become an unhealthy accompaniment of her daily experience. But she continued to give high priority to her walks with friends, especially the gay men she had always enjoyed as her buddies and drinking partners. Chris also gave much time to staying in touch with her family, but the driving force that had kept her so happily in the spotlight for three decades, the direct approval she received from live audiences, was gone for good. It was not simply the loss of applause that she missed: it was also the loss of the emphatic reminders that she was not only an approved person, but a beloved person, that hurt her so much. Christine had long been a chain smoker and her occasional binge drinking dated back to her job-searching days in Hollywood in the late 1940s. But now, the smoking and drinking were becoming forces in her life that, while obviously important to her, made Chris a far less attractive person to be around.

One very close friend explained that after about 1980, Chris often started drinking soon after she got up, usually in the late morning, and that she would have a drink in her hands during much of the remainder of the day and into the evening; she was smoking several packs a day.[15] Chris could become nasty, hostile, and mean when she was drinking. Several of her friends called it a pattern of becoming "bitchy" after too much Scotch or vodka. During this period, according to one eye witness, when she was about to board a flight to San Francisco for a talk show appearance "she was obviously a little drunk, and she complained about everything."[16] Once aboard the aircraft, "she continued to drink and when we took a cab into the City, she insisted that the driver stop at a liquor store so she could buy several bottles of booze." That evening, her friend explained, Chris was the guest of honor at a party hosted by a well-known psychologist where she proceeded to drink a good deal more, then raised her voice in anger to tell her host that he was not behaving properly in his sex life. "She was cursing, screaming, shouting, and raking her host over the coals in front of many guests because she didn't approve of his boyfriend at the time."[17] In contrast, no one ever mentioned that any of her public appearances or show business performances had been compromised by alcohol. Stanton Bahr,[18] her Long Island buddy, said she always tried to refrain from drinking until sundown, but there are many indications that the control of alcohol intake became a more serious problem during the final five or six years of her life. It even interfered with some of her highly valued family relationships.

In 1984, Copenhagen entrepreneur and documentary film maker, Teit Ritzau, wrote Chris asking her to participate in a transgender film. She replied in a short, handwritten letter that she'd like nothing more than to "walk the streets of Copenhagen again."[19] This was an undisguised way to encourage an invitation to Denmark. Ritzau had received a grant for the making of the film and after inviting her he rolled out the red carpet, paying for travel and booking her into a very expensive hotel. He had arranged for her to be met at the airport by Dr. Georg Stürup. Chris had been asked to bring contracts, documents of all kinds, old passports, and photographs for possible use in the documentary. But Ritzau was surprised at the cost of air freight for the many boxes she'd brought, weighing over 100 pounds. It was these materials that became the first of three donations of Jorgensen papers to the Danish Royal Library.[20]

Ritzau's documentary film contrasted Christine's story with that of a cross dresser, then concluded with an interview with a female to male transsexual. Psychiatrist Preben Hertoft was a consultant and co-author of a book that accompanied the film. The shots of Christine simulating her nightclub act reveal her well out of practice, singing a bit off key, and weighing considerably more than she did three years earlier at the Freddy's gig. The footage is of interest as it shows her at the end of her career, and this performance, shot in a Copenhagen nightclub that Ritzen had rented for a sound stage, may be among the last motion pictures of her in performance. In Ritzau's staged nightclub "audience" were many of her Danish relatives, Miss Elsa Sabroe, and some of the medical personnel who had assisted her thirty-one years earlier. Unfortunately, copies of *Paradise Is Not For Sale* have not been available for many years. Ritzau had hoped one of the American cable networks would air the documentary, but some considered it too sexy and off-beat, while others wrote it off as not sexy enough. The copy I viewed is owned by Dr. Preben Hertoft.

The Danish Royal Library was established by the King of Denmark in the middle of the seventeenth century and has grown into a major national treasure. It houses information resources unmatched by the finest libraries of many countries far larger than Denmark. The library is located at the waterfront on the site of a historic naval facility on Copenhagen's east side. While the physical facilities have changed a good deal over the past 350 years, it is still located close to where it began. The new building is a five-year-old "glass jewel" along the waterfront, and it is considered one of the architectural masterpieces of modern Europe.

In 1984, the library director, upon learning from Dr. Hertoft of Jorgensen's possible interest in leaving her personal papers and photographs in Copenhagen, arranged a display depicting the Christine Jorgensen life story, and adjoining this, a parallel display of Hans Christian Andersen, one of Denmark's most honored authors.[21] This tactic, of course, was an undisguised but entirely successful attempt to charm Christine and encourage the gift of her personal papers. It worked. When Christine visited the temporary display in the foyer of the old library, she was highly impressed to discover the distinguished company with whom she had been placed. The first installment of her personal papers and photographs were then donated, and she may have unrealistically believed that some kind of Christine Jorgensen Room would be established. According to Hertoft, this was not something that had been promised. Christine tended to believe that she was an exceptionally important historical figure.[22] A second batch of materials that had been used in the documentary film was contributed in 1985 at the urging of Preben Hertoft. Following Chris's death in 1989, a final set of materials was assembled by Brenda Lana Smith, her housemate during the final six months of her life, and this was sent to the Royal Library in accordance with Christine's wishes. Unfortunately, while the collection is very extensive, it does not include much material dealing with Chris's personal life or family correspondence. It is not likely these materials have survived.[23] While Christine was careful to preserve hundreds of pieces of memorabilia, newspaper articles, receipts, theater programs, family snapshots, and matchbook covers, it is likely that she destroyed all of the correspondence with her parents. Whatever the truth of the matter, these materials do not appear to exist. At the time of her mother's death, Chris's personal correspondence would almost certainly have been at the Massapequa home they shared. We are left to wonder whether these papers survived until Mrs. Jorgensen died, and if they did, what ultimately was done with them.

Chris was very reliable about sending birthday and Christmas cards to her friends and relatives, and thank-you notes as well. But the few letters that have survived were seldom for family members and very few of them reveal anything personal. Among her papers there are very friendly but businesslike letters to Alfred Kinsey, Harry Benjamin, Christian Hamburger, Georg Stürup, and Louise Lawrence,[24] but they reveal nothing of the personal, emotional life of Christine.

The most candid letters she wrote, which reveal her handling of anger, were sent to attorneys, tax consultants, actress-writer Lois Kibbee, publisher Paul Eriksson, filmmakers Teit Ritzau and Edward Small, and the doctors who were trying to help her with her cancer problems. These letters reveal more of Chris as the angry, demanding, somewhat childish, accusatory, litigious, and unpleasant person that she became when frustrated by what she perceived as unfairness. The irritation and threats she revealed in this correspondence, often compounded with her own poorly formulated legal opinions, seldom, if ever, led to any financial gain although they surely served to ventilate her feelings.

Her dealings with Ritzau offer another example of how Jorgensen sometimes expressed intense anger toward a colleague who had befriended her. In 1986 Chris was trying to develop a television special about her life story based on a so-called "no-holds-barred" interview. Supposedly, she would tell all of her long-hidden secrets. Upon writing her proposal, she realized some of the materials she had donated to the Danish Royal Library might be of value. However, when she wrote to Ritzau and Hertoft asking them to help her retrieve some of the personal papers given to the Royal Library, they explained that this was against the policy of the library. Christine became furious with Ritzau who had published a book to go along with his documentary:

> Concerning your book, I never gave you permission to use any photos or letters . . . you simply took what you wanted . . . Please do not breach my contract or you will force me into other actions. I am seriously considering canceling my permission for the Royal Library to have my archives . . . You may show this letter to Preben [Hertoft]. He is also involved.[26]

Despite her threats aimed at Ritzau, Christine soon dropped the matter; none of the donated materials were returned, and as so often happened, the "no-holds-barred" television proposal never saw the light of day. This became another example of the many conflicts that ripped apart some of Chris's relationships.

A tradition Christine enjoyed very much was her annual "Christmas in July" party. Her close friend, Stanton Bahr, told me she'd gotten the idea for this event from him. For several years, all of her many friends would be invited to her home for this party. They would fill the garden room along the entire rear of her home, spilling into the back yard. The conversation was lively along with plentiful food and beverages. The guests included friends, relatives, a few transsexuals, many neighbors, some newspaper columnists, and numerous show business people. Chris knew the importance of keeping your name in the news, and of stimulating possible sources of employment, so parties like this were a way to keep in touch with her extensive list of friends. She was a lively hostess and the star of her own parties. Usually, there would be over 100 guests, including a few gay and lesbian activists with whom she had worked on AIDS prevention projects. There were also people interested in supporting public libraries, and a few social workers and psychologists, but it was mainly a show business crowd. Large parties, like the Christmas in July event, exemplify Chris's extroversion and her enjoyment of people. One niece put it this way: "Christine was always a party waiting to happen."[26]

One of her closest friends was a transsexual lady, Sister Mary Elizabeth, whom she had met in the early 1980s. Formerly married and the father of a son, Sister Mary Elizabeth has the unique history of having served in the Navy for seventeen years before being involuntarily discharged when she began taking female hormones. Then, after being trained as a paralegal, she was recruited to join the U.S. Army Reserve where she served about a year-and-one-half. While in the Reserve, she performed personnel duties not unlike the Fort Dix assignment of Pfc. George Jorgensen forty years earlier. Upon joining the military she had provided a full account of her transsexual status, and of course, passed the induction physical examination. She liked her assignment, and her work record was excellent, but she was again involuntarily discharged a few months before her twenty-year pension was earned. Higher authorities had decided that she should not have been inducted. Sister Mary Elizabeth recalls[27] lending Christine "my old combat boots and some of my women's army uniform . . . " for her performance either in 1983 or 1984 at Anaheim's Grand Dinner Theater. Again on stage, Christine used her quick-change routines with break-away costumes, darting behind a screen and emerging with a new costume. The show was well received. This was one of her final theatrical performances.

During this period, the ever-rising cost of home ownership along with her modest monthly living expenses stretched Chris's cash flow to the breaking point. As we've noted, she was relieved to have housemates who would share the expenses. In the mid-1980s, as her health problems grew more serious, she asked her close confidant, Stanton Bahr, to marry her with the hope of acquiring better health insurance than she was capable of purchasing.[28] The plan was seriously considered by each, but for various reasons her health insurance difficulties would not have been resolved by such a marriage, and the matter was dropped. Chris and Bahr never applied for a marriage license, but he was ready to become her husband if this would have afforded her better health insurance. After describing this, Bahr asked: "What are friends for?"

By the end of 1984, Christine was looking for ways to reduce her fixed expenses, so along with other economies she withdrew from membership in Actors Equity.[29] Her dreams of a Broadway or Hollywood theatrical career had not been realized, and she was feeling a financial pinch since both her nightclub and college speaking gigs had ended. She had been very frugal in some ways, while at other times she seemed capable of spending substantial sums while barely aware of it. Stan Bahr, who supported her as closely as any family member, put it this way:

> She was just not good at handling money. People were always asking her to invest, in a restaurant, a chain of beauty shops, and even a medical practice, but these all lost money. She made some good real estate investments, but she didn't hold on to those properties.[30]

After returning from her 1984 documentary filmmaking in Copenhagen, Chris wrote to Bahr to say she had decided to put her house up for sale. Feeling at loose ends, she wanted to make a major change, but she had no real plan of what the next move might be. She had considered living in Europe for a few years, or possibly moving to Florida. Christine seemed uncertain of what she wanted in her future, or where she might live, but as it turned out, she did not put her house up for sale until the summer of 1986. She explained in her 1984 letter to Bahr[31] that she was planning to ask $225,000 for her home, a substantial price at the time. Her letter asked him for his suggestions about her next step, and whether they might buy homes in Florida close to each other. A few Jorgensen relatives were on the West Coast, but there were also some in Florida.

Throughout 1985, Christine was living in her Laguna Niguel home, actively recruiting renters to take responsibility for one side of the house. This 3,000-square-foot residence was more than a place to live. It symbolized two important things. First, her home helped to sustain her conviction that she was a significant public figure deserving respect and admiration. This was a spacious home for a distinguished and successful person. Chris thought of herself as ranking in importance alongside the most honored of the nation's high achievers, such as Dr. Jonas Salk, who lived a few miles further down the coast in La Jolla. Speaking to friends, she compared her fame to his more than once. She had been highly successful as a nightclub entertainer and as a college lecturer, and she viewed this elegant home as evidence of her success. Her assets were far greater than any other members of the Jorgensen family, and her spacious, sun-filled home helped to remind her that she had achieved both fame and respectability. Second, the Laguna Niguel property also symbolized financial and personal security at a time when she was beginning to feel a monthly financial squeeze, in part due to troubling medical bills. For this world traveler, her home in a neighborhood of handsome properties signified the stability, public recognition, and sense of importance she had worked so hard to achieve. She loved her home, but all of this was coming to an end.

During the early months of 1986, Chris continued to take long walks with her gay friends and she spent many afternoons in the bars of Laguna Beach, drinking and sharing stories with her many friends. But this lifestyle was stretching her monthly income to the breaking point, and that summer she put her house up for sale. It sold for $225,000.[32] Chris rented a comfortable three-bedroom apartment in San Clemente, a charming coastal community close to Laguna Niguel, and not far from President Nixon's former estate overlooking the Pacific. Compared to her former residence, Christine told her niece that she considered it "ticky-tacky."[33] It was not "tacky," but it was a major adjustment from living in the home she had loved. With little expectation of any new source of income, Christine was giving more attention to her investments and the control of her expenses. Although the apartment was a big step down from her former home, it was much more economical than owning a residence.

But for Christine, the highly disturbing changes in her life went beyond moving to a new place to live. Without warning, she noticed blood in her urine. She then telephoned Sister Mary Elizabeth to obtain a referral to a physician, and soon thereafter she was diagnosed with cancer of the bladder. At once she began a therapeutic regimen involving medication and chemotherapy. Home alone, she fell and broke her arm resulting in a quick trip to an emergency room. Very soon, a dispute arose concerning the medical evaluation and treatment of this injury. Chris directed her attorney to bring suit against some of her doctors and the hospital where she had been treated; this legal action made the newspapers, but the case was later dropped.[34]

At the outset of these health difficulties, Chris kept trying to stir up some business with the help of her friend, Christopher Basinger, a devoted fan. They tried to develop a television project based on the theme of Hollywood Legends. Her idea was to present biographies of major Hollywood figures of the past, but like many story proposals in the film capital, the project did not get off the ground. Ironically, in February of 1986 Christine bought forty-six orchestra seats at Los Angeles' Ahmanson Theater to entertain a group of her friends at a musical production called "Legends" which had nothing to do with her earlier project. It was her way to thank many close friends. Now and then, Christine enjoyed making a grand gesture. It served to signal her power, her status, and the breadth of her many friendships.

In June 1986, Christine was interviewed for a *Los Angeles Times* article designed to bring the public up to date about her life. Her health was not the main topic, although she was already seriously ill. Chris managed to again mention how "shocking" it had been to supposedly have some disloyal person reveal her story of transsexuality to the *New York Daily News* in 1952. As she had so many times before, she told the reporter that she couldn't imagine who would do such a thing.[35] Throughout the following year, living alone, she continued a series of cancer treatments including additional chemotherapy. During that year, the press learned of her cancer and in an optimistic interview Chris told a newsman she was "going to beat it."[36] She concluded the interview optimistically: "If I die tomorrow, I wouldn't think life owed me anything."

In February 1988, Christine agreed to be a luncheon speaker at the second national meeting of the International Foundation for Gender Education. Chris only requested one thing for this Chicago meeting: an ample supply of liquor was to be provided. Dressed attractively and in high spirits, Chris's luncheon speech sparkled with timely humor, often poked fun at herself as well as the audience of 150 cross dressers, then ended in a surprising finish as she proclaimed: "and remember, I'm the only person in this room to have a legitimate reason for wearing a wig!"[37] She then flipped off her wig revealing a near-bald head amid the roaring cheers and applause of the men in dresses, nearly all of whom were wearing wigs. She had imitated the classic culmination of many female impersonation acts from the days of vaudeville.

Physically, mentally, and emotionally, life became more difficult for Christine during 1988, although she was determined to mobilize her strength and collaborate on an autobiography encompassing her entire life. She wanted to title this: *After the Ball.*[38] She viewed this as an important unfinished work, and she believed there was a story to be told that should be revealed. A New York literary agent put her in touch with Raymond Strait, a former cabaret singer who had written several biographies of Hollywood personalities, including Bob Hope, Rosemary Clooney, and Abbot and Costello. Years earlier, Strait had been a personal assistant to Jayne Mansfield for more than a decade. He and Chris agreed to tape record a series of interviews to be used as the core of a biography, and, hopefully, to divide any proceeds from the publication of a book. At this point, I assume Christine was more concerned about her place in history than in earning money from a biography. As she had done previously, Chris referred to this as a "no holds-barred" account of her life, but Strait soon found that she had little to say that had not been previously told. When he asked personal questions, especially concerning her romantic relationships, Chris waved him off, saying, "that's something I don't intend to get in to."[39] Working together for several sessions in her San Clemente apartment, Strait was surprised by her appearance. To him she appeared:

> Frumpy . . . like a school marm except that she preferred to wear shorts and a T-shirt . . . and she was extremely paranoid. She was worried that I'd ask a question, then after she'd respond, I'd say "Gotcha," and she was also worried whether I had been followed to her apartment. She didn't want people to know where she was living.

All of their interviews took place while Chris was ill, although no one realized she had only a few months to live. It is understandable that since Strait had met her under the most difficult circumstances she had ever faced, he saw a less patient, less cordial, less attractive and more complaining Christine than she had been before her illness. "She seemed to me an aging, bitter woman who resented that she had not been accorded the fame and recognition she believed was coming to her," he said. Chris became increasingly impatient in her dealings with Strait and following an argument she insulted him. He then told her off and the relationship ended.[40] Chatting with me at lunch, Strait explained: "She repeatedly compared herself to some of the most famous American heroes and scientists." Soon thereafter, she directed her attorney, Donald Segretti, of Watergate fame to have Strait send her his tape recordings which Strait refused to do.[41]

It would be a mistake to assess Raymond Strait's impressions of Chris without recognizing her health difficulties. Throughout her life, those who knew her described a far more engaging and generous person than Strait came to know. But it is important that even when her illness is taken into account, Christine revealed her sense of not being fully appreciated for what she believed she had accomplished as a transsexual pioneer.

Chapter 24

The Final Year

Christine may have overestimated her own importance as a national icon, confusing her fame as the first celebrity transsexual with the high esteem a nation may accord its most distinguished citizens. Her name will always be linked to the early medical management of transsexuality, and her perseverance and courage in quest of the dream to achieve a new identity as a woman should not be discounted. But an honest assessment of her celebrity would not put her close to the recognition America accords its most famous citizen-heros.

As a nationally recognized personality, Christine Jorgensen's flame burned with exceptional brilliance for about thirty years, but her fame was entirely attributable to her popularity as a transsexual entertainer, not her singing, dancing, or acting. She lived an exemplary public life, and she had good reason to feel a sense of pride as a transsexual pathfinder. It is therefore unfortunate that toward the end of her life she looked back with disappointment, convinced that the honors and recognition that were due had never been delivered. Putting aside the decades of high earnings, a motion picture film that had honored her, and her success as a college and university speaker, a voice inside of Chris told her all of that was not enough. In her view there had never been sufficient recognition and proof of her respectability. Perhaps in the recesses of her mind were distant echoes of the kids in the Bronx, teasing and taunting her, and calling her "Goose." She seems to have experienced a somewhat disappointing quest for proof of respectability; all the applause and all the money had not been enough.

Chatting with Stan Bahr in an ice cream shop in Massapequa fifteen years after Chris's death, I asked him if there were any unfulfilled aspirations she might have shared with him. "No," he first explained, and then he added: ". . . she might have hoped to receive

Becoming a Woman: A Biography of Christine Jorgensen
© 2008 by The Haworth Press, Taylor & Francis Group. All rights reserved.
doi:10.1300/5896_24

some kind of formal recognition from the nation of Denmark, like Brenda Smith did—maybe some sort of title or something like that, and now and then she commented on whether she would merit a star along the Hollywood Boulevard Walk of Fame." Stan added: "She could have had the star, but it would have called for an investment of about $5,000."[1]

Toward the end of 1988, Christine urged Sister Mary Elizabeth to share her three-bedroom San Clemente apartment and to help pay the rent and other expenses, but at the time, Mary had made other arrangements in the Midwest.[2] Instead, Mary suggested she invite a friend, Brenda Lana Smith, to join her. Christine had never met Brenda, an English-born, genial, fifty-five-year-old resident of Bermuda, who had lived in Southern California during her gender transition and re-assignment surgery four years earlier. In Bermuda, Brenda had served as the honorary Danish Consul for a decade, services for which Queen Margrethe II would bestow a knighthood in 1979. The title is: Ridder af Dannebrogorden. Roughly translated, this means Knight of Denmark. Brenda Lana Smith's own story has some interesting twists and turns.

Writing years later, Brenda Smith described herself as having been a lifelong closeted cross dresser with an unremitting feminine gender identity that culminated with her undergoing male-to-female genital reconstruction in 1984. A longtime resident of Bermuda, her twenty-nine-year marriage had ended in divorce, and she was also estranged from her son and daughter. Brenda hoped to become an American citizen or legal resident alien. Hence, for all of these reasons the idea of coming here to assist Christine appealed to her. With the encouragement of Sister Mary Elizabeth, a series of telephone calls were made to Christine, mainly at the initiative of Brenda Smith, who had never met Jorgensen in person. After several conversations conducted over fourteen months, Christine invited Brenda Lana to move in to one of her three bedrooms and to share some of the living expenses. Upon arriving in southern California, Brenda learned that the housing arrangement she preferred was not available. Therefore, somewhat as a "happenstance," after giving Christine very short notice, Brenda arrived on her San Clemente doorstep on October 18, 1988. It was not Brenda's top priority, but the arrangement proved helpful to both. They dined that evening at a fine restaurant, The Rose and Crown, and a close friendship developed.

The appearance of Chris's apartment concerned her new friend: She found it "unkempt" with newspapers and crossword puzzles scattered everywhere, and the "well-worn furniture" somewhat threadbare. What distressed Brenda most was something Chris had not mentioned: her bladder cancer had spread to her right lung and she appeared to be "far from well."[3] Chris explained that she had been driving herself to Mission Viejo Hospital for "deep radiation treatments." The following morning, after arising four hours before Chris came to breakfast, Brenda took stock of her surroundings. There was much evidence that Chris had been drinking heavily, just as Brenda had observed the night before, and her oversized reclining chair along with the caftans she liked to wear revealed many cigarette holes. Summing up her impression, Brenda considered the apartment to be "rather pathetic for what one would consider the world-famous Christine Jorgensen would be living in . . . ." To her, Chris seemed to be "camping out."

That evening, after Chris had polished off a string of vodkas over ice, Brenda made several telephone calls to Southern California friends explaining that she was back in town. This annoyed Christine as they were both sitting in the living room, and she was trying to watch television. Unpleasantly, Chris told her that henceforth she should use the telephone in her bedroom. Her manner was sufficiently harsh to remind Brenda that she had been warned of Chris's propensity for belligerence after an evening of drinking. She explained that Chris had become "well oiled" on that evening. Since Chris arose at eleven each morning, and Brenda preferred to get up at seven, she had ample time to straighten up the apartment and get organized for the day. According to Brenda Smith, "Upon waking, Chris would reach for a Carlton menthol cigarette, the first of a very large number, then pull on a caftan and drink the lukewarm combination of coffee and chocolate milk I had prepared."

Usually, Chris did not enter into conversation until she had finished her breakfast and scanned a newspaper. Brenda concluded that she had a hangover almost every morning. Should she be enjoying a television program, Chris would point and utter: "Do you mind?"

Christine seldom shared much of her childhood with others, but she did reminisce with Brenda about her growing-up years in the Bronx, and her enjoyment of wearing her sister's dresses in the house on Dudley Avenue. It was similar to the account of childhood cross dressing she had described to Dr. Hamburger in 1950. When telling Brenda of her first years as Christine, she noted that "she had been asexually cocooned in a predominantly gay environment since her transsexual change."[4] However, Chris seemed to have especially enjoyed her romantic interludes with straight men, such as Sergeant Bill Calhoun, "Jim" Knox, and attorney Moton Holt. Although she had many good friends who were transsexuals or gay men, none of these appear to have led to sustained romantic attachments.

Judging from Brenda Lana Smith's unpublished narrative of her six months with Christine, the two seemed to have gotten along nicely, typically sharing the cost of afternoon drinks in local bars and splitting the tab for dinners at their favorite restaurants. They were both on tight budgets. During the early months of 1989, Chris was still driving her white 1972 Cadillac Fleetwood sedan along Pacific Coast Highway, stopping here and there to call upon gay buddies who had become supportive friends, passing time over drinks, and keeping up with her many medical appointments. Even with the ever-present reality of her serious cancer difficulties, Chris was doing all she could to sustain the lifestyle she had come to enjoy, but each month became more of a challenge. She was reluctant to surrender any of the pleasures and friendships of her high-energy daily life; this typically meant staying up until the early hours of the morning. Brenda Smith seemed fully capable of maintaining the pace. But Chris's drinking and uneven money management throughout the later part of her life stood out as problems. Brenda respected Christine and they were good friends, but looking back, she provided this candid comment:

> while always frugally looking for a bargain, she was readily prepared to handsomely open her pocketbook for something she wanted . . . especially, good service or, when in an inebriated evening's haze she went about setting the world straight . . . a lonely imperious haze that for some twenty-odd years had . . . when we finally met . . . damn near drained her pocketbook dry.[5]

Following Christine's death, Brenda Lana Smith moved to England. Smith was exceptionally forthcoming and cooperative in providing information for this biography and in putting me in touch with many of Christine's friends.

The two daughters of Christine's sister, had been born in the early 1950s and, along with the three Courtney sisters,[6] they filled the roles of the children Christine never had. She was also on excellent terms with nearly all of her aunts and uncles. In the late 1980s, one of Dorothy's daughters lived in California, and she had visited her "Aunt Chris." These were typically happy family visits, with the children rambling about Chris's Laguna Niguel home. But difficulty arose when the children observed Chris drinking, sometimes accompanied by loud and inappropriate language. Although included in Chris's will, her differences with her aunt along with her outspoken style nearly led to her exclusion.

Dolly visited Christine in San Clemente during April 1989 and realized that Chris's condition was critical. It was a sad reunion for the Jorgensens for it was clear that Christine's cancer had become terminal. When they visited for the last time, it was especially difficult for them to say good-bye. Christine's bladder cancer now also involved her lungs as well as three inoperable brain tumors. She died in a coma on May 3, 1989, three weeks before her sixty-third birthday. Brenda Smith had been with her, almost continuously, during those final days. Along with Chris's medical team, Brenda Smith and the relatives had done all anyone could do to assist her during the traumatic and painful final months of her life.

Now, Brenda had the duty of listing all of the items and assets in Christine's estate, and of distributing her personal possessions in accordance with her wishes. They divided the tea cups and ashtrays, the souvenirs from world travels, the jewelry and the oil paintings. The extensive inventory was well organized, room by room, with each item carefully described. After Dorothy's daughters decided which family member should receive the various personal items, Brenda noted the decision with the initials of the recipient beside each item. Some of the most valuable jewelry was in a safe deposit box. A small box of special keepsakes was set aside for Peggy Olsen. As may be seen at times like this within many families, there was more than a little tension between Brenda Lana Smith and the relatives. There was tension over the whereabouts of a video camera and a ring. According to Smith, these issues were resolved when a good friend of Christine's, Jackie Napalitano, explained that Chris has previously given the camera to her daughter. The ring, Brenda explained, had been given to her in front of several "creditable witnesses."[7] There were five beneficiaries who divided the proceeds of Christine's retirement account. Reportedly, they each received about $16,000.[8]

Never one to pass up a party, Christine had asked Brenda to arrange such an event after her death. The invitation list was based on Christine's address books, and 270 acceptances were received. However, seventy of these failed to show up for the party resulting in 200 attendees. The afternoon event was held on June 11, 1989, at the Crown House restaurant in Laguna Niguel.[9] Dolly did not make the trip from the East Coast, but Stan Bahr, Christine's long-time Long Island friend attended. He had often stayed with Christine during his vacations in California, and she stayed with him when in the New York area. The guests, many of whom were show business or newspaper people, enjoyed the wine Chris had planned, and many recollections were recounted. It was a joyful afternoon event, starting at two and ending at five. The distinguished gender researcher-psychiatrist, Richard Green, and his wife, Melissa Hines, attended along with a few of the people who had worked on Edward Small's 1970 movie. After all had been heard, Brenda Smith, poised, attractive, and experienced in public speaking, read the personal comments Dolly had sent:[10]

To the friends gathered to remember Chris: Greetings.

Not being with you in person, I thought I might greet you by way of this message which I have asked Brenda to read to you.

Most of you have known Chris since 1969 when she moved to California. But I pose this question: Was there life for Chris before California? You bet there was! Here are a few highlights.

I remember when our grandparents returned from a trip to Denmark in 1927. They brought a stuffed dog for the newest grandchild. Puffy was on Chris's bed when she died—a lifelong companion.

I remember a 4th of July when we kids set off firecrackers at the Danish beach club off Long Island Sound in the Bronx. I envied Chris's toy cannon that sounded louder than a base drum to my young ears.

See that Christmas tree over there? Chris's fascination for the Christmas tree started when she was about seven. I recall many a difference of opinion as to how to decorate the tree—but when it came to the lights, that was Chris's forte.

I remember our parents, cousins, aunts and uncles all dancing around the tree on Christmas Eve, singing carols in English and Danish.

I remember the Bon Voyage party on the ship when my brother sailed for Denmark, to return three years later as Christine.

The wonderful support our parents gave Chris during those first tumultuous months after she returned from Denmark (and how that) endeared them to both of us.

I remember when Chris was named "Woman of the Year" by the Scandinavian Society and the party Chris had for the cast of *Oh, Dad,* a summer stock company on Long Island in which she had a leading role.

I remember meeting Bea Lillie at Chris's home, and the time I accompanied her to a luncheon at Irving Berlin's New York apartment. Even now, I can visualize my young daughters parading in the living room in Auntie Chris's theatrical costumes.

There were the swimming pools that went from small to medium to large as her nieces grew. And the girl's young friends who loved to join them at Auntie Chris's home. Then there was the shared sadness of the loss of both of our parents within 18 months of time of each other.

Chris has been an important part of my life for 63 years. She presented me with challenge, opportunity, excitement, some frustration and a good measure of love. I join others of you who will miss her.

"Hell-O!" [Should be said the way Chris would have on the other end of the telephone.]

A few weeks ago I saw Chris for the last time when both of my daughters and I visited her in San Clemente. I'd like to close with the last words I spoke to Chris that I am sure she heard; they were, "God be with you." I wish the same for all of you.

Thank you all for being here.

    Dolly

Christine had expressed a wish to have her ashes sprinkled either in the sea off Hawaii or just off the Southern California coast. The nieces, Stan Bahr, and Brenda Smith[11] decided to keep the procedure personal and less complicated by performing this ceremony in the surf at San Clemente, not far from where Chris had lived. They saw no need to involve a large group of people or the scheduling of boats. The four held hands and cried together as they waded into the frothy, cool, Pacific Ocean to bid farewell to Christine Jorgensen in the afterglow of a shimmering, golden sunset. Standing in the surf, in semi-darkness, they sprinkled the ashes into the sea. As they turned and walked to their car they could hear children on the beach, laughing and playing in the cooling sand. It was a long way from the children's games George had known a half-century earlier on Dudley Avenue and at the Askov Hall beach club.

None of Chris's relatives, not even the executor of her estate, thought much about the formality of filing a death certificate, a duty typically handled by the undertaker. Therefore, Brenda Smith was stunned to examine this document a week or two later when copies arrived by mail from the County Recorder's Office. In California, a death certificate consists of a single page identifying the deceased, the names of the parents, the birthplace, the date and place of death, the cause of death, and the certification of the physician in attendance. But it was not the death certificate that took Brenda's breath away, it was the appended affidavit, attached as a second page. This official record had a surprise ending that forever linked George and Christine in the records of the State of California: The affidavit read:

CHRISTINE JORGENSEN (Also Known As) GEORGE WILLIAM JORGENSEN, JR.[12]

Very likely, Christine arranged this when she contracted for her cremation in 1979. Her motivation for including her birth name may have been that one or more life insurance policies remained in George's name; we know this was true for one policy administered by the Veteran's Administration.[13] This affidavit is just a piece of paper, a document that became an official record of Christine's identity, but it seemed like a peculiar final twist in the life of the world's best known transsexual. It was a reminder that the kid who was rejected and teased by his boyhood neighbors in the Bronx, never fully eliminated every vestige of his male identity. But the significance and identity of Christine Jorgensen goes well beyond the official records of the State of California. She left an enduring legacy, for Jorgensen and her doctors broke new ground and set in place the trail markers for transsexual change. As decades pass, the names and celebrity of her Danish physicians may fade, but among transsexuals the name of Christine Jorgensen will never be forgotten.

Bibliography

American Psychiatric Association. (2002). *Diagnostic and Statistical Manual of Mental Disorders (Edition IV-TR).* Washington, DC: American Psychiatric Association.

Benjamin, H. (1953). Transvestism and transsexualism. *International Journal of Sexology, 7,* 12-14.

Benjamin, H. (1966). *The Transsexual Phenomenon.* New York: Julian Press.

Bentler, P. M. (1976). A typology of transsexualism: Gender identity theory and data. *Archives of Sexual Behavior, 5,* 567-584.

Blanchard, R. (1985). Typology of male-to-female transsexualism. *Archives of Sexual Behavior,* 14, 247-261.

Blanchard, R. (1989). The concept of autogynephilia and the typology of male gender dysphoria. *Journal of Nervous and Mental Disease,* 177, 616-623.

Brierley, H. (1979). *Transvestism: Illness, perversion, or choice.* New York: Pergamon.

Buhrich, N. (1976). A heterosexual transvestite club. Australian and New Zealand *Journal of Psychiatry,* 10, 331-335.

Bullough, B., Bullough, V. L., & Elias. (1997). *Gender blending.* Amherst, NY: Prometheus Books.

Bullough, V. L. (1994). *Science in the bedroom: A history of sex research.* New York: Basic Books.

Bullough V. L., & Bullough, B. (1993). *Cross dressing, sex, and gender.* Philadelphia: University of Pennsylvania Press.

Chauncey, G. (1994). *Gay New York: Gender, urban culture, and the makings of the gay male world.* New York: Basic Books.

Christenson, C. V. (1971). *Kinsey: A biography.* Bloomington, IN: Indiana University Press.

Colapinto, J. (2000). *As nature made him.* New York: Harper Collins.

De Kruif, P. (1945). *The male hormone.* New York: Harcourt, Brace.

Devor, H. *FTM: Female to male transsexuals in society.* Bloomington: Indiana University Press.

Diamond, M. (1997). Human Sexual Development. In F. Beach (Ed.), *Human Sexuality in Four Perspectives* (pp. 22-61). Baltimore: Johns Hopkins University Press.

Diamond, M., & Sigmundson, K. (1997). Sex reassignment at birth: A long-term review and clinical implications. *Archives of Pediatric and Adolescent Medicine. 150,* 298-304.

Becoming a Woman: A Biography of Christine Jorgensen
© 2008 by The Haworth Press, Taylor & Francis Group. All rights reserved.
doi:10.1300/5896_25

Dillon, M. (1946). *Self: A study in ethics and endocrinology.* London: William Heinemann.

Docter, R. F. (1988). *Transvestites and Transsexuals: Toward a theory of cross-gender behavior.* New York: Plenum Press.

Docter, R. F. (2004). *From man to woman: The transgender journey of Virginia prince.* Northridge, CA: Docter Press.

Ekins, R., & King, D. (2005). Virginia Prince: Pioneer of transgendering. *International Journal of Transgenderism. 8,* (4).

Feinbloom, D. (1976). *Transvestites and Transsexuals.* New York: Dell.

Gathorne-Hardy, J. (1998). *Sex: The measure of all things.* Bloomington, IN: Indiana University Press.

Gebhard, P. H. (1965). *Sex offenders: An analysis of types.* New York: Harper and Row.

Gebhard, P. H., & Johnson, A. B. (1979). *The Kinsey Data: Marginal tabulations of the 1938-1963 interviews conducted by the Institute for Sex Research.* Philadelphia: W. B. Saunders.

Gillies, H. D., & Millard, R. D. (1957). *The principles and art of plastic surgery.* Boston: Little, Brown.

Hamburger, C. (1953). The desire for change of sex as shown by personal letters from 465 men and women. *Acta Endocrinologica, 14,* 363-376.

Hamburger, C., & Sprechler, M. (1951). The influence of steroid hormones on the hormonal activity of the adenohypophysis in man. *Acta Endocrinologica, 7,* 167-195.

Hamburger, C., Stürup, G. K., & Dahl-Iverson, E. (1953). Transvestism: Hormonal, psychiatric, and surgical treatment. *Journal of the American Medical Association, 152,* 391-396.

Hines, M. (1993). Hormonal and neural correlates of sex-typed behavioral development in human beings. In M. Haug,, R. E. Whalen, C. Aron, and K. L. Olsen (Eds.), *The development of sex differences and similarities in behavior* (pp. 131-149). Boston: Kluwer Academic Publishers.

Hoyer, N. (1933). *Man into woman: An auththentic record of a change of sex.* New York: Dutton.

International Foundation for Gender Education, P. O. Box 540229, Wayland, MA 02454-0229.

Jones, J. H. (1997). *Alfred C. Kinsey: A public/private life.* New York: Norton.

Jorgensen, C. (1967). *Christine Jorgensen: A personal autobiography.* New York: Paul S. Eriksson.

Kinsey, A. C., Pomeroy., & Martin, C. E.(1948). *Sexual behavior in the human male.* Philadelphia: W. B. Saunders.

Kinsey, A. C., Pomeroy, W. B., Martin, C. E., & Gebhard, P. H. (1953). *Sexual behavior in the human female.* Philadelphia: W. B. Saunders.

Memorial for Harry Benjamin. 1986). *Archives of Sexual Behavior, 17,* 24-25.

Meyerowitz, J. (2002). *How sex changed: A history of transsexuality.* Cambridge: Harvard University Press.

Money, J., & Ehrhardt, Anne. (1972). *Man and Woman: Boy and Girl.* Baltimore: The Johns Hopkins University Press.

Pomeroy, W. B. (1960). *Dr. Kinsey and the Institute for Sex Research.* New York: The Free Press.

Schaefer, L. C., & Wheeler, C. C. (1995). Harry Benjamin's first ten cases (1938-1953): A clinical historical note. *Archives of Sexual Behavior, 24,* 73-93.

Smith, B. L. (1991). *a'top a dung hill.* Unpublished manuscript.

Starup, J. (1973). Christian Hamburger. *Acta Endocrinologica, 75,* 1-2.

Stoller, R. J. (1968). *Sex and gender.* New York: Julian Press.

Werther, R. (1922). *The female-impersonators.* New York: Arno Press. Reprinted 1975.

Notes

Abbreviations

CJ indicates either the name of Christine Jorgensen or her autobiography: Jorgensen, C. (1967). *Christine Jorgensen: A personal autobiography.* New York: Paul S. Eriksson, Inc. The associated page numbers in the notes refer to the hardback edition.

DRL refers to the Christine Jorgensen Collection held by the Danish Royal Library in Copenhagen, Denmark.

Chapter 1

1. Herein, a cross dresser is defined as a heterosexual male who periodically derives pleasure from dressing as a woman, often for the purpose of sexual gratification, at least in his early history. It is an inexact term.

2. Herein, a transsexual is defined as a person living entirely and continuously in the gender role opposite his or her biological sex, regardless of hormonal or surgical intervention. We never refer to intersex persons as transsexuals.

3. For a description of support groups for cross dressers: in England see Brierley, H. (1979). *Transvestism: Illness, perversion, or choice.* New York: Pergamon; in New Zealand see Buhrich, N. (1976). A heterosexual transvestite club. *Australian and New Zealand Journal of Psychiatry, 10,* 331-335; in America see Feinbloom, D. (1976). *Transvestites and Transsexuals.* New York: Dell. Virginia Prince was instrumental in the establishment of these groups in America, Canada, England, Australia, and Sweden. This story is told in a biography of Prince: Docter, R. F. (2004). *From Man to Woman: The transgender journey of Virginia Prince.* Northridge, CA: Docter Press.

4. Personal communication, Sister Mary Elizabeth, OSM, San Clemente, California. September 30, 2003 and September 1, 2004.

5. Personal communication, Alison Laing, April, 2003.

6. I have attempted to imitate CJ's speaking style as I heard it that evening. She manifested a strong in-charge presence.

7. For example, as noted by Yvonne Cook Riley, personal communication, April 29, 2005.

8. See Meyerowitz, J. (2002). *How sex changed: A history of transsexuality.* Cambridge: Harvard University Press.

9. Today, the terms transvestite and cross dresser are used synonymously. Jorgensen's return to America led to clarification of this terminology. See Benjamin,

doi:10.1300/5896_26
269

H. (1953). Transvestism and transsexualism. *International Journal of Sexology, 7,* 12-14. Transsexuals continue to be defined somewhat differently in legal, medical, behavioral, and street parlance. The essence of transsexuality involves both a sustained conviction that one must live entirely in the gender role opposite his or her biological sex, and continuous occupancy of that gender role. In Western nations, surgical or hormonal body alteration to change gender appearance is often elected, but in many cultures this is not an option.

10. The prevalence of transsexuality in America and elsewhere has not been extensively studied and remains controversial. For example, Lynn Conway has provided an analysis concluding that in male-to- female cases the prevalence is at least one in 2,500 and possibly as frequent as one in 500 (http://www.lynnconway.com/). She provides arguments against the far smaller prevalence data cited by the American Psychiatric Association: *Diagnostic and Statistical Manual of Mental Disorders (Edition IV-TR).* (2002). Washington, DC: American Psychiatric Association.

11. Benjamin, H. (1966). *The transsexual phenomenon.* New York: Julian Press. Benjamin described six variations of gender deviance on a scale he labeled Sex and Gender Role Disorientation and Indecision (Males), ranging from Pseudo Transvestite through the True Transsexual. In present language his scale represents variations in fetishism, the intensity of feminine gender identity and the motivation to live continuously in the gender role of a woman. For other taxonomic formulations see Bentler, P. M. (1976). A typology of transsexualism: Gender identity theory and data. *Archives of Sexual Behavior, 5,* 567-584 or Blanchard, R. (1985). Typology of male-to-female transsexualism. *Archives of Sexual Behavior, 14,* 247-261.

12. For examples, the sexual aspects of cross dressing and transsexualism have been described by Benjamin (1966), and by Blanchard (1989). See: Blanchard, R. (1989). The concept of autogynephilia and the typology of male gender dysphoria. *Journal of Nervous and Mental Disease, 177,* 616-623.

13. For example: Stoller, R. J. (1968). *Sex and gender.* New York: Julian Press.

14. Interview with Stanton Bahr, November 29, 2003.

15. In her autobiography, Jorgensen provided many examples of her youthful romantic relationships with men, but never characterized these as homosexual or as involving overt sexual activity. The idea of being classified as a homosexual was repulsive to George as a youth. For example: "I was repulsed at the thought of homosexuality but I was definitely attracted to men." *The Pitt News,* September 18, 1972. Looking back on her teenage years and young adulthood, Christine consistently described herself as always having felt she should have been a girl or a woman.

16. For example, during the first twelve months of her nightclub act (1953-1954), Jorgensen documented income of at least $170,000. CJ papers. DRL. There is no public record of her annual income thereafter, although the decline of revenue was noted in her autobiography. During her final decade, she relied on income from investments. Personal communication, Stanton Bahr, March 27, 2004.

17. Concerning the distinction between transvestism (cross dressing) and transsexualism see Benjamin (1953). After 1953, the term sex change continued to be used as a key search word by the Library of Congress for several years.

18. Concerning the causes of transsexuality, nearly all researchers have assumed the possibility of a biological predisposition coupled with gender-specific social learning. However, there is no factual basis to prove specific causal factors. For a re-

view see Bullough V. L., & Bullough, B. (1993). *Cross dressing, sex, and gender.* Philadelphia: University of Pennsylvania Press.

19. For a review: Hines, M. (1993). Hormonal and neural correlates of sex-typed behavioral development in human beings. In M. Haug, R. E. Whalen, C. Aron, and K. L. Olsen (Eds.), *The development of sex differences and similarities in behavior* (pp. 131-149). Boston: Kluwer Academic Publishers.

Chapter 2

1. Telephone interview with Bruce Silver, childhood friend of George Jorgensen Jr. April 18, 2004.
2. Interview with Diane Osborne, March 30, 2004. Interview with Mr. and Mrs. Robert Andersen, March 29, 2004.
3. Interview with Mr. and Mrs. Robert Andersen, March 29, 2004.
4. Interview with Mr. and Mrs. Vincent Manno who were close friends of the parents of Christine Jorgensen, March 28, 2004.
5. Interview with Diane Osborne, March 30, 2004.
6. Interview with Mr. and Mrs. Robert Andersen, March 29, 2004.
7. Interview with the Andersens, March 29, 2004.
8. Interview with the Mannos, March 28, 2004. Interview with Marilyn Courtney, March 27, 2004.
9. CJ, 10.
10. CJ, 8.
11. Interview with Mr. and Mrs. Robert Andersen, March 29, 2004.
12. Interview with the Andersens, March 29, 2004.
13. Interview with Sister Mary Elizabeth, September 30, 2003.
14. Interview, Mr. and Mrs. Vincent Manno, March 27, 2004.
15. Interview, Mr. and Mrs. Robert Andersen, March 29, 2004.
16. Interview, Marilyn Courtney, March 28, 2004.
17. CJ, 110. Adjusted for the present value of the dollar, Dolly loaned her brother the equivalent of about $2,500.
18. Interview, Diane Osborne, 2004.
19. Interview with anonymous close friend of CJ, 2003.
20. There are several letters to CJ from her sister among the Jorgensen papers. DRL.
21. Interview with the Mannos, March 28, 2004.
22. Interview with Diane Osborne, March 30, 2004.
23. Interview with the Andersens, March 29, 2004.
24. Ibid.

Chapter 3

1. In 1953 the present owner of the residence purchased the property from CJ's parents. He requested anonymity and does not encourage visitors.
2. CJ, 10.
3. CJ, 11.
4. CJ, 12.

5. Interview with the Andersens, 2004.

6. Interview with Danny Riley (pseudonym), schoolmate and childhood acquaintance of George Jorgensen Jr., March 28, 2004.

7. Interview with Danny Riley, 2004. Telephone interview with Bruce Silver, 2004.

8. Interview with Danny Riley, 2004.

9. Several of the relatives and friends of Christine Jorgensen reported a marked change of personality upon her return to the United States in 1953. Interview with Marilyn Courtney, March 27, 2004.

10. A pseudonym, I assume.

11. CJ, 16.

12. CJ, 18.

13. Interview with the Andersens, 2004.

14. As noted by Meyerowitz (2002), CJ's autobiography contains several self descriptions concerning "prudish" sexual attitudes. See chapters 3-6 in the Jorgensen autobiography. See Meyerowitz, J. (2002). *How sex changed: A history of transexuality.* Cambridge: Harvard University Press.

15. For CJs efforts to "pass" as a heterosexual young man see Chapters 3-6 in her autobiography dealing with De Molay membership, her months at RKO-Pathé, and service in the US Army. Passing as a heterosexual male was the preferred mode of public presentation for George Jr. until his adoption of a more androgenous appearance in 1950-1952.

16. CJ, 17.

17. As an adult, Christine Jorgensen recorded her height in U.S. passports as either 5'6" or one-half inch taller.

18. CJ. The first three chapters of the Jorgensen autobiography (1967) emphasize his childhood self-perception as the frail, lonely, outsider with ever-stronger feminine identification.

19. Interview with the Andersens, 2004.

20. CJ, 20.

21. Interview with the Andersons, 2004.

22. Hamburger, C., Stürup, G. K., & Dahl-Iverson, E. (1953). Transvestism: Hormonal, psychiatric, and surgical treatment. *Journal of the American Medical Association, 152,* 391-396.

23. Letter from CJ to his sister, Dorothy, c. 1943. DRL.

24. CJ papers. DRL.

25. For example, letters from Jorgensen to Stanton Bahr concerning possible relocation following the sale of her Laguna Niguel residence. 1986. DRL.

26. Meyerowitz, 2002.

27. Before about 1970, most newspapers reported little about homosexuals or their support groups. In New York, the coverage of Halloween "drag" balls was an exception.

28. From a memoir: Smith, B. L. (1991). *a'top a dung hill.* Unpublished manuscript.

29. Hamburger, C., Stürup, G. K., and Dahl-Iverson, E. (1953). Transvestism: Hormonal, psychiatric, and surgical treatment. *Journal of the American Medical Association, 152,* 391-396.

30. Personal communication, Brenda Lana Smith, November 18, 2003.

31. Telephone interview with Paul S. Eriksson, October 26, 2004.

32. Personal communication from Sister Mary Elizabeth, 2003.

33. Interview with the Andersens, 2003.

34. Interview with Danny Riley, 2004.

35. CJ, 27.

36. These feelings of having a feminine gender identity were described to Christian Hamburger. Hamburger et al., 1953.

37. Personal communication, anonymous A. c. April 8, 2004.

38. CJ, 34.

39. Christine cited several different weight estimates for her early adult years.

40. Meyerowitz, (2002).

41. The 1944 self-photo of George Jr. as a mature gentleman appears in the Jorgensen autobiography. The 1944 photograph believed to have been taken at the Photographic Institute with a lab towel over George's shoulder was later used in publicity releases to illustrate his appearance as a male. The *New York Times* used the later picture in their Jorgensen obituary.

42. Jorgensen autobiography. Part of a set of photographs, pages not numbered.

43. De Molay photograph, Jorgensen collection. DRL.

Chapter 4

1. CJ, Chapters 5-10.

2. Werther, R., pseudo. (1922). *The female-impersonators.* New York: Arno Press. Reprinted 1975.

3. Chauncey, G. (1994). *Gay New York: Gender, urban culture, and the makings of the gay male world.* New York: Basic Books.

4. Kinsey, A. C., Pomeroy, W. B., & Martin, C. E.(1948). *Sexual behavior in the human male.* Philadelphia: W. B. Saunders.

5. Gebhard, P. H., and others of the Institute for Sex Research. (1965). *Sex offenders: An analysis of types.* New York: Harper and Row. Also, Gebhard, P. H., & Johnson, A. B. (1979). *The Kinsey data: Marginal tabulations of the 1938-1963 interviews conducted by the Institute for Sex Research.* Philadelphia: W. B. Saunders.

6. CJ, 93. CJ and Angelo appear to have been referring to: Hoyer, N. (1933). *Man into woman: An authentic record of a change of sex.* New York: Dutton.

7. Dillon, M. (1946). *Self: A study in ethics and endocrinology.* London: William Heinemann. Dillon did not reveal his own transsexual transition while describing an endocrinolgical hypothesis of the roots of gender identity formation in females seeking to become men.

8. CJ, 31.

9. CJ, 33.

10. CJ, 33.

11. CJ, 34.

12. CJ, 35.

13. In a series of passport applications, Christine Jorgensen gave her height at 5'6" and at other times as one-half inch taller.

14. CJ's Army notebook, 1946. DRL.

15. These persistent feelings are almost invariably reported by transsexuals-in-process.

16. CJ's Army notebook, 1946. DRL.

17. CJ, 37.

18. Ibid.

19. Hamburger et al., (1953).

20. CJ, 29.

21. Meyerowitz, J. (2002). *How sex changed: A history of transexuality.* Cambridge: Harvard University Press.

22. CJ, 30.

23. CJ, 38.

24. CJ, 39.

Chapter 5

1. CJ, 44.

2. CJ, 46.

3. CJ, 48.

4. CJ, 50.

5. CJ, 52.

6. CJ, 59.

7. CJ letter to parents and relatives, courtesy of Marilyn Courtney. June 4, 1947. In this signature, George omitted the final e from his name. Most of his letters through July, 1952 were signed, Brud.

8. CJ, 58.

9. CJ, 60.

10. For a history of hormonal research see Bullough, V. L. (1994). *Science in the bedroom: A history of sex research.* New York: Basic Books.

11. CJ, 61.

12. CJ, 61.

13. CJ, 61.

14. CJ, 62.

15. CJ, 62.

16. CJ, 62.

17. CJ, 6.

Chapter 6

1. CJ, 68.

2. CJ, 70.

3. CJ, 70.

4. CJ, 71.

5. CJ, 71.

6. CJ, 71.

7. Meyerowitz (2002) *How sex changed: A history of transexuality.* Cambridge: Harvard U. Press. First suggested that psychologist and hormone researcher Frank A. Beach of Yale University might have been the so-called "psychiatrist" Jorgensen

met with in New Haven. If this is correct, Beach would almost certainly have been able to give Jorgensen bibliographic leads concerning "sex changes." Beach was most likely also the source of a November 1949 letter to Jorgensen advising him that the "treatment" he sought, a change of sex, might be available in Sweden. CJ, 94. Prior to the final edit of CJ's autobiography, the manuscript named "Dr. Gray" as the New Haven doctor. For unknown reasons the pseudonym of Dr. Grayson was substituted for Dr. Gray. An unpublished additional segment of the partial letter from the New Haven doctor quoted in the autobiography on page 94 urged Jorgensen to stay in touch with him, suggesting that this man had given Jorgensen more attention than is described in the autobiography. Manuscript of CJ autobiography in possession of the author, through the courtesy of Warren Bayless and Paul S. Eriksson.

8. CJ, 74.
9. CJ, 75.
10. CJ, 78.
11. De Kruif, Paul. (1945). *The male hormone.* New York: Harcourt, Brace.
12. De Kruif, (1945), 189.
13. CJ, 79.
14. CJ, 80.
15. CJ, 80.
16. CJ, 81.

Chapter 7

1. CJ, 91.
2. CJ, 86.
3. CJ, 86.
4. CJ, 86.
5. Hamburger et al., (1953).
6. CJ, 86.
7. CJ, 88.
8. CJ, 94.
9. CJ, 94.
10. Joanne Meyerowitz informed me that she had discovered a letter among the Harry Benjamin papers at the Kinsey Institute from a Swedish surgeon stating that he had been involved with some of the earliest sexual reassignment surgeries during the 1920s. The letter explained that this surgery was done in Sweden. Personal communication, 2005.
11. CJ, 94.

Chapter 8

1. Helen Johnson had married prior to December 1952.
2. CJ photographs. DRL
3. Interview with Jesper Hamburger, March 28, 2004. For biographical information concerning Christian Hamburger's contributions as Editor of *Acta Endocrinologica,* see: Starup, J. (1973). Christian Hamburger. *Acta Endocrinologica, 75,* 1-2.
4. CJ, 100-103. Also, Hamburger et al., (1953).

5. According to Jesper Hamburger, his father preferred tea. Personal communication, 2004.

6. The CJ autobiography refers to Mrs. Hamburger serving refreshments, but his son, Jesper Hamburger, told me the entire family was away except for his father. Interview with Jesper Hamburger, March 28, 2003.

7. Hoyer, (1933). The German language edition appeared in 1931.

8. Also, Hamburger, C. & Sprechler, M. (1951). The influence of steroid hormones on the hormonal activity of the adenohypophysis in man. *Acta Endocrinologica, 7,* 167-195.

9. Hamburger et al., (1953).

Chapter 9

1. CJ, 111-112.

2. Hamburger et al., (1953), p. 353.

3. Hamburger et al., (1953), p. 354.

4. Photographs of Christine's chest taken in 1953 reveal the swelling Hamburger mentioned; very little breast development had occurred. Photographs provided by anonymous B, May, 2004. Authenticity confirmed by author.

5. Personal communication from Brenda Lana Smith who provided a nearly nude photograph of CJ showing C-cup-sized breasts. There is no proof that Jorgensen received breast implants, but this seems very likely in view of the ample breast size shown in this photograph. It is very unlikely that such development was achieved through continued use of estrogenic hormones. Undated photograph, c. 1980. May 26, 2005.

6. Hamburger et al., 1953, 354.

7. CJ, 112.

8. Letter from CJ to Stürup, undated, c. August, 1951. DRL.

9. Ibid.

10. Ibid.

11. Interview with Jesper Hamburger, March 28, 2004.

12. Ibid.

13. Correspondence: Henrik Hamburger to author, November 11, 2003. Christian Hamburger died in 1992.

14. CJ, 111.

15. CJ, 107.

16. From copy of 1952 U.S. passport. DRL.

17. CJ, 110.

18. The 1952 contract between CJ and the Hearst organization is among her papers. DRL.

Chapter 10

1. CJ, 122.

2. CJ, 123-126.

3. Transcript of an extensive 1984 interview of CJ by Teit Reitzen provided by Preben Hertoft, 1984.

4. This meeting was described in various news reports on December 1, 1952. Additionally, a participant who was present but prefers to remain anonymous described the proceedings to me. Personal communication, 2004.

5. This statement is from the *American Weekly* life story series published by the Hearst newspapers. *Los Angeles Examiner,* March 8, 1953. Similar accounts of the passport application process are given in Jorgensen's autobiography (1967).

6. Telephone interview: John Hotchner, Office of Passport Services, U. S. Department of State. March 22, 2004. According to Hotchner, the initiative for adding sex identification to U. S. passports came from recommendations in 1977 by an association of international air carriers urging uniform descriptive information on these documents.

7. In a series of articles questioning CJs authenticity as a woman, Alvin Davis also questioned whether the U.S. ambassador to Denmark had done more than she should have to assist Jorgensen. See: Davis, A. The Truth About "Christine" Jorgensen. The *New York Post,* April 6, 1953.

8. News reports concerning CJ's relationship with William Calhoun were extensively reported in the press: United Press, December 5, 1952; Associated Press, December 5, 1952; *San Francisco Examiner,* March 29, 1953. The letter from Calhoun to CJ that appears to request money for his silence is among her papers. Whether he actually intended such a proposition is unclear. DRL.

9. CJ papers. DRL.

10. Richendorff described his role in breaking the Jorgensen story in Denmark in a *Los Angeles Times* article: Aug. 9, 1954, p. 19.

11. Ritzau interview, c. May, 1984. Provided to the author by Preben Hertoft.

12. CJ did not make it easy to track her adult romantic life. She described close relationships with Howard Knox, the only man to whom she was engaged, Sergeant Bill Calhoun who found her highly attractive, Patrick Flanigan who remained married while urging CJ to marry him, and attorney Moton B. Holt with whom she became intimate for over a year.

13. From mail addressed to CJ while a patient in the Danish Royal Hospital, November, 1952. DRL.

Chapter 11

1. *New York Daily News,* December 1, 1952.

2. Davis, A. The Truth About "Christine" Jorgensen. The *New York Post,* April 6, 1953.

3. An early print of this photograph (full-length, right arm horizontal) includes a notation by Jorgensen that she had created both the clothing and the photograph herself. It was one of several pictures sent to her parents with her June 8, 1952 letter. Jorgensen Collection. DRL.

4. CJ, 151.

5. Christine had become acquainted with Tony Whitehouse, foreign general manager of Hallmark Productions, Inc., a theatrical booking agency. Whitehouse was based in London. In his January 15, 1953, letter to Jorgensen he urged her to meet with Kroger Babb, president of Hallmark, to negotiate the showing of her film, *Denmark,* and a public speaking tour in the United States. CJ, Box I, DRL.

6. *New York Daily News,* December 1, 1952.

7. The Veterans Administration refused to change the name on an insurance policy issued to George Jorgensen Jr. during his Army service. Letter from VA among the CJ papers. DRL.

8. *New York Daily News,* December 2, 1952. Jorgensen's explanatory letter to her parents (June 8, 1952) was quoted extensively in the press and positioned her as both a victim of a "glandular disorder" and possibly of a vague intersex condition.

9. For example, *Los Angeles Times,* December 2, 1952, p. 8. This article referred to Christine's return " . . . with a U.S. woman's passport . . . "

10. Jorgensen often told reporters how shocked and distressed she had been to have her story revealed.

Chapter 12

1. *Los Angeles Times,* August 9, 1954, p. 19. In her autobiography, Jorgensen described her experiences with several news reporters, but never mentioned Henrik Rechendorff or Paul Ifversen. Neither were her court appearance or Rechendorff's subsequent article mentioned.

2. We have no reason to disbelieve Rechendorff's account. However, a search of the newspaper he said he had published in, *Berlinske Tidende,* for the six months prior to December 1, 1952 did not turn up his article.

3. Thorkild Behrens, *Scope,* May, 1953.

4. Paul Ifversen, *New York Daily News,* December 2, 1952.

5. In an article, Ifversen explained that Jorgensen had given him the entire sex change story while being sworn to secrecy. *New York Daily News,* December 2, 1952. The Danny Kaye event is described in CJ's autobiography. A helpful reporter is mentioned but not named.

6. Ifversen, *New York Daily News,* December 2, 1952.

7. Personal communication from Vern Bullough, 2003.

8. Personal communication from Stanton Bahr, 2003.

9. Behrens, 1953.

10. The contract and Hearst payments to Jorgensen are among the CJ papers. DRL.

11. Jorgensen did not state who bought and delivered her new outfit for the December 11, 1952 press conference. Apparently, the Junker-Jensen's did not come to her hotel prior to this press affair. I have therefore assumed that Elsa Sabroe assisted her on December 11.

12. Forchhammer had been the dealmaker for the Hearst papers. We assume he had a major role at this press event. In her autobiography, CJ describes him in friendly terms. Later in December 1952 he saw her frequently and escorted her to a party.

13. Many newspapers in this country carried the December 11, 1952 article and photographs.

14. CJ, 159.

15. The photographs of Jorgensen's departure from Kastrup Airport appear candid, but they were acquired as part of a staged press event prior to her flight.

Chapter 13

1. In her autobiography, Jorgensen acknowledged taking a "sip" of a Bloody Mary after being urged to do so by Irmis Johnson. CJ, 186.

2. *Time,* February 23, 1953.

3. *San Francisco Examiner,* February 13, 1953.

4. *New York Journal American,* February 13, 1953.

5. Jorgensen's statement became the most frequently heard words from this press event, carried worldwide by motion picture news films. Her manner seemed confident, yet courteous. Millions of movie goers viewed these news reports in which she presented herself as a totally convincing woman.

6. Interview with Robert Andersen. March 27, 2004.

7. *Time,* February 23, 1953. Adjusted for inflation, today her suite would cost about $300 per day.

8. See the International News Service article on Jorgensen's return to New York, February 12, 1953.

9. *Time,* February 23, 1953.

10. CJ never admitted to having surgical breast implants, but as previously noted, she probably did. In 1977 she told her then boy friend, attorney Moton Holt, that "what you see above the waist is not all mine." Interview with Moton Holt, December 26, 2004.

11. *Los Angeles Times,* December 1, 1952.

12. *Los Angeles Times,* December 2, 1952.

13. *Los Angeles Times,* December 3, 1952.

14. *Los Angeles Times,* December 7, 1952.

15. *Los Angeles Times,* December 11, 1952.

16. *Los Angeles Mirror,* December 2, 1952.

17. The five-part series was attributed to Christine Jorgensen but actually written by a Hearst staffer, Irmis Johnson. It ran in the *American Weekly,* a Sunday supplement of the Hearst newspapers, beginning February 15, 1952, and for each of the following four Sundays. The articles are extensively illustrated by the photographs of Jens Junker-Jensen, Christine's Copenhagen friend.

18. *Los Angeles Examiner,* subheadline from Part I of the life story series, February 15, 1953.

19. CJ, 207-208.

20. Hamburger et al., (1953).

21. See the Introduction to CJ's 1967 autobiography.

22. CJ, 194. The autobiography gives extensive details of Jorgenen's New York celebrity social life during 1953.

Chapter 14

1. The six articles written by Alvin Davis for the *New York Post* were adequately researched and factually accurate, but his interpretation of the facts was colored by a single conclusion: Jorgensen, in Davis's view, was simply a castrate male. Davis did

not give consideration to allowing a "sex change" person to occupy a legitimate space in our society. While an important and not uncommon dissent in 1953, this view did not hold up over time. The articles appeared as follows: A. Davis, *The New York Post,* April 6, 1953, pp. 3 and 16; April 7, 1953, pp. 4 and 44; April 8, pp. 4 and 56; April 9, 1953, pp. 4 and 18; April 10, pp. 4 and 34; April 12, 1953, pp. 4 and 24.

2. Christine Jorgensen, Hearst newspapers, *American Weekly* series, Part II, March 15, 1953.

3. *Modern Romance* magazine, Christine Jorgensen: Is she still a man? August, 1953.

4. Hamburger, C. (1953). The desire for change of sex as shown by personal letters from 465 men and women. *Acta Endocrinologica, 14,* 363-376.

5. This copy of Hamburger's letter without the name of the addressee somehow came into the possession of Alvin Harris, a San Francisco lingerie fetishist. Harris corresponded with many transgendered men and was a close friend of Louise Lawrence who had her own network of cross dresser correspondents. Harris later gave his extensive collection of transgender materials to his friend, Richard Wheeler. Following Harris' death, Wheeler donated the materials to the Special Collections Department of the library of California State University, Northridge.

Chapter 15

1. Letter, Yates to CJ, 1953. DRL.

2. *Time Magazine,* April 20, 1953.

3. *Los Angeles Herald & Express,* May 7, 1953, p. A-3.

4. *Los Angeles Times,* May 7, 1953.

5. *Los Angeles Herald & Express,* May 7, 1953.

6. *Los Angeles Times,* May 8, 1953.

7. *Los Angeles Mirror,* May 7, 1953.

8. Ibid.

9. Ibid.

10. Ibid.

11. *Los Angeles Herald & Express,* May 7, 1953.

12. As previously noted, photographs of CJ's unclothed body taken in 1953 support this description. Authenticity of the photographs confirmed by author.

13. There is no record of Al Lyon's words. We offer this invention as an approximation.

14. Hammond, F. The Los Angeles Times, May 9, 1953.

15. Williams, D. The Los Angeles Times, May 8, 1952.

16. *New York Journal American,* May 9, 1953.

17. Harrison, C. *Los Angeles Herald & Express,* May 9, 1953.

18. Associated Press, May 9, 1993.

19. CJ papers. DRL.

20. CJ papers. DRL.

21. Las Vegas Sahara Hotel cancellation correspondence, c. May, 1953. DRL.

Chapter 16

1. Charles Yates to CJ, correspondence, May 20, 1953. DRL.

2. Interview with Vincent and Georgiana Manno who observed her 1950s performances in New York City. March 26, 2004.

3. The preservation and labeling of these family pictures would be a worthwhile project.

4. Schaefer, L. C., & Wheeler, C. C. (1995). Harry Benjamin's first ten cases (1938-1953): A clinical historical note. *Archives of Sexual Behavior, 24,* 73-93.

5. Benjamin, (1966).

6. Memorial for Harry Benjamin (1986). Remarks by Christine Jorgensen. *Archives of Sexual Behavior, 17,* 24-25. Jorgensen contributed her comments by telephone.

7. Charles Yates to CJ, correspondence, c. May, 1953. DRL.

8. Notations by CJ concerning a few singing lessons, c. April, 1953. DRL.

9. A grandson of Myles Bell who carries his name provided this family information. Telephone conversation with Myles Bell, February, 2004.

10. Obituary of Charles Yates among clippings of CJ, undated. Newspaper unknown. c, 1955. DRL.

11. Believed to be an unpublished song. The lyrics can be heard on Teit Ritzau's 1984 film: *Paradise Is Not for Sale.*

12. We have inferred this from the advice of several vaudeville performers.

13. Meyerowitz, J, (2002). *How sex changed: A history of transexuality.* Cambridge: Harvard U. Press.

14. CJ file, Kinsey Institute on Sex, Gender, and Reproduction. 1953.

15. CJ file, The Kinsey Institute on sex, Gender, and Reproduction. 1953.

16. Kinsey, A. C., Pomeroy, W. B., & Martin C. E. (1948). *Sexual behavior in the human male.* Philadelphia: W. B. Saunders. p. 639.

17. Jones, J. H. (1997). *Alfred C. Kinsey: A public/private life.* New York: Norton.

18. Gathorne-Hardy, J. (1998). *Sex: The measure of all things.* Bloomington, IN: Indiana University Press.

19. Christenson, C. V. (1971). *Kinsey: A biography.* Bloomington, IN: Indiana University Press.

20. Pomeroy, W. B. (1960). *Dr. Kinsey and the Institute for Sex Research.* New York: The Free Press.

21. Kinsey et al, (1948).

22. Kinsey, A. C., Pomeroy, W. B., Martin, C. E., & Gebhard, P. H. (1953). *Sexual behavior in the human female.* Philadelphia: W. B. Saunders.

23. Interview with the Mannos, 2003.

24. Locations of nightclubs, contract data, and dates for 1953 and 1954 appearances were derived from records in the CJ papers, DRL. For other years, see the CJ autobiography.

25. Many examples of contracts are among the CJ papers. DRL. Correspondence between CJ and various nightclub owners sometimes includes remarks concerning "bar tabs." CJ papers. DRL.

26. Brenda Lana Smith has pointed out that the opening date was probably August 5, because in 1953 August 9 was a Sunday. Personal communication. May 27, 2005.

27. Notations of CJ found among her financial records. DRL.

28. A collection of news clippings concerning Patrick Flanigan is among the CJ papers at the Kinsey Institute on Sex, Gender, and Reproduction.

29. CJ used the abbreviation, "Flannery," when referring to Flanigan within her family. Personal communication, Marilyn Courtney, March 27, 2004.

30. *San Francisco Examiner,* April 17, 1954.

31. CJ papers, undated. DRL.

32. Remarks by CJ, Harry Benjamin Memorial, 1986.

Chapter 17

1. CJ, 250.

2. CJ, 250.

3. Personal communication, Sister Mary Elizabeth, November 2003.

4. Letter from Yates to CJ, August 23, 1954. DRL.

5. *True Confessions* magazine, September, 1954.

6. CJ, 262.

7. The play was: *To Dorothy with Love.*

8. Personal communication from Brenda Lana Smith who noted these heavy-duty zippers on costumes CJ had worn. May 27, 2005.

9. CJ, 272.

10. Letter from CJ to Kinsey. Kinsey Institute for Research on Sex, Gender, and Reproduction, Indiana University, 1955.

11. Letter from Kibbee to CJ, December 31, 1969. DRL.

12. Letter from CJ to Kinsey, Kinsey Institute, 1955.

13. Identified as Betty Walton in the CJ autobiography.

14. The *Chicago Sun Times,* July 15, 1956.

15. CJ, 281.

16. Personal communication from Brenda Lana Smith, May 27, 2005. Smith believes CJ needed to establish intent to become a Danish citizen to become eligible for various medical services in Denmark. If so, it is not clear why CJ remained silent about this in her autobiography.

17. Letter from CJ to her tax consultants in Washington, DC, c. 1957. DRL.

18. 33 1/3 rpm. recording, R. Russell and CJ, 1957. In her autobiography, CJ stated her interviewer was "Nipsey Russell," CJ, 255. For unknown reasons, the record jacket gives the name of her interviewer as R. Russell. In the 1950s, Russell had appeared in some musical reviews but was little known. Russell died in 2005. The Internet Movie Data Base.

19. These policy changes are described by Meyerowitz, J. (2002). *How sex changed: A history of transsexuality.* Cambridge: Harvard U. Press.

Chapter 18

1. Identified as John Traub in CJ's 1967 autobiography.
2. CJ, 288.
3. Ibid.
4. CJ, 288-289.
5. CJ, 289
6. The *New York Daily Mirror,* April 6, 1959.
7. CJ, 290.
8. Ibid.
9. CJ, 293.
10. The *Chicago American,* September 8, 1959.
11. Personal communication, Stanton Bahr, March 26, 2004.

Chapter 19

1. Country Style Living, *Massapequa Post,* April 2, 1959.
2. Identified in the CJ autobiography as Betty Walton.
3. Gillies, H. D., & Millard, R. D. (1957). *The principles and art of plastic surgery.* Boston:.Little, Brown.
4. CJ notes and records from the 1950s and 1960s. DRL.
5. Personal communication from Diane Osborne, March 28, 2004.
6. Receipts and financial records, 1955. DRL.
7. *Long Beach Independent,* April 9, 1960.
8. Ibid.
9. Relatives and friends unanimously report Christine preferred this daily schedule throughout her adult life.
10. CJ, 300.
11. Ibid.
12 . CJ, 303.

Chapter 20

1. CJ, 308.
2. Elizabeth Finken, personal communication, October 19, 2006.
3. Ibid.
4. CJ papers. DRL.
5. Over several years, CJ sustained a cordial friendship with Hy Gardner, his wife, and family.
6. As quoted in CJ's advertising brochure. Attributed to Ben Gross of the *New York Daily News.* Undated. DRL.
7. As quoted in CJ's advertising brochure. Attributed to Hy Gardner. Undated. DRL.
8. This person may have been identified as "Roger," a so-called fast-rising film director in the five-part life story series published in the *American Weekly.*

9. Correspondence from unnamed secretary of a film director to CJ. Undated. c. 1965. DRL.

10. CJ, 317.

11. The CJ and Lamparski interview is available on the internet: www.queer musicheritage.com/aug200a.html. This site gives an incorrect 1967 date for the interview. This may have been the date it aired on radio station WBAI. The interview was recorded prior to April 1966.

12. Colapinto, J. (2000). *As nature made him.* New York: Harper Collins.

13. Money, J., & Ehrhardt, Anne. (1972). *Man and woman: Boy and girl.* Baltimore: The Johns Hopkins University Press.

14. Diamond, M., & Sigmundson, K. (1997). Sex reassignment at birth: A long-term review and clinical implications. *Archives of Pediatric and Adolescent Medicine. 150,* 298-304.

Chapter 21

1. Letter from Lois Kibbee to CJ, December 31, 1969. DRL. Kibbee wrote that Jorgensen had paid Irmis Johnson $5000 for a supposedly "worthless" biography based on the *American Weekly* five-part series.

2. Interview with Warren Bayless, November 9, 2004.

3. For Kibbee's career history see her obituary, New York Times, April 7, 1995.

4. Personal communication, June Bennett Larsen, November 10, 2004.

5. Ibid.

6. Ibid.

7. Interview with Warren Bayless, November 9, 2004.

8. Telephone interview with Warren Bayless, April 20, 2004.

9. Correspondence from Warren Bayless to Howard Cady, September 19, 1966. From the files of Jorgensen's publisher, Paul S. Eriksson.

10. Interview with Warren Bayless, April 20, 2004.

11. Howard Cady later served as the copy editor of Kibbee's Jorgensen manuscript, as requested by CJ.

12. Copy of Bantam royalty report for 1974 in possession of author, courtesy of Paul S. Eriksson.

13. Personal communication, Paul S. Eriksson, January 14, 2004.

14. Clipping of a brief note from *Daily Variety.* Undated. c. 1971. DRL.

15. Correspondence from CJ to nightclub owners and booking agents, c. 1967-1970. DRL.

16. *San Francisco Examiner,* October 18, 1967. 6E.

17. Correspondence from Eriksson to his lawyers during 1971. Files of Paul S. Eriksson.

18. Letter from Kibbee to CJ, December 31, 1969. DRL.

19. Interview with Mr. and Mrs. Robert Andersen. March 29, 2004.

20. The Olsen and Jorgensen relationship was explained by Brenda Lana Smith in her memoir, *a'top a dung hill.* According to Brenda Smith, Olsen had become a Jorgensen fan. Smith, B. L. (1991). *a'top a dung hill.* Unpublished manuscript. p. 108.

21. Interview with Bayless, April 20, 2004.

Chapter 22

1. In a three-volume unpublishèd story of his life, Small listed 117 feature films he had produced. Edward Small Collection, University of Southern California Cinema-Television Library. Undated. c. 1973.

2. Small's obituary in *Daily Variety* said he had produced "more than 200" films. *Daily Variety*, January 26, 1977.

3. Small biography, Part III, 375.

4. Telephone interview with Malcom Marmorstein, April 13, 2004.

5. Ibid.

6. Versions of screenplays for the Jorgensen film are among the Edward Small Collection, University of Southern California Cinema-Television Library. The collection includes extensive documentation and photographs dealing with the Jorgensen film.

7. Small biography, Part III, 376.

8. Meyerowitz, J. (2002). *How sex changed: A history of transexuality.* Cambridge: Harvard U. Press.

9. Letter from Benjamin to CJ, August 19, 1969. Kinsey Institute on Sex, Gender and Reproduction.

10. Personal communication from Warren Bayless, April 21, 2005.

11. *The Christine Jorgensen Story* as a feature film fell well short of a "truthful narrative." For Small's comments, see his biography, Part III, 377.

12. Personal communication, Marilyn Courtney, January 14, 2004.

13. Small biography, Part III, 377.

14. Small reportedly told Jorgensen that the film had lost money, which appears to have been accurate. He had paid himself a $150,000 producer's fee for assembling the project and supervising the making of the movie. This documentation is part of the record of the Los Angeles Superior Court lawsuit brought by CJ against the Bank of America and others, filed September 7, 1977. Case Number: C 212 284.

15. Personal communication, Stanton Bahr, March 26, 2004.

16. Production records, *The Christine Jorgensen Story,* a part of the Edward Small Collection, University of Southern California Cinema-Television Library. 1970.

17. *Philadelphia Enquirer,* July 10, 1970. Perhaps Christine mentioned *Gone with the Wind* as this was said to be her favorite movie.

18. See Rapper obituary, *New York Times,* December 30, 1999.

19. Library of the Screen Writers Guild, Los Angeles, California.

20. Kids of the Kingdom state they have no record that John Hansen was ever a member of the group.

21. Edward Small Collection, University of Southern California Cinema-Television Library. Undated. c. 1973.

22. Edward Small Collection, University of Southern California Cinema-Television Library. Undated biographical notes.

23. *New York Daily News,* July 25, 1970.

24. *The New York Times,* July 25, 1970.

25. The *San Francisco Chronicle,* July 25, 1970.

26. *Daily Variety,* June 4, 1970.

27. The *Washington Post,* September 19, 1970.

28. Interview with Diane Osborne, (pseudonym) March 30, 2004.

29. The *San Francisco Examiner & Chronicle,* September 26, 1971.

30. Extensive documentation of the deal between Small and United Artists became part of the court record in CJ's lawsuit against the Bank of America and others.

31. CJ's lawsuit against the Bank of America et al., 1977.

32. *Daily Variety,* January 6, 1971.

33. Interview with attorney Moton B. Holt, Sacramento, California, December 26, 2004.

34. Holt explained to CJ that no evidence had been discovered to sustain Jorgensen's belief that Small had withheld money she deserved to share. He urged her to drop the suit. Interview with Holt, 2004.

35. Ibid.

36. Holt explained that the California Bar advised him that when an agreement had been reached to "drop a case" that he obtain a written agreement from the client. Interview with Holt. December 26, 2004.

37. CJ papers. DRL.

38. Sales brochures, CJ papers. DRL.

39. Contracts between CJ and her booking agency show she typically received about $1,000 per lecture, but she sometimes told news reporters that her fee was as much as $2,500. CJ collection. Undated notes and letters, c. 1972. DRL.

40. Personal communication, Marilyn Courtney, March 27, 2004.

41. Courtney, 2004.

42. Interview with Robert Andersen, March 29, 2004.

43. Personal communication from Brenda Lana Smith, September 9, 2004. Smith's observations were incorporated in her own transsexual memoir: (1991). Unpublished manuscript. Partial copy in possession of the author through the courtesy of Brenda Lana Smith. Unpublished. Undated manuscript. c. 1990-1991.

Chapter 23

1. Interview with Marilyn Courtney, March 27, 2004.

2. Ibid.

3. Ibid.

4. Ibid.

5. Ibid.

6. Ibid.

7. Ibid.

8. Courtney, 2004. CJ's sister, Dorothy, was said to have made a distinction between the "make believe" or show business life of Christine and "real life."

9. Courtney, 2004.

10. Telephone interview with executor, March 16, 2004.

11. CJ collection. DRL.

12. Courtney, 2004.

13. CJ collection. DRL. Author and date unknown. c. 1981.

14. Courtney, 2004.

15. Personal communications with Sister Mary Elizabeth, 2003 and 2004.

16. Telephone interview, anonymous friend of CJ, 2004.

17. Ibid.

18. Interview with Stanton Bahr, March 26, 2004.

19. CJ collection, c. 1984. DRL

20. Interview with Preben Hertoft, December 10, 2003.

21. Ibid.

22. For example, CJ revealed her somewhat lofty self-assessment to Brenda Lana Smith when she spoke of the possibility of being honored with a commemorative star on Hollywood's Walk of Fame. Smith, B. L. (1991).

23. According to all living relatives, there is no collection of CJ's correspondence or personal records other than what she gave to the Danish Royal Library. As noted, many other Jorgensen materials are held by the Kinsey Institute and California State University, Northridge library.

24. The Louise Lawrence story is told by Joanne Meyerowitz, (2002) *How sex changed: A history of transexuality.*

25. Letter, CJ to Ritzau, March 4, 1985, Box 9. DRL.

26. Personal communication with Marilyn Courtney, November 10, 2003.

27. Personal communication with Sister Mary Elizabeth, September 1, 2004. Her navy service included eleven years of active duty, and seven years in the Reserve.

28. Interview with Stanton Bahr, March 27, 2004.

29. Letter, CJ to Actors Equity, c. 1984. CJ collection. DRL.

30. Interview with Stanton Bahr, 2004.

31. Letter from CJ to Stanton Bahr, 1984. DRL.

32. CJ provided a second mortgage of $30,000 to facilitate the sale of her residence. The purchaser subsequently refused to pay the interest on this mortgage until CJ reimbursed him for disputed repairs. Following her death, CJ's attorney reportedly paid $5,000 to settle these claims although CJ had instructed that this should not be done. Personal communication, Brenda Lana Smith, April 4, 2005.

33. Interview with Diane Osborne, March 30, 2004.

34. Personal communication with Brenda Lana Smith, April 3, 2004.

35. *Los Angeles Times,* June 22, 1986.

36. *Enquirer,* date unknown. c. 1986.

37. Author's observations and notes. February 1988.

38. CJ letter to Jack Romano of Bantam Books. January 2, 1985. DRL.

39. Interview with Raymond Strait, March 23, 2004.

40. The break up of their collaboration is described in the CJ papers. DRL.

41. Raymond Strait told the author he believes he has these tape recordings but he was not able to locate them.

Chapter 24

1. Interview with Stanton Bahr, March 27, 2004.

2. Interview with Sister Mary Elizabeth, 2004.

3. Smith, 2003. 98.

4. Smith, 2003. 102-110.

5. Smith, 2003. 90.

6. The three Courtney sisters were the third cousins of Christine Jorgensen.

7. Personal communication, Brenda Lana Smith, May 31, 2005.

8. Mae Henri Lewis (deceased) was the long-time housekeeper for the Jorgensen family.

9. The signed commemorative register for the memorial get-together contains the names of 147 persons; about fifty attendees did not sign the register. DRL.

10. Transcript of Dorothy Jorgensen's remarks provided by Brenda Lana Smith, 2003.

11. According to the niece, Brenda Lana Smith took responsibility for carrying out CJ's wishes including the distribution of her ashes. Interview with niece, March 30, 2004.

12. Death certificate, Country Recorder of Orange County, California. May 8, 1989.

13. Letter, CJ to U. S. Veteran's Administration. Date unknown. c. 1980. CJ collection. DRL.

Index